Plan Recognition in Natural Language Dialogue

ACL–MIT Press Series
in Natural Language Processing

Aravind Joshi, editor

Speaking: From Intention to Articulation
Willem Levelt

Plan Recognition in Natural Language Dialogue
Sandra Carberry

006.3 C177p

Plan Recognition in Natural Language Dialogue

Sandra Carberry

A Bradford Book
The MIT Press
Cambridge, Massachusetts
London, England

This book was set in Computer Modern by The MIT Press and printed and bound in the United States of America.

Library of Congress Cataloging-in-Publication Data

Carberry, Sandra.
  Plan recognition in natural language dialogue/Sandra Carberry.
    p.   cm.—(ACL–MIT Press series in natural language processing)
  "A Bradford book."
  Includes bibliographical references.
  ISBN 0-262-03167-1
  1. Artificial intelligence. 2. Linguistics—Data processing. 3. Pattern perception. I. Title. II. Series.
  [DNLM: 1. Artificial Intelligence. 2. Models, Theoretical. 3. Pattern Recognition. Q 335 C263p]
Q335.C28   1990
006.3—dc20
DNLM/DLC
for Library of Congress   89-13580
                                                                                CIP

Contents

Preface

If computer systems are to attain their full potential as cooperative, helpful assistants in problem solving and decision making, then they must be able to communicate as effectively with humans as humans communicate with one another. For the most part, current natural language systems treat each query as an isolated request for information, with little use of the dialogue context within which the query occurs. This book addresses the problem of developing computational strategies for assimilating an ongoing dialogue and reasoning on the acquired knowledge to facilitate cooperative and effective interaction.

One way in which a natural language system can assimilate dialogue is by inferring the underlying task-related plan motivating an information seeker's queries. This book critically examines plan inference in natural language systems and its historical roots in other disciplines and describes significant models of the plan inference process. It presents the details of my own process model for incremental plan recognition in information-seeking dialogues. This system assimilates a new utterance by hypothesizing domain goals that might represent the specific aspect of the task on which the information seeker's attention is now centered and by using focusing heuristics to select the hypothesized domain goal that has the most coherent relationship to the existing dialogue context. Thus the system dynamically infers new goals and integrates them into the plan structure, thereby incrementally expanding and adding detail to its beliefs about what the information seeker wants to do.

In a cooperative information-seeking dialogue, the information provider is engaged in helping the information seeker construct a plan for his underlying task. However, naturally occurring communication is both incomplete and imperfect. Not only does the information seeker fail to explicitly communicate all aspects of his goals and partially constructed plan for achieving these goals, but also his utterances are often imperfectly formulated. They may be ill-formed in the strict syntactic or semantic sense, or they may present pragmatic problems in understanding. However, analysis of naturally occurring dialogue suggests that the information seeker expects the information provider to reason with her acquired knowledge about what the information seeker is trying to accomplish, in order to understand many of the information seeker's faulty utterances and enable the dialogue to continue without interruption.

This book demonstrates the utility of reasoning on a model of the information seeker's plans and goals by presenting computational strategies for interpreting two kinds of problematic utterances: utterances that violate the pragmatic rules of the system's world model and intersentential elliptical fragments. My strategy for handling pragmatically ill-formed utterances relies on the system's beliefs about the information seeker's underlying task-related plan as the primary mechanism for suggesting potential interpretations and thereby considers only interpretations that are relevant to what the system believes the information seeker is trying to accomplish. These suggested interpretations must then be evaluated on the basis of semantic criteria and relevance to the current focus of attention in the dialogue. This strategy is superior to previous approaches because it uses a model of the established dialogue context to identify and address the information seeker's perceived intentions and needs.

To understand an elliptical fragment, a listener must recognize the discourse goal that the speaker is pursuing and identify how the speaker's fragmentary utterance is intended to further that discourse goal. I argue that the dialogue preceding an elliptical fragment establishes expectations about discourse goals that a speaker might pursue and that understanding intersentential ellipsis is heavily dependent on these discourse expectations. My ellipsis interpretation strategy is a top-down procedure utilizing expectations gleaned from the preceding dialogue to suggest discourse goals that the speaker might be expected to pursue. If the aspect of the speaker's plan highlighted by his elliptical fragment can produce a coherent interpretation relevant to a suggested discourse goal, then the fragment is recognized as intending to accomplish that discourse goal, and the appropriate interpretation is produced. Interpretation of elliptical fragments appears to rely heavily on conversational expectations and focus of attention, and this approach captures such discourse knowledge. In addition, it is the first ellipsis-resolution strategy to address recognition of the speaker's discourse goal.

Unfortunately, current models of plan inference make a number of restrictive assumptions that limit their ability to handle naturally occurring dialogue. This book discusses these limiting assumptions and describes research directed toward a more robust plan-inference framework. It argues that since communication is imperfect and the system's reasoning processes are fallible, the system must be able to detect disparities between its inferred model and the actual plan under construction by the information seeker and repair its model whenever possible. It presents a four-phase approach to the problem of model disparity that was motivated by an analysis of naturally occurring information-seeking dialogues. In addition, it highlights several important areas of current and future research.

Thus the overall goals of the book are to (1) present and critically analyze the important ideas in plan recognition, (2) describe the details of one research effort directed toward modeling the user's plans and goals and reasoning on the acquired knowledge to increase system robustness, and (3) suggest directions for future work.

Many people have influenced this work. Foremost among these was Ralph Weischedel, my Ph.D. thesis advisor, who provided the encouragement and motivation for successful research, helped to focus my work along fruitful paths, and has always been a ready source of constructive suggestions. I would also like to thank Aravind Joshi, the editor of this series, for his encouragement in developing this manuscript and his invaluable advice. Over the years, a number of other people have contributed to this research with their comments and suggestions. I would particularly like to thank Kathy Cebulka, Dan Chester, Brad Goodman, Kathy McCoy, Martha Pollack, Alan Pope, and Lance Ramshaw. In addition, I am grateful to Dan Chester for his work on DIALS, the Delaware Intelligent Advisory Language System, into which the computational strategies described in this book are being incorporated. And I would like to thank the AI group at the University of Delaware for providing a forum for stimulating discussion and my family for their patience and understanding when the research and manuscript consumed countless hours of my time.

Portions of this work were partially supported by a grant from the National Science Foundation IST-8311400, by a subcontract from Bolt Beranek and Newman Inc. of a grant from the National Science Foundation IST-8419162, and by a grant from the University of Delaware Research Foundation. This work has also been aided by research-equipment grant CCR-8612706 from the National Science Foundation. The author's current research is supported by National Science Foundation grant IRI-8909332. Any opinions, findings, and conclusions or recommendations expressed in this material are those of the author and do not necessarily reflect the views of the National Science Foundation.

Plan Recognition in Natural Language Dialogue

1 Introduction

When two individuals participate in an information-seeking dialogue, the information provider uses the context within which each query occurs to interpret the query, determine the desired information, and formulate an appropriate response. This context consists of more than mere knowledge of the previous questions and answers. A cooperative participant uses the information exchanged during the dialogue and his knowledge of the domain to hypothesize a model of the information seeker and dynamically adjust and expand the model as the dialogue progresses.

A model of an information seeker may have several components, including representations of the following:

- The underlying task motivating the information seeker's queries and his partially developed plan for accomplishing the task

- The *plan construction* or *problem-solving goals* that the information seeker is pursuing to further expand and instantiate his task-related plan, such as comparing alternative ways of achieving a subgoal

- The information seeker's *discourse* or *communicative goals*, such as answering a question or seeking clarification

- The information seeker's likes and dislikes

- The information seeker's beliefs

- The information seeker's level of expertise in the domain

While all of these are important, my concern has focused on the first three. As demonstrated by Cohen, Perrault, and Allen, users of question-answering systems "expect more than just answers to isolated questions. They expect to engage in a conversation whose coherence is manifested in the interdependence of their often unstated plans and goals with those of the system." ([CPA81] page 245)

For the most part, natural language interfaces currently treat each query as an isolated request for information, with little use of the dialogue context within which the query occurs. I am concerned with how a natural language system can assimilate an ongoing dialogue and use the resulting knowledge to increase its robustness. The architecture I envision for an intelligent robust system, portions of which have been implemented and are now being integrated into the Delaware Intelligent Advisory Language System (DIALS), is illustrated in figure 1.1.

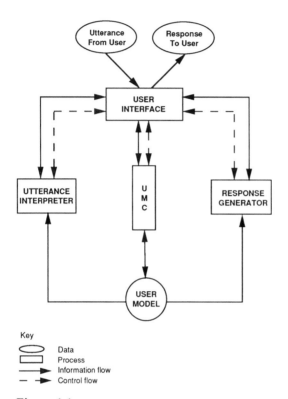

Figure 1.1
Architecture for an intelligent robust natural language system

The user model represents the system's assimilation of the dialogue and contains information about the user and the current dialogue context that can increase the system's ability to engage in effective communication. All utterances between user and system pass through a user interface. When the user interface receives an utterance from the user, an utterance interpreter is invoked; it reasons on the utterance and the user model to identify the user's intended meaning and returns it to the interface for subsequent processing. Once a user's utterance is understood, the user-modeling component, UMC, must update the user model to reflect the affect of this new utterance on the system's beliefs about the user and the current dialogue context. Then the response generator is invoked; it reasons on the intended meaning of the user's utterance and the user model to construct a response that addresses the user's perceived needs. The user-modeling component must then update the user model to reflect the system's response.

This book investigates one dimension of the dialogue assimilation process: the modeling of the plans and goals motivating an information seeker's queries. Chapter 2 critically examines plan inference in natural language systems and its historical roots in other disciplines. Chapter 3 then presents a process model for dynamically inferring from an ongoing dialogue the information seeker's task-related plans and goals. Plan recognition has proven important both in understanding natural language utterances and in generating cooperative responses. Chapters 4 through 6 illustrate its impact on language understanding by presenting computational strategies that reason on the system's inferred model of the information seeker's plans and goals in order to handle two kinds of problematic utterances: utterances that violate the pragmatic rules of the system's world model and intersentential elliptical fragments. Unfortunately, current models of plan inference make a number of assumptions that limit their ability to handle naturally occurring dialogue; chapter 7 discusses these limitations and describes research directed toward a more robust plan inference framework. Chapter 8 summarizes research on process models of plan inference and the role of plan recognition in natural language processing, highlighting several important areas of current and future research. Thus, the overall goals of the book are to (1) present an overview of the important ideas in plan recognition, (2) describe the details of one research effort directed toward modeling the user's plans and goals and reasoning on the acquired knowledge to increase system robustness, and (3) suggest directions for future work.

1.1   Information-Seeking Dialogues

An *information-seeking dialogue* contains two participants, one seeking information and the other attempting to provide that information. Analysis of naturally occurring dialogue suggests that when a human being plays the role of information provider in such a dialogue, that person generally attempts to infer the underlying task-related plan motivating the information seeker's queries and to use this plan to understand subsequent utterances and provide cooperative, helpful responses.

The underlying task motivating the information-seeking dialogue may be executed concurrently with the dialogue, in alternation with it, or subsequent to it. If one's task is simply to learn about the domain, one's information-seeking queries accomplish this task concurrent with the dialogue. Apprentice-expert dialogues exemplify situations in which task execution may alternate with the dialogue. In such domains the apprentice seeks help from an expert in performing a specific task and appraises the expert on his progress in completing aspects of the task. Task execution occurs alternately with portions of the dialogue: the apprentice may perform part of the task, discuss his progress with the expert, request help regarding the next steps, perform those steps, describe his current status, and so forth.

In the third type of dialogue the information seeker requests information in order to construct a plan for a task that will be executed at some time in the future. Such tasks include expanding a company's product line, purchasing a home, pursuing a degree at a university, or even taking a vacation. This class of dialogues represents the kind of interaction that a user might have with an expert consultation system. In some cases only a partial plan will be constructed, with further details filled in later. For example, during his freshman year at a university, a student may only construct part of his plan for earning a degree, leaving other aspects of the plan to be fleshed out in subsequent years.

Dialogues in which the underlying task-related plan is being constructed for subsequent execution differ from the other classes of information-seeking dialogues in that the speaker's queries are not tightly constrained by the order in which the individual actions comprising the task must be executed. For example, in an apprentice-expert dialogue the apprentice describes his progress and requests help as he is attempting to perform a task. One expects the order of these utterances to reflect the order in which the actions comprising the task are performed. Such constraints do not exist in cases where the plan will be executed in the future. For example, a client interacting with a travel agent might first plan hotel accommodations and theater attendance in New York before inquiring about ways to reach New York, even though travel to New York will occur before attending a New York theater in a temporal ordering of actions in the resultant plan.

1.2   Classes of Dialogues

Information-seeking dialogues may be classified as either *top-down* or *bottom-up*. In a top-down dialogue, the information seeker directly communicates his underlying task at the outset of the dialogue and then proceeds to formulate queries relevant to constructing a plan for accomplishing the task. The following is an example of a naturally occurring top-down dialogue:

Speaker 1: I am trying to get to New York. Does this road lead to Route 13?

In the first utterance the speaker conveys his underlying task, and in the second utterance he formulates an information-seeking query in order to construct a plan for accomplishing this task of getting to New York City. If the information provider believes that Route 13 is a good way of getting to New York City, her response is likely to consist of directions for reaching that highway. On the other hand, if the information provider does not believe that finding Route 13 is a step in a good plan for traveling to New York City, then her response is likely to suggest alternative routes. This is the case in the following response to the above query:

Speaker 2: If you want to go to New York City, your best bet is to go about 2 miles down this road, get on I-95, and then follow the signs directing you to New York.

In both cases, the human information provider appears to direct her response to what she believes is the task underlying the information seeker's queries.

In a bottom-up dialogue the information seeker does not directly communicate his overall task but instead formulates queries relevant to subtasks within the overall task, constructs plans for accomplishing these subtasks, and builds his plan from the bottom up. The following is an example of a naturally occurring bottom-up dialogue:

Speaker 1: Do you know what computers the elementary schools are using?

Speaker 2: (responds with the brands of computers being used in the elementary schools in the area)

Speaker 1: I saw a [Brand X] computer advertised in the newspaper. Is $89 a good price for it?

Speaker 2: Yes, but prices are falling rapidly. However, if you are thinking of getting it for Sarah [a fourth grader], I don't really think you will be happy with it because ...

Although the information seeker did not directly communicate her overall task of purchasing a computer system to further her daughter Sarah's educational opportunities, this was inferred by the information provider from the dialogue and knowledge about the information seeker. The information provider then responded by addressing not only the information seeker's query but also the information seeker's inferred task.

Top-down dialogues seem to occur when the information seeker has little knowledge about how to proceed in the domain and is willing to relinquish control of the dialogue to the information provider. Bottom-up dialogues seem to occur when the information seeker believes he is already knowledgeable about the domain and wants to maintain control of the dialogue and fill in those parts of his partially constructed plan that are not yet complete. In both cases human beings seem to use the information seeker's inferred task-related plan in the subsequent dialogue.

Thus one way in which human beings appear to assimilate dialogue is by inferring the *underlying task-related plan* motivating an information seeker's queries. The resulting model of what the speaker wants to accomplish seems to play a major role in providing cooperative responses, as illustrated in the above dialogues, and in interpreting subsequent utterances, as will be shown in a later section.

1.3   Plan Inference in Information-Seeking Dialogues

In both top-down and bottom-up dialogues, a plan inference system must build its model of the information seeker's plan incrementally as the dialogue progresses. At the outset of a dialogue the information seeker's purpose in requesting information is unknown. In most cases his complete plan cannot be determined during the first part of a dialogue. Instead, potential goals must be inferred from individual utterances and integrated into an overall plan structure, which will thereby incrementally expand and add detail to the system's beliefs about what the information seeker wants to do.

If the information seeker initiates a top-down dialogue, his overall task will be explicitly conveyed during the first few utterances. However, the details of how he intends to accomplish this task remain unknown. For example, the initial utterance "I want to earn a Bachelor of Arts degree." conveys the speaker's underlying task of earning a degree, specifically, a Bachelor of Arts degree, but omits the details of how the speaker plans to accomplish the task. These details may often be inferred from subsequent utterances, such as "What are the requirements for a computer science major?"

On the other hand, if the information seeker initiates a bottom-up dialogue, his overall task is not communicated during the first few utterances. Instead, the information seeker communicates the identity of subtasks within the overall task and may refrain from explicitly mentioning the overall task during the course of the dialogue. For example, the utterance "What are the prerequisites for CS360?" might allow one to infer that the information seeker is considering enrolling in CS360 or that he wants to generate a set of course descriptions, perhaps for a department handout. Not only is his current focused goal ambiguous, but also the higher-level goal motivating each individual goal may be unclear. For example, even if we determine that the information seeker wants to enroll in CS360 (computer architecture), we still do not know whether he is pursuing a computer science major or is trying to satisfy the requirements of a digital systems option in electrical engineering. Such higher-level goals may be communicated in subsequent utterances or may be inferred from the dialogue by relating several subtasks. For example, if the College of Arts and Science has a set of group distribution requirements and the College of Engineering has not, then the utterance "Will any of my computer science courses satisfy the Group 4 distribution requirements?" eliminates from consideration the plan for majoring in electrical engineering, since satisfying the Arts and Science group distribution requirements is inconsistent with it. Thus a model of the information seeker's underlying task-related plan may be expanded in overall scope by relating individual utterances to the existing inferred plan context.

Since a complete plan for the information seeker cannot be inferred during the first part of a dialogue, the task-related plan motivating the information seeker's utterances must be inferred and built incrementally as the dialogue progresses. For each new utterance, my approach is to do the following:

- Relate the utterance to the system's domain knowledge in order to hypothesize a set of domain-dependent subgoals and associated subplans that represent aspects of tasks on which the speaker's attention might be currently focused in light of this isolated utterance

- Relate these potential subgoals and subplans to the system's existing beliefs about the information seeker's overall plan in order to identify the specific subgoal and subplan on which his attention is currently centered

- Appropriately expand the existing inferred plan for the speaker so that it includes this new subgoal and subplan

The subtask on which the speaker's attention is centered changes during the course of a dialogue. If a natural language system is to recognize a speaker's intentions, it must track his focus of attention in his plan structure. In my model, local and global contexts are differentiated. The local context is the subgoal and associated subplan on which the speaker's attention is currently focused. This local context is particularly important because it provides the strongest expectations for subsequent utterances. The global context includes higher-level goals and plans that produced the current local context. The context mechanism distinguishes local and global contexts and uses these to hypothesize new speaker goals from the current utterance. Chapter 3 describes my model of plan inference.

1.4   The Use of Inferred Plans in Interpreting Utterances

In a cooperative information-seeking dialogue, the information provider is engaged in helping the information seeker develop a plan for his underlying task. The information seeker is expected to communicate whatever information is necessary for the information provider to fulfill her helping role in the dialogue. On the other hand, the information seeker expects the information provider to assimilate the dialogue, infer from it much of what the information seeker wants to accomplish, and use these inferences to understand the information seeker's queries.

This presumption that a cooperative listener will infer the speaker's underlying task-related plan and use it to interpret utterances is the basis of much humor. Consider, for example, the following short dialogue from the movie *SPLASH* between a man and a somewhat dense member of a boat crew:

Man: I was dropped off on the wrong side of the beach and I was wondering if you could take me over to the island?

Crew: Well, uh, we're not, we're not going, we're just, we're tacking the boat. We're not going out there.

Man: Well, have you seen anyone else along this beach?

(An intervening dialogue about what the crew was doing)

Dense crew member: There's a guy down the beach that runs people out to the island.

Man: What's the name?

Dense crew member: The guy or the island?

The last utterance is humorous because of the failure of the crewman to interpret the utterance "What's the name?" cooperatively, that is, to recognize the speaker's task-related plan communicated in the preceding dialogue and use it in interpreting subsequent utterances.

Previous research work has illustrated the importance of the speaker's underlying task-related plan in interpreting definite noun phrases [Gro77b], verb phrases [Rob81], and indirect speech acts [PA80]. In addition, understanding two kinds of utterances that occur in an information-seeking dialogue—pragmatically ill-formed utterances and intersentential elliptical fragments—also depends heavily on this inferred plan.

1.4.1 Pragmatic Ill-Formedness

Pragmatic knowledge about the world, represented in a *world model*, includes structural information (such as objects, their attributes, and relationships in which the objects can participate), extensional information (such as actual instances of objects and the values of their attributes), and integrity constraints on attribute values and relationships. To understand and properly respond to an utterance, a listener must relate it to what she believes is the world model used by the speaker in formulating the utterance [Jos82]. As long as the listener does not have evidence to the contrary, she will generally assume that many of her beliefs about the world are also those of the speaker and interpret utterances with respect to these beliefs.

Similarly, a natural language system must understand utterances using its model of the world. An utterance can be syntactically and semantically well-formed but violate the structural properties or integrity constraints of the system's world model. This does not necessarily mean that the user has an incorrect view of the world or even one that differs from the system's view; it only means that the semantic representation of the user's utterance does not conform to the system's world model. I will say that such an utterance is *pragmatically ill-formed*. Consider, for example, a real estate domain in which individual apartments can be rented and houses, condominiums, and apartment buildings can be sold. The query "Which apartments are for sale?" illustrates an intensional failure, since its semantic representation contains the proposition

Sale-status(_x:&APARTMENT, FOR-SALE)

and therefore erroneously presumes that objects of type apartment can be sold.

Pragmatically ill-formed utterances can occur if the user's beliefs about the world contradict those of the system or if the user is careless in formulating the language of his intended statement or query. Consider again the query "Which apartments are for sale?" The query may exhibit a misconception on the part of the user, namely, that single apartments are sold. On the other hand, the user and the system may have similar beliefs about the world, but the user may have been careless in making his utterance and inadvertently used the term *apartment*, when he meant *condominium* or *apartment building*. Another kind of language carelessness that can result in pragmatic ill-formedness is the tendency of speakers to short-cut the complete formulation of an intended query and to rely on the established context for proper interpretation. For example, suppose that Dr. Smith is a university faculty member and the information seeker utters the query "When's Smith meet?" In a university world model there is no direct relation between faculty members and times. However, faculty members teach sections of courses, present colloquia, and chair committees, all of which have scheduled meeting times. Depending on the context established by the preceding dialogue, the speaker might mean "What are the meeting times of sections of the course taught by Dr. Smith?" "What is the meeting time of the colloquium given by Dr. Smith?" or "What is the meeting time of the committee chaired by Dr. Smith?"

Unfortunately, pragmatically ill-formed utterances occur frequently in natural language dialogue. Information seekers often exhibit misconceptions about the world [McC86] or inadvertently use incorrect terminology. In addition, shortcuts in the use of language appear prevalent and ingrained. Carbonell [Car83] conducted an empirical study to ascertain whether users could comfortably interact with a natural language system that constrained them to the use of complete utterances, adherence to the topic, and avoidance of complex syntactic structures. Whenever a user violated the constraints, a standard error message noted the violation and reminded the user of the limitations on acceptable utterances. Interestingly, subjects found it easy to avoid complex syntactic structures but repeatedly violated the constraint on employing only complete utterances. Carbonell summarized the results of this experiment as follows:

> *Terseness Principle:* Users insist on being as terse as possible, independent of communication media or typing ability.
> ([Car83] page 165)

So the question arises, How should a natural language system handle pragmatically ill-formed utterances? I contend that the answer to this question depends on the cause of the pragmatic ill-formedness and the importance of any exhibited misconceptions. If the ill-formed query leads the system to believe that the user has a serious misconception, the system should explicitly correct the misconception; otherwise, the system's silence may be seen by the user as confirming his false presumptions [Jos82]. What is viewed as serious or important depends on the listener's goals. Since a parent has the goal of educating his child in the proper use of language, he may view a misconception about grammar as important. Similarly, since an information provider has the goal of helping the information seeker construct a plan for his underlying task, misconceptions that affect the information seeker's ability to construct or carry out his plan will be viewed as important. Several research efforts have followed this approach. Mays [May80a,May80b] proposed that the system respond to a misconception by providing information about the structure of the system's world model. His response strategy was to abstract the erroneously presumed relation and to give the user a list of classes that could participate in the stated relation and a list of relations in which each of the stated classes could participate. McCoy [McC86] generated a natural language response that not only corrected the misconception but also addressed aspects of the user's knowledge that might have produced it.

On the other hand, suppose that the pragmatic ill-formedness resulted from a language error or a minor unimportant misconception. Then a natural language system could respond in one of three ways:

- It could educate the user by correcting all errors.

- It could display a set of possible interpretations from which the user might select his intended query.

- It could attempt to discern the user's intent in making the utterance and respond accordingly.

The first two response strategies detract from an information seeker's ability to formulate a plan in two ways: by slowing his information-seeking with additional dialogue and by causing him to give less attention to his problem-solving goals in order to concentrate more on the preciseness of his utterances. I contend that a natural language system should follow the third strategy. Analysis of naturally occurring dialogue suggests that when given a pragmatically ill-formed query, human listeners often answer a related modified query that is well-formed with respect to the listener's world model and is believed to represent the speaker's intent or satisfy his perceived needs. This modification generally depends on the context established by the preceding discourse. Consider, for example, the following two sequences of utterances:

Speaker 1: I'd like to own my own residence, but I don't like a lot of maintenance. Which apartments are for sale?

Speaker 1: We'd like to invest between $30 and $50 million. Which apartments are for sale?

The context established by the first utterance in each sequence affects how a human listener might respond. In the first case the human listener might interpret the query as "Which condominiums are for sale?" and in the second case as "Which apartment buildings are for sale?" Unless a natural language system attempts to deduce what the user meant to say and responds accordingly, the dialogue cannot be considered natural, since the system will be unable to understand utterances easily handled by human listeners.

Other researchers have addressed variations of this problem [Cha78, Kap79, Sow76], but each analyzed utterances in isolation from the preceding dialogue. They thus failed to address the speaker's perceived intentions in making an utterance. I claim that the system must consider its beliefs about the information seeker's task-related plan in understanding and responding to pragmatically ill-formed queries, and I have developed a strategy that reasons about this plan to recognize the speaker's intent or at least satisfy his perceived needs. Chapter 4 describes my interpretation strategy.

1.4.2   Intersentential Ellipsis

Incomplete utterances are common in communication between humans. They range from sentences that fail to include all requisite semantic information to syntactically incomplete sentence fragments. Experiments with the REL natural language interface to a database of ships and cargoes indicate that approximately 10 percent of user utterances are elliptical [Tho80]. In many cases these utterances cannot be understood in isolation but must be interpreted within the established context. Precisely how this should be done is a difficult problem for natural language systems.

One suggestion is that the problem be avoided in man-machine communication by training human users to employ only syntactically and semantically complete utterances. However, this does not appear to be feasible, as shown by Carbonell's empirical study [Car83] described earlier. Even if it were possible to train users to avoid incomplete utterances, these restrictions would be undesirable. Constraining man-machine communication to only a subset of the utterances normally employed by humans would force users to give less attention to their problem-solving goals in order to concentrate more on the preciseness of their utterances. In addition, it appears that fragmentary utterances are not merely a result of sloppy communication. They are often used to accomplish discourse goals that would require more effort to convey with a complete sentence. For example, in the following dialogue from [FD84], Speaker 2's fragment expresses doubt about the proposition stated by Speaker 1.

Speaker 1: The Korean jet shot down by the Soviets was a spy plane.

Speaker 2: With 269 people on board?

A complete sentence such as "Was the Korean jet shot down by the Soviets a spy plane with 269 people on board?" fails to adequately communicate the doubt conveyed by the previous fragment. This objective can be accomplished only with a more complex sentence that marks the discourse goal, such as "How can you think that the Korean jet shot down by the Soviets was a spy plane, when it had 269 people on board?"

Thus a robust natural language interface must handle the kinds of incomplete utterances normally used by humans. To do otherwise is to prohibit communication that humans regard as natural and therefore to detract from their ability to communicate as effectively with machines as they do with one another.

I have studied the problem of understanding one class of incomplete utterance: intersentential ellipsis. An *intersentential elliptical fragment* is the use of a syntactically incomplete sentence fragment, along with the context established by the preceding dialogue, to communicate a complete thought and accomplish a speech act. As noted by Allen [All79], this kind of utterance differs from other forms of ellipsis in that interpretation often depends more heavily on the listener's beliefs about the speaker's underlying task-related plan than on preceding syntactic forms. For example, the fragment in the second sentence below can be understood correctly only if it is interpreted within the context of the speaker's goal as communicated in the first sentence: "I want to cash this check. Small bills only, please."[1] Thus the listener's assimilation of the preceding dialogue plays a major role in the interpretation of fragmentary utterances. In addition, real understanding requires identification of the speaker's discourse goal, such as expressing surprise in the example about the Korean airline.

I have developed a pragmatics-based computational framework that coordinates many knowledge sources, including discourse expectations, inferred beliefs, and the information seeker's inferred task-related plan, to produce a rich interpretation of ellipsis. Elliptical fragments are comprehended by identifying both the aspect of the information seeker's task-related plan highlighted by the fragment and the conversational discourse goal fulfilled by the utterance. Chapters 5 and 6 describe my interpretation strategy.

1.5   The Corpus of Dialogues

To develop the hypotheses and strategies presented in this book, dialogues from many different domains were analyzed. Two sets of transcripts were available: one from a radio talk show during which callers sought investment advice and the other from terminal sessions during which users queried a database of ships using the REL natural language interface [Tho80].[2] In addition to transcripts of other radio talk shows on real estate and animal care, two sets of transcripts of student advisement dialogues were also collected. The first set was obtained from tapes of actual students obtaining advice; in this case the students knew they were being taped but did not know the specific objectives of the research. The second set consisted of transcripts of terminal-terminal dialogues during which students sought advice from a simulated expert advisement system. In addition, naturally occurring dialogues were often transcribed as they occurred in everyday information-seeking settings.

Many of the examples presented in this book were extracted from these dialogues; others are based on hypothetical dialogues for a particular domain.

---

[1]The fragment "Small bills only, please." could be interpreted in several ways. It might be a command to one's subordinates to limit the charges on their expense accounts or a stipulation regarding the characteristics of the birds ordered for the zoo, as well as a request for small-denomination paper money.

[2]The transcripts of the radio talk show on investments were provided by the Department of Computer and Information Science of the University of Pennsylvania.

1.6   Outline of the Book

Chapters 2 and 7 are a critical examination of plan inference in natural language dialogue systems. Chapter 2 explores the roots of plan recognition work in previous research on planning, the philosophy of language and meaning, and focusing; it describes significant models of the plan inference process and provides the background for the rest of the book.

Chapter 3 describes my process model for incrementally inferring from an ongoing dialogue a model of an information seeker's underlying task-related plan. This plan inference framework has been implemented in a system called TRACK, which operates in a university domain containing information on degree requirements, policies, courses, and related items. Chapter 3 contains working examples from this system.

Chapters 4 through 6 are concerned with how a model of the user's plans and goals can contribute to a more robust natural language interface. Chapter 4 is devoted to pragmatically ill-formed utterances. It presents a strategy for interpreting one kind of pragmatically ill-formed query. The strategy utilizes the information seeker's inferred task-related plan to suggest variants of his actual utterance that are relevant to what the system believes the information seeker is trying to accomplish and which may capture his intended meaning or at least satisfy his needs. This interpretation framework has been implemented for the aforementioned university world model and is illustrated by examples from this and other domains.

Chapters 5 and 6 are devoted to intersentential elliptical utterances. Chapter 5 reviews related work and argues that interpretation of intersentential elliptical fragments must coordinate many knowledge sources, including the information seeker's anticipated discourse goals and inferred task-related plan. Chapter 6 presents my interpretation framework, a top-down strategy that utilizes expectations about the information seeker's discourse goals to guide interpretation of elliptical fragments. It defines a set of discourse goals that can be pursued via elliptical fragments in an information-seeking dialogue and describes how elliptical fragments highlight aspects of the information seeker's task-related plan. My process model understands intersentential elliptical utterances by identifying the discourse goal that the speaker is pursuing in uttering the fragment and by interpreting the fragment relative to this discourse goal and the highlighted plan components. This pragmatics-based interpretation framework, limited to ten discourse goals, has also been implemented for the aforementioned university world model. Many of the examples presented in chapter 6 are from this implementation.

Current models of plan inference maintain several restrictive assumptions that limit their ability to handle naturally occurring dialogue. Chapter 7 examines research directed toward a more robust plan inference framework. It describes recent work by Pollack [Pol86b,Pol87b] which includes a new plan inference paradigm that treats plans as mental models and removes the assumption that the information seeker has no misconceptions about the domain. It then examines other recent research on models of plan recognition that can make generalized and default inferences and can handle less than ideal dialogues. Chapter 8 briefly explores other language problems, besides understanding pragmatically ill-formed input and intersentential elliptical fragments, that have been addressed by reasoning on a model of the user's plan, and highlights several important areas of current and future work.

2 Models of Plan Recognition

Suppose that you saw an empty car with a missing tire parked along a highway and half a mile down the road you came upon three young children led by a man carrying a baby and rolling a tire. It is quite likely that you would offer the five people a ride to the next service station and perhaps even offer to wait for their tire to be fixed and drive them back to the stranded car. But what motivated your behavior? In all likelihood you deduced that the stranded car belonged to the man, that he had a flat tire with no spare on hand, that he was taking the tire to be fixed so that he could return to the car and continue on his way, and that the children were following him because he was afraid to leave them unattended in the car. In so doing, you engaged in *plan recognition*, that is, you inferred a plan that you believed the man had constructed in order to achieve his goal of getting to his destination.

Thus to some extent *plan recognition* is the inverse of *planning*. In planning, an agent attempts to formulate a sequence of actions that will achieve a goal; in plan recognition an agent attempts to reconstruct from the available evidence a plan that was previously constructed by another agent. Evidence includes both an agent's observed actions (including utterances) and expectations about his likely goals. This chapter discusses the roots of plan recognition work and describes several major research efforts. Chapter 7 then continues the presentation by examining research directed toward removing the restrictive assumptions of these first-generation models of plan inference.

2.1 Plans and Plan Recognition

2.1.1 Planning versus Plan Recognition

Both planning and plan recognition are mental phenomena and produce cognitive structures. According to Pollack [Pol86a], a plan represents an agent's beliefs and intentions about achieving a goal, but it need not be correct, and the agent need not actually execute it. The agent must believe that each action in the plan is essential to the plan's success, that each action is executable, and that executing the plan will achieve the goal for which the plan was developed [Pol86a]. Similarly, a *recognized plan* represents the recognizing agent's beliefs about the plan constructed by the planning agent. Since these are different agents, their knowledge and beliefs need not be the same, and the plan constructed by the planning agent may not be the plan that the recognizing agent would have constructed in the same circumstances. The recognizing agent may believe that the planning agent has included unnecessary actions in his plan, that not all of the actions are executable, that the plan is an inefficient or ineffective means of achieving the planning agent's goal, or that the plan will have disastrous side effects [JWW84]. In addition, since the recognizing agent is not free in inferring the planning agent's plan to construct any plan she wishes but instead must attempt to get inside the planning agent's mind, the recognizing agent's model of the planning agent's plan may be wrong.[1]

For these reasons, plan recognition is an even more difficult task than planning. Yet people appear to do such processing and even expect machines to do it. Cohen, Allen, and Perrault [CPA81] undertook a study of users interacting with an actual question-answering system (PLANES [Wal78]) and an expert simulating an ideal version of the system. They demonstrated that "users expect more than just answers to isolated questions. They expect to engage in a conversation whose coherence is manifested in the interdependence of their often unstated plans and goals with those of the system" ([CPA81] page 245). To achieve this expected behavior, it is necessary for a system to recognize and reason about the goals and plans motivating its human users.

2.1.2 Kinds of Plans

There are several different kinds of plans that appear to play a role in communication. The first kind of plan is constructed to achieve some domain goal, such as vacationing in Hawaii, earning a college degree, or repairing a broken appliance. I will call such plans *task-related plans.* As illustrated in the example of the man with a flat tire, recognizing an agent's task-related plan is useful in generating cooperative, helpful responses [AP80].

Agents often need help in constructing their task-related plans, and they often get this help by engaging in an information-seeking dialogue with another person. An important feature of different kinds of information-seeking dialogues is whether the task-related plan is being executed during the course of the dialogue or whether the dialogue is being used to construct a plan for future execution. Apprentice-expert dialogues, in which an apprentice seeks advice from an expert while performing a task, exemplify situations in which task execution and the information-seeking dialogue are closely connected. On the other hand, a large percentage of interactions with database management systems,

---

[1] As stated by Pollack, "inferring another agent's plan means figuring out what actions he *has in mind*" ([Pol86b] page 208).

decision support systems, and expert systems are typical of situations in which the task is not being performed during the system's interaction with the user. For example, in consulting a travel agent, an information seeker is often formulating a plan for taking a future vacation. In this kind of dialogue the information seeker's queries are not tightly constrained by the order of execution of the steps of the underlying task, as in apprentice-expert dialogues.

In attempting to formulate a task-related plan, an agent can construct and execute a metaplan for developing his task-related plan. I will call this second kind of plan a *plan-construction* or *problem-solving metaplan* [Ram89a]. For example, in planning how to satisfy a humanities requirement for a college degree, an agent might decide to fully investigate a plan for taking one particular course before moving on to investigate a plan for taking a different course, or he might choose to investigate the two plans in parallel. At the end of chapter 6, I will argue that recognizing an information seeker's plan-construction metaplan is necessary in interpreting elliptical fragments.

A third kind of plan is the *discourse* or *communicative plan* that an agent constructs and executes with the goal that the resulting utterance have some intended effect on his listener. We will see that recognizing an agent's communicative goals plays a central role in understanding natural language; in particular, it is crucial in understanding indirect speech acts and interpreting elliptical fragments.

2.1.3   The Plan-Recognition Context

Pollack [Pol86a] differentiates plan recognition situations according to the influence the planning agent exerts on the plan inference process. She notes that the planning agent can be *actively uncooperative*, *passive* (or passively uncooperative in Pollack's terms), or *actively cooperative*. An actively uncooperative planning agent will try to thwart the recognizing agent's inference of his plan, as a businessman might attempt to do in adversarial negotiations. A passive planning agent will be unconcerned about whether his plan is recognized, and an actively cooperative planning agent will intend for the recognizing agent to recognize his plan from his actions.

Cohen, Allen, and Perrault distinguished between these latter two plan recognition contexts [CPA81]. They equated a passive situation with unobtrusively observing an agent through a keyhole and referred to plan inference in passive and actively cooperative contexts as *keyhole recognition* and *intended recognition* respectively.   Although keyhole recognition is useful in generating unsolicited advice, intended recognition is essential in communicative situations [CPA81], since the listener must identify the intended meaning of a speaker's utterance.

Plan recognition has dealt almost exclusively with passive and actively cooperative interactions, and recent research has concentrated more heavily on actively cooperative situations than on passive ones. There appear to be several reasons for this:

- It is difficult to obtain and analyze transcripts of naturally occurring interactions in which an agent is actively uncooperative. Few people will admit that they were being deliberately deceptive, and one must be certain that actions identified as attempts to thwart plan inference were intended as such and were not merely instances of accidental miscommunication.

- Plan recognition should be easier if the planning agent is not trying to thwart the inference process, and even easier if the planning agent intends the recognizing agent to infer his plan [CPA81,Pol86a]. In the latter case the planning agent's actions will be planned with the recognizing agent's task in mind. When the planning agent decides to perform an action, he will have reasoned about the recognizing agent's knowledge and beliefs and how the recognizing agent will interpret his action and will have selected an action that he believes will enable the recognizing agent to accurately infer his plan.

- There are more useful applications involving cooperative and passive agents than uncooperative ones. Expert consulting and tutoring are two examples of actively cooperative interaction. Plan inference systems for these domains have addressed such problems as generating helpful responses [AP80], recognizing and responding to ill-formed plans [Pol86b], and generating useful definitions [SC88]. Help systems are an example of passive situations in which the user is merely observed and unsolicited advice is provided. Implemented systems have generated suggestions intended to help the user of an operating system accomplish his inferred goals [Fin83] and have provided helpful advice in an office environment [CLM84].

- Plan inference in actively cooperative situations (intended recognition) provides insight into communication and the use of language. Systems employing intended recognition have addressed such various language problems as understanding indirect speech acts [PA80], understanding pragmatically ill-formed input [Car87a, Car87b] handling clarification subdialogues [LA87], and interpreting ellipsis [AP80,Lit86b,Car89b].

Although a few research efforts have modeled plan recognition in adversarial settings, such as naval warfare [AFFH86,AFH89], the published results indicate that these models do not yet account for attempts by a planning agent to confuse the recognizing agent and prevent recognition of the planning agent's intended plans and goals.

2.2   Roots in Other Disciplines

Plan recognition research has built on work in other areas, most notably planning, philosophy of language and meaning, and focusing. The representations used in models of plan recognition are based on those developed for robot planning and problem solving. In addition, recent work has used concepts (like metaplans) that have been successfully applied in planning systems. Many philosophers have been interested in communication, and the work of Austin [Aus62], Grice [Gri57,Gri69,Gri75a], and Searle [Sea70,Sea75] has had a major impact on intended plan recognition. Austin proposed that language be viewed as action and defined *speech acts*, or actions performed with an utterance. Grice investigated the relationship between utterances and meaning and claimed that the meaning of an utterance is the effect that a speaker intends the utterance to have on the listener by virtue of the listener's recognition of that intent [Gri57,Gri69]. Searle postulated conditions for successfully executing one kind of speech act, the illocutionary act, and claimed that identifying the meaning of an indirect speech act requires inferences by the hearer that use knowledge of speech acts, principles of cooperative conversation, and background knowledge shared with the speaker.

Research on intended recognition has adopted this view of language, action, and meaning. It has represented utterances as the realization of planned actions, the speech acts. Building on the representational formalisms and plan construction strategies developed for planning systems, it has attempted to develop computational processes that model the reasoning necessary to recognize that part of the speaker's plan containing the executed speech act and so thereby to deduce the speaker's intentions.

To incrementally construct a speaker's task-related plan from multiple utterances, plan recognition systems must identify the intended relation-

ship of a new utterance to the existing dialogue context. To develop such
process models, researchers drew on earlier work on focusing in task dialogues [Gro77a,Rob81], focusing in anaphora resolution [Sid83a], and
focusing in language generation [McK83]. Building on the hypothesis
that speaker and hearer must maintain the same focus of attention in
the dialogue in order to avoid miscommunication [Gro81], researchers
developed focusing heuristics that ordered expectations about shifts in
the speaker's focus of attention within the plan structure. Since these
expectations are mutually known, one can intend a listener to recognize
such shifts when they occur and to correctly identify the relationship of a
new utterance to the partial plan inferred from the preceding utterances.

The next sections present the important developments in each of these
three areas, emphasizing their impact on plan recognition research in
natural language systems.

2.3 Basic Plan Recognition

Research in plan recognition has been strongly influenced by ideas developed in the context of planning systems. This section describes early
planning systems whose impact can be seen in subsequent models of
plan inference. It informally illustrates how a planning system might
construct a plan containing a speech act and presents the planning/plan-
recognition formalism of Cohen, Allen, and Perrault for generating and
recognizing speaker plans.

2.3.1 Planning Systems

Early models of planning   Several formalisms have been proposed
for modeling how actions can change the world. One of the classic approaches is the situation calculus introduced by McCarthy and Hayes
[MH69]. A situation can be viewed as a time period during which the
world remains unchanged, and it is described by a set of predicate calculus well-formed formulas, or wffs. McCarthy and Hayes regarded actions
as functions that transformed the world from one situation to another,
and each action was modeled by a set of implications. The left side of
each implication was a conjunction of atomic formulas specifying conditions that had to be satisfied in the situation existing at the time the
action was executed; the right side of each implication was a conjunction of atomic formulas specifying characteristics of the world in the new
state resulting from execution of the action. Thus the situation calculus
could be viewed as a discrete temporal model in which the situations

formed the discrete points at which the world was modeled and in which transitions between situations occurred instantaneously.

Green [Gre69] proposed a planning system that used formal deduction strategies (in his case, resolution theorem proving) to construct plans using a situation calculus. Each formula contained a state variable indicating a particular situation in which that formula was true. The initial state was represented as a set of wffs describing all relevant characteristics of the world. The goal state was represented as a set of wffs with an existentially quantified state variable. Actions were represented by formulas describing world conditions under which an action could be performed and also describing how executing the action would transform the world from one situation to another. Resolution theorem proving was used to deduce a contradiction from the negation of the goal state and in the process to generate the sequence of actions that would transform the initial state into the goal state.

A major problem with the situation calculus is that one must formulate not only an assertion indicating changes to the world upon execution of each action but also assertions specifying all world characteristics that remain unchanged. This has been termed the *frame problem*, and it is a severe impediment to planning systems based on theorem proving. The need to develop a planner unencumbered by the frame problem, along with a desire to build a robot problem solver that could solve problems requiring complex world models, was a major motivation behind the work on STRIPS [FN71].

STRIPS was a radically different *state-space approach to planning*, and its influence can be seen in most subsequent research on planning and plan recognition. In a state-space approach, a problem is represented by descriptions of an *initial state*, a desired *goal state*, and a *set of operators* that transform one state into another. The planner must search for a sequence of operators that transform the initial state into a goal state. The identified sequence of operators represents a plan for solving the problem.

STRIPS represented the initial and goal states by sets of wffs. Operators were associated with primitive actions that could be performed if certain preconditions were satisfied. Operators were modeled by listing the preconditions of their action as wffs and by specifying how execution of the action associated with the operator would change the world. This was accomplished by an add list of atomic formulas that would necessarily become true upon executing the action and a delete list of atomic formulas that would necessarily become false. The frame problem was addressed by assuming that existing world characteristics not affected by the add and delete lists remained unchanged. Below is illustrated a

typical block-world STRIPS operator for putting one block on another
block.

Put-on(_x, _y)
Preconditions:
    Holding(_x)
    Clear(_y)
Add list:
    On(_x, _y)
    Hand-empty
Delete list:
    Holding(_x)
    Clear(_y)

STRIPS built on the *means-end analysis* used in an early general
problem-solving system called GPS [EN69]. GPS computed a set of differences between the state of the world associated with a partial solution
to a problem and the goal state, and it directed its search for a solution
by considering operators that reduced these differences. STRIPS used
a similar approach. In many cases the differences could be computed in
STRIPS as the set of propositions that held in the goal state but not in
the state associated with the partial solution. However, since some goal
propositions might be implied by the propositions in the state associated with the partial solution (in which case the planner need not plan
to accomplish them) or by propositions in the add list of operators (in
which case satisfying the latter propositions would result in satisfying
the goal propositions), STRIPS used a more sophisticated approach. It
attempted by means of resolution theorem proving to prove the goal
propositions from the world state associated with a partial solution, and
it used the clauses in the unsuccessful proof as differences that had to
be eliminated.

STRIPS matched the difference propositions against the add lists of
the operators to determine which actions might bring these characteristics into existence. If the preconditions of a selected action were not
currently satisfied, the same process was recursively used to plan actions
that would bring about a world state in which the preconditions were
true. Once an operator with satisfied preconditions was selected, the
recursive planning process terminated, and the sequence of generated
actions could be entered into a partial plan. The world state resulting
from executing these actions was then computed, and the planner attempted to remove any remaining differences between the current world
state and the goal state.

A partial plan can be viewed as an initial state, a goal state, and a
sequence of operators whose associated action sequence can be applied to
some world, called the *source world*, and will transform it into a second

world, called the *object world*. A STRIPS-type planner is thus really searching through a space of partial plans, terminating when it finds one in which the source and object worlds are the initial state and goal state respectively.

Hierarchical and nonlinear planning   Although STRIPS investigated only a fraction of the nodes in the space of partial plans, it still considered many sequences of actions that failed to produce a solution. This was because it attempted to fill in details of subparts of a plan before generating an overall plan that would be a solution to the problem, and it committed itself very early in the planning process to the ordering of actions in the final plan. The first deficiency resulted from the STRIPS control structure. Selection of an operator caused the planner to immediately begin devising plans for satisfying the operator's preconditions. Consequently, STRIPS constructed a fully detailed plan for reaching a world state in which the relevant operator could be applied *before* it ascertained that the operator was part of a complete plan for solving the problem in question. This process was equivalent to planning a vacation by first planning the details of getting to the airport. The effort expended on these details will be wasted if the complete plan eventually involves driving rather than flying.

The second deficiency resulted from the fact that even partial plans produced by STRIPS were fully linearized. The order of actions in a plan was based on the order in which operators were selected to reduce differences during the planning process, with the exception that action sequences generated to achieve preconditions of a selected action were positioned immediately preceding the selected action. Occasionally an operator selected to reduce a difference between the current state and the goal state would also have the undesirable effect of undoing the positive changes achieved by operators applied earlier or would be inapplicable because of changes to the world induced by earlier operators. To use an example from Sacerdoti [Sac77], if one wants to paint both a ceiling and a ladder, painting either one reduces the difference between the initial state and the goal state, but a successful plan for painting both the ceiling and the ladder entails painting the ceiling first. Consequently, much of STRIPS's backtracking was caused by premature ordering of actions in the plan.

Sacerdoti addressed these problems in successive planning systems: ABSTRIPS [Sac74] and NOAH [Sac75,Sac77]. In ABSTRIPS he introduced the notion of a hierarchy of abstraction spaces. An abstraction space was a representation of a domain and problem that ignored details unimportant at that level of abstraction. ABSTRIPS planned a solution in the highest, or most general, abstraction space, then expanded the details of the solution at successively lower levels of abstraction. Thus a plan whose details were being attended to was guaranteed to represent a solution to the original problem if the details could be successfully worked out. If the details at a particular abstraction level could not be worked out, the planner could still backtrack to a higher level, propose an alternative plan at that more general level of abstraction, and then attempt to work out its details.

Since ABSTRIPS's efficiency was highly dependent on its ability to propose skeletal plans whose details could be successfully filled in at lower levels of abstraction, it also modified the STRIPS evaluation function. STRIPS chose an action for inclusion in the partial plan solely on the basis of how much the operator associated with the action reduced the difference between the current state and the goal. No consideration was given to how difficult it would be to get to a world state in which the operator could be applied, that is, how difficult it would be to satisfy the preconditions of the operator. Since for ABSTRIPS these preconditions represented details that needed to be filled in, its evaluation function took into account both an estimate of the difficulty in reaching a goal state after application of an operator (based on how much the operator reduced the difference between the current state and the goal state) and an estimate of the difficulty in reaching a state in which the operator could be applied (based on how difficult satisfying the operator's preconditions was likely to be).

The ABSTRIPS representation scheme enabled each abstraction space to use the same world model. This was accomplished by assigning criticality values to each literal in the preconditions of an operator and allowing the planner to examine only those literals whose criticality values were equal to or greater than the level of abstraction at which the planning was being done. Thus requirements that should be treated as details at a particular abstraction level had lower criticality values and were effectively hidden from view. At each level of abstraction the skeletal plan was expanded in detail by constructing skeletal plans for satisfying preconditions visible at that level of abstraction. Below is a typical ABSTRIPS operator for a travel domain. Criticality values precede each precondition.

Take-bus-trip($\_$x, $\_$y)
Preconditions:
    4:At($\_$x)
    ($\exists$ $\_$z)[5:Is-bus($\_$z) $\wedge$ 5:Origin($\_$z, $\_$x) $\wedge$ 5:Destination($\_$z, $\_$y)]
    2:Have-ticket($\_$x, $\_$y)
Add list:
    At($\_$y)

(a) Travel-west and Dry-clothes

Figure 2.1
A NOAH plan network. (*a*) Initial plan. (*b*) Refinement of initial plan.

Delete list:
  At($\_x$)
  Have-ticket($\_x$, $\_y$)

Sacerdoti noted that though actions in a plan are executed linearly one after another, a mental plan is nonlinear, as it contains many sets of actions with no relative ordering. He hypothesized that a planner would be more powerful if it constructed nonlinear plans, ordering the actions only when necessary to prevent conflict or enhance efficiency. The result was NOAH [Sac75,Sac77], a *hierarchical nonlinear planning system.*

NOAH's representation of actions included add and delete lists specifying the results of successfully executing an action at its level of abstraction and procedural knowledge expressing how an action could be broken down into a partially ordered set of more primitive actions. Thus NOAH introduced the idea of action decomposition; that is, it considered an action as consisting of a *body* of more primitive goals and actions. As with ABSTRIPS, NOAH expanded a plan at successively more detailed levels of abstraction. It did this by replacing actions in a plan with the bodies of their operators and using the add and delete lists to update the world model to reflect the result of execution at this more detailed level of abstraction. But whenever possible NOAH generated parallel actions. For example, if refinement of an action in a plan specified that two conceptually independent actions be performed (such as clearing the tops of two blocks), then they were positioned parallel to one another in the expanded plan. The end result was a plan represented as a partially ordered network of actions. Figure 2.1a illustrates an initial plan for traveling west and drying one's clothes if one is on the east side of a river and one's only resources are an old wooden raft, a paddle, and some matches. Figure 2.1b gives a refinement of the plan in which the conjunctive goal has been split into two independent parallel actions and each of these actions has been expanded into a set of more detailed actions.

Constructive critics analyzed the expanded plan after each refinement, and proposed sequencing some actions and instantiating certain variables. The critics were constructive in that they placed further constraints on the plan instead of debugging an already constrained plan. Critics might suggest linearizing part of a plan to resolve conflicts among actions or to remove redundant actions, or they might suggest replacing a variable with an existing plan object to improve efficiency. For example, figure 2.2a presents a further refinement of the plan network shown in figure 2.1b. The actions Chop-raft and Ride-raft-across-river in figure 2.2a potentially conflict because once one chops up the raft for firewood, one no longer has it to ride across the river. Therefore, a NOAH critic would detect that the effect of Chop-raft negates a precondition of Ride-raft-across-river and propose restructuring the plan so that the raft is ridden across the river before it is cut up for firewood. The revised plan is shown in figure 2.2b. Further analysis by critics would detect that the raft could not be carried west and suggest restructuring the plan in figure 2.2b so that Walk-westward followed the Chop-raft, Set-raft-afire, Dry-clothes-by-fire sequence.

STRIPS-type operators, hierarchical abstraction, and nonlinear planning have been used in many subsequent planning systems. In later sections we will see how they have influenced plan recognition, particularly the representation of actions and the structure of the inferred plan.

2.3.2   Planning in Language Generation

Grosz [Gro79] illustrated that a single utterance may be intended to accomplish goals of several different types, including task-related goals, communicative goals, and social goals. One approach taken in modeling the generation of natural language utterances has been to hypothesize that utterances are formulated and executed as part of a plan to accomplish an agent's goals. This was the approach suggested by Bruce [Bru86], who viewed utterances as a kind of social action, an action that took into account and affected such mental attitudes as belief and intention. Other researchers have pursued this paradigm. For example, Hobbs and Evans [HE80] postulated a plan-based model of conversation, and Appelt [App82,App85] developed a model for planning natural language referring expressions.

If one adopts the view that utterances are actions, it is reasonable to attempt to model them by using STRIPS-type operators. In addition, if one adopts a plan-based approach to language generation, then

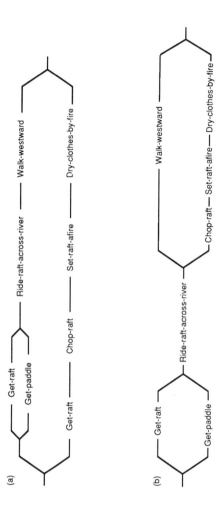

Figure 2.2
NOAH plan networks. (*a*) Further refinement of plan. (*b*) A plan constrained by critics.

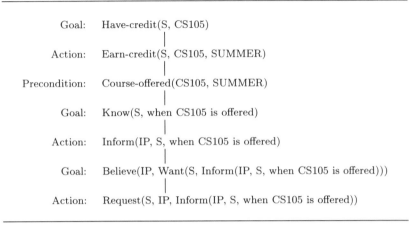

Figure 2.3
A sample plan including a request

one might model the generation of such utterances by using planning techniques developed in work on robot planning and problem solving. This approach, based on Searle's formulation of speech acts [Sea70], was taken by Cohen [CP79] and Allen [All79].

To see how an utterance might be entered into a plan, consider a student who has a goal of having credit for CS105, an introductory computer science course. One way of accomplishing this goal is to take it during the summer. Therefore, this action could be entered into the student's partial plan, and next the student might consider making certain that the action's preconditions are satisfied. One precondition is that CS105 be offered during the summer. So the student might adopt the goal of knowing which semesters CS105 can be taken in, which in turn could be accomplished by someone telling the student this information. Under certain conditions an agent can get another person to give him information by making the other person believe that the agent wants him to so inform him, and this reasoning might lead the student to enter a request action into his plan.

This partial plan is depicted in figure 2.3. It contains both goals to be accomplished and actions to be performed. Note that some of the actions have the student (S) as the agent of the action, whereas others have an information provider (IP) as the agent. This illustrates a partial plan some of whose constituent actions are executed before the plan is complete and in fact oftentimes *must* be executed before the plan can be completed. For example, the information that the student hopes to obtain by executing the request will enable him to determine whether to alter the plan or continue expanding it. For example, if CS105 is not offered during the summer, the student will need either to change the semester during which CS105 is taken or to replace taking CS105 with a different action (for example, earning credit by exam). In addition, there may be other preconditions to taking CS105 that have not yet been considered.

2.3.3   The Planning/Plan-Recognition Formalism of Cohen, Allen, and Perrault

Phil Cohen and James Allen, students of Ray Perrault, developed a plan-based approach to the generation and recognition of speech acts that has influenced all subsequent research in the area. Cohen formulated a planning system for modeling the possible intentions leading to the execution of a speech act [CP79]. Allen built on the foundations laid by Cohen. He extended Cohen's planning formalism and definition of speech acts in terms of STRIPS operators, inverted Cohen's plan-construction rules to produce inference rules for recognizing plans, added a control mechanism for guiding the search through the space of possible plans, and, most important, addressed the problem of recognizing the intentions that a speaker intends to convey in making a particular utterance [AP80,PA80].

Allen used an extension of the STRIPS and NOAH formalisms to represent operators associated with actions. Each operator (actually an operator schema) consisted of a *header* with constraints (called applicability conditions) on instantiation of its parameters, a set of *preconditions* for execution of the associated action, a *body* containing actions to be performed or goals to be achieved, and an *effect list* of propositions representing changes to the world resulting from execution of the action. The preconditions corresponded with preconditions on the original STRIPS operators, and the effects replaced the STRIPS add and delete lists. As in NOAH, with the addition of operator bodies hierarchical abstraction was possible, since higher-level actions could be decomposed and planned for in increasingly greater detail; however, little use was made of this ability in Allen's system.

Allen's *plan-construction inference rules* were intended to model the inferences that could be made about how a planning agent might expand an incompletely specified plan. In STRIPS the only two such inferences were the following:

1. If the planning agent has a goal of achieving proposition P and the operator associated with action A has P on its effect list, then the planning agent might insert action A into his plan.

2. If the planning agent wants to perform an action A for which proposition P is a precondition, then the planning agent might insert a goal of achieving P into his plan.

The first accounts for planning an action that achieves a desired goal, and the second accounts for planning to satisfy the preconditions of a selected action by treating them as new goals to be achieved. In NOAH a third inference was possible, one that accounted for planning to perform an action by performing its refinement:

3. If the planning agent wants an action A performed, then he might insert into his plan the body of the operator associated with A; that is, he might want the actions performed and the goals achieved that are in the body of A.

In Allen's system the planning agent could plan for other agents to execute actions. In addition, not all of the knowledge accessible to the planning agent was given in the operator descriptions and propositions describing the world: the planning agent could obtain additional information by asking another agent to provide it. Consequently, Allen's system contained additional plan-construction inference rules [AP80]. The first group of such rules, applicable to planning actions in general, included the following:

4. If the planning agent wants an action performed for which he is not the agent, then he might include in his plan a goal of getting the agent of the action to desire the action.

5. If the planning agent wants another agent to have a goal of achieving a proposition P, then the planning agent might include in his plan a goal of getting the other agent to believe that the planning agent wants the proposition achieved.

These two rules enable planning for other agents to perform actions. The first concerns the intentionality of actions: if one wants another agent to perform an action, then it is necessary to cause him to want the action. The second was based on an assumption of cooperativeness underlying the dialogues studied by Allen: if one agent wanted another agent to have a goal, then it was necessary only to cause the second agent to believe that the first agent desired the goal for the second cooperative agent to adopt it also.

The second group of plan-construction inference rules enabled the planning agent to plan to acquire information needed to determine where his plan should be further expanded or to identify the referents of descriptive terms:

6. If the planning agent has a goal of achieving a proposition P, then the planning agent might include in his plan a goal of knowing whether P (or $\neg P$) is currently satisfied.

7. If the planning agent has a goal of achieving a proposition P and P contains a descriptive term T, then the planning agent might include in his plan a goal of knowing the referent of T.

Both of these inference rules assume that the planning agent does not already know the desired information.

In addition, one more rule was necessary to model how a planning agent might plan for someone else to plan:

8. If the planning agent wants another agent to want W_1 and the planning agent believes that the other agent's wanting W_2 would lead him to want W_1, then the planning agent might include in his plan a goal that the other agent want W_2.

For example, if P is a precondition of an action A, then wanting A will lead an agent to want P. Therefore, if a planning agent wants another agent to want P, the planning agent need only plan for the other agent to want A, and the other agent by his own planning will want P. The planning agent can apply this rule to his other inference rules and plan to accomplish his own goals by causing another agent to have desires that cause the other agent to plan.

With these inference rules one can model how a planner *might* plan to achieve a particular goal. As noted by Allen, these are only *plausible* inferences. They model how the planner might proceed but say nothing about what the planner actually does. This is why I have used *might* in stating each of the rules.

From evidence of a user's plan, such as knowledge about an action in the plan, one should be able to invert the plan-construction rules and reason about the possible plans that might have led to execution of the action. This inversion process was used by Allen to produce a set of *plan-deduction inference rules:*[2]

1. If the planning agent wants an action and proposition P is an effect of the action, then he might want P.

2. If the planning agent has a goal of achieving a proposition P that is a precondition of an action A, then the planning agent might want A.

3. If the planning agent wants a constituent of the body of an action A, then the planning agent might want the action A.

4. If the planning agent wants another person to want an action for which the other person is the agent, then the planning agent wants the action.

5. If the planning agent wants another agent to believe that the planning agent has the goal of achieving proposition P, then the planning agent might want the other person to have a goal of achieving proposition P.

6. (a) If the planning agent wants to know if a proposition P is true, then the planning agent might want P to be satisfied.

   (b) If the planning agent wants to know if a proposition P is true, then the planning agent might want $\neg P$ to be satisfied.

7. If the planning agent wants to know the referent of a descriptive term T, then the planning agent might want to satisfy a proposition P that contains the term T.

8. If the planning agent wants another agent to want W_2 and the planning agent believes that the other agent's wanting W_2 would lead him to want W_1, then the planning agent might want him to want W_1.

Each of these is the inverse of the corresponding rule in the set of plan-construction inference rules. Note that rule 6 is broken into two plausible inferences. As Allen points out, a person may want to know if a proposition P is true when he in fact wants P to be false, as illustrated by the query "Have I been found guilty?"

---

[2]Recall that the plans under consideration, as illustrated in figure 2.3, need not be completely specified, since it may be necessary to execute an action in the plan in order to decide how to expand it further.

2.3.4   The Plan-Deduction Process

In deducing a planning agent's plan, the recognizing agent should use all of the available evidence. Part of this evidence consists of the action or sequence of actions that the planning agent is observed executing. The other part consists of any knowledge that limits the goals that the planning agent might be trying to achieve. Allen's system assumed a limited domain in which the planning agent's goals were severely restricted. The setting in his implementation was that of an information agent in a train station, and it was assumed that the planning agent's goal was either to meet or to board a train.

Allen's model of plan recognition combined backward chaining from the limited goals that an agent might pursue and forward chaining from the single action that the agent was observed performing. A partial plan consisted of two parts: (1) a possible goal and the portion of a plan constructed from it by means of plan-construction rules, called an *expectation*, and (2) an observed action and the portion of a plan deduced from it by means of the plan-deduction rules, called an *alternative*. At the start of the plan recognition process, N partial plans were constructed by pairing each of the N possible goals with the single observed action. But once the chaining process was begun, the partial plans were expanded, and a partial plan could generate copies of itself if mutually exclusive lines of inference were possible. For example, if the alternative of a partial plan indicated that the planner wanted to know if proposition P was true, then it might be the case that the planner wanted P to be true or that the planner wanted $\neg P$ to be true. The partial plan whose alternative motivated the inferences would be copied, and each of the two inferences would be used to expand one of the plans.

Chaining terminated when the alternative and expectation of a partial plan merged sufficiently into a single connected plan, which was taken to be the plan whose partial execution produced the observed action. In reality, Allen's system appears to have made relatively little use of backward chaining from expectations and instead relied primarily on forward chaining from the alternative. But this is really not surprising, since the initial alternative, which consisted of an observed action, was better specified than the initial expectation, which consisted of a parameterized possible goal, and the deductions that could be made in a forward direction were generally more limited than the inferences that could be made in a backward direction.

Allen's model of plan recognition searched through a space of partial plans for the plan motivating the agent's observed action. If one views a partial plan as a node in the search space, the rating assigned to a partial plan estimates the likelihood that further inferencing on it will eventually lead to the observed agent's plan. The control heuristics directing this search consisted of heuristics applicable to plan recognition in general and also heuristics appropriate for intended plan recognition.

The first set of control heuristics for general plan recognition assumed rational behavior by the planning agent. Partial plans representing irrational behavior had their ratings decreased. These included partial plans that contained an executing action with a false precondition or an action whose effect would already be true when the action was performed. Such plans represent irrational behavior because an agent would not normally try to execute an action that was doomed to fail because its preconditions were not satisfied or that would produce a result of no consequence.

Other heuristics increased the ratings of partial plans whose expectations and alternatives appeared to be moving toward well-specified plans. For example, the rating of a partial plan was increased if object descriptions in its expectation and alternative were unifiable or if application of an inference rule expanded the expectation or alternative.

Allen used the concept of nonlinear planning developed in the NOAH system. His partial plans were directed graphs of propositions, actions, and plan bodies, with the arcs specifying the relationships between nodes as inferred from the plan-construction and plan-deduction rules. For example, enable arcs might link several propositions to an action, thereby specifying that the propositions must be satisfied before the action is executed but not specifying an order for achieving the propositions themselves. Thus a planning agent's plan could be recognized without knowing the exact sequence in which the planning agent intended to carry out all of the plan's constituent actions.

We have not yet addressed an important aspect of Allen's model of plan recognition: the recognition of speaker intention. The system as currently described models keyhole recognition, but not intended recognition. A description of the remainder of Allen's model must be preceded by a discussion of philosophical work on meaning, intention, and speech acts.

2.4   Roots in Philosophy

I have said that a plan-based approach to language understanding treats utterances as actions executed as part of a plan for accomplishing a goal. In communicative situations the listener must identify the *intended meaning* of a speaker's utterance [CPA81]. Allen claimed that this could be accomplished by recognizing the goals and plans that a speaker intends to convey with an utterance [PA80]. This strategy of treating utterances as actions and equating the meaning of an utterance with the goals and plans that the agent intends to convey is based on work in philosophy, most notably that of Austin, Grice, and Searle.

Austin's historic work [Aus62] led to utterances being viewed as actions. Austin noted that some utterances, instead of representing a statement that could be evaluated as true or false, actually constituted, or were at least an integral part of, performing an action. He called such utterances *performatives*. For example, consider the utterances "I appoint you chairman" and "I bet you $10 that my team will win the tournament." Although one can argue about whether the named action of appointing or betting is successfully carried out, the utterances cannot be said to be true or false statements.

In investigating performatives and the actions that they accomplish, Austin found that other requirements besides merely uttering the appropriate words often had to be met before an action could be said to have been performed. He claimed that there must be an accepted procedure for performing the action, that the procedure must include making the utterance, that the appropriate participants must correctly and completely carry out the procedure under the appropriate circumstances, and that the participants must have the requisite thoughts, feelings, intentions, and subsequent conduct. For example, uttering "I appoint you chairman" cannot be said to be an appointment unless the speaker has the power to make such appointments. Similarly, uttering "I bet you $10 that my team will win the tournament" does not constitute a bet unless the bet is accepted by the other party. Austin claimed that these requirements were not unique to actions performed by means of utterances but in fact were shared by actions in general. For example, one can silently bet at a blackjack table in a casino by merely placing an appropriate sum of money at the appropriate spot on the table and proceeding to play the cards dealt. However, if one is not seated in a chair designated for players, then placing a sum of money on the table would not constitute betting, since the criterion of an appropriate circumstance is not met.

Austin tried to distinguish performatives from other utterances. He eventually concluded that all utterances, even statements that could be evaluated as true or false, constituted actions, which he called *speech acts*. He claimed that there are three distinct ways in which making an utterance constitutes performing an action. In making an utterance, one performs a *locutionary act* of uttering something, an *illocutionary act* in intentionally doing something by means of the utterance, and often a *perlocutionary act* as a result of the consequences of the utterance. For example, uttering "The eye of the hurricane is expected to pass over us" constitutes not only the locutionary act of speaking the words but also the illocutionary act of warning if that is the speaker's intention. Austin referred to the function of the utterance, in this case a warning, as its *illocutionary force*. Other examples of illocutionary force include a request, a promise, and an order. In addition to the locutionary and illocutionary acts of speaking and warning, the above utterance might also constitute the perlocutionary act of scaring if the utterance had that effect on the listener. Austin claimed that although the speaker determines his locutionary and illocutionary acts, the perlocutionary act performed by making an utterance is beyond the speaker's control.

Actions can fail, and merely performing a locutionary act does not necessarily accomplish the intended illocutionary act. For the latter to succeed, the listener must recognize the meaning of the utterance and its function. Therefore, it is necessary to distinguish between actually performing a speech act and unsuccessfully attempting to perform one.

If utterances are viewed as actions, it is reasonable to expect that the meaning of an utterance should have something to do with the action being performed. The work of Grice [Gri57,Gri69] took the first step in this direction by associating meaning with recognition of the speaker's intention, that is, with recognition of what the speaker is trying to do with the utterance. Searle [Sea70,Sea75] expanded on this by providing the groundwork for explicating how this recognition of intention takes place.

Grice [Gri57] claimed that the meaning of an utterance on a particular occasion is the effect that the speaker intends to produce in the hearer by virtue of the hearer's recognition of that intent. So the meaning of the utterance "The eye of the hurricane is expected to pass over us" might be different if uttered by a speaker hurriedly attempting to vacate a beach house or if uttered by a speaker safely ensconced in an underground concrete shelter, since the intentions communicated by the speaker will differ in the two situations.

However, it is unclear whether Grice was equating *effect* with the *illocutionary* or *perlocutionary effect* of an utterance. Searle [Sea70] argues convincingly that meaning must be related to illocutionary effect. According to Searle, many utterances have no associated perlocutionary act yet do have meaning.[3] In addition, perlocutionary effects cannot be achieved by means of recognition of the speaker's intention since they are beyond the speaker's control.

Searle [Sea70] set out to explain how an utterance could be recognized as performing a particular illocutionary act. He claimed that communicating via language was a form of *rule-governed behavior* and that illocutionary acts could be specified by a set of necessary and sufficient conditions for their successful performance. These conditions consisted of the following:

Input-output conditions: conditions representative of communication under normal circumstances, such as the requirement that speaker and hearer are both fluent in the language

Propositional content conditions: required features of the proposition contained in the utterance. For example, a warning must predicate a future situation or event, and a promise must predicate a future act of the speaker.

Preparatory conditions: conditions that must hold before the act can be performed. For example, a preparatory condition for a promise is that the speaker believes that the hearer wants him to do the predicated action, whereas a preparatory condition for a warning is that the speaker believes the predicated event will adversely affect the hearer.

Sincerity conditions: conditions on genuine and honest performance of the action. For example, the sincerity condition for a promise is that the speaker plans to do the predicated action.

Essential conditions: conditions expressing how the speaker intends the utterance to be taken. For example, the essential condition for a promise is that it count as placing the speaker under an obligation to perform the predicated action, and the essential condition for a warning is that it count as an attempt to let the hearer know that the predicated event may have adverse consequences.

In addition, Searle included two additional unnamed conditions that state that the speaker intends to bring about the essential condition by means of the hearer's recognition of that intent and that an utterance is an instance of a particular illocutionary act if and only if all of the above-mentioned conditions of the act are satisfied.

In his early work [Sea70], Searle postulated the existence of *illocutionary-force-indicating devices* that convey what illocutionary act

---

[3]Searle gives the example of greeting someone by saying "Hello."

an utterance constitutes. These devices include such features as punctuation and verb mood as well as explicit performative verbs. Searle derived a set of rules, corresponding to the conditions on illocutionary acts, that specify when one of the force indicators for a particular illocutionary act can be used.

In his later work [Sea75] Searle amended this treatment and associated illocutionary-force-indicating devices only with the literal interpretation of an utterance. He argued that an utterance could have both a literal and an indirect illocutionary force, that the indirect force might be primary and the literal force only secondary, and that a primary illocutionary act does not rely on deficiencies in the secondary act associated with the literal interpretation. He contended that an explanation of the meaning of an indirect speech act must be based on inferring done by the hearer using knowledge of speech acts, principles of cooperative conversation [Gri75a], and background knowledge shared with the speaker. Searle presented an example suggesting how this inferencing is done, but Allen was the first to devise a computational strategy for recognizing the intended illocutionary force of an utterance.

2.5   Recognition of Intention

As described so far, Allen's model of plan recognition performs keyhole recognition but does not address recognition of speaker intention. Intended plan recognition is the recognition of the plan that the agent intends to convey by his observed action. Beliefs of the form "RA Believes PA Wants X" are insufficient for intended plan recognition, since they fail to capture what the planning agent (PA) intends the recognizing agent (RA) to believe that the planning agent wants. Therefore, intended plan recognition must work with beliefs of the form "RA Believes (PA Wants [RA Believes (PA Wants X)])"

Allen's model of plan recognition accommodated reasoning with nested beliefs by including an inference rule of the following form:

> If the recognizing agent and planning agent share the knowledge that the recognizing agent's belief that the planning agent wants X will allow the recognizing agent to infer that the planning agent wants Y, then from a belief that the planning agent wants the recognizing agent to believe that the planning agent wants X, the recognizing agent can infer that the planning agent wants it to believe that the planning agent wants Y.

For example, suppose that Jim and Mary share the knowledge that from a belief that Jim wants the car moved, Mary can infer that Jim wants her to move the car. Then if Mary believes that Jim wants her to believe that he wants the car moved, Mary can infer that Jim wants her to believe that he wants her to move the car. Consequently, intended plan recognition is modeled with inferences based on shared beliefs; one cannot believe that an agent intends that an inference in his plan be recognized unless one believes that both participants believe they share the knowledge on which the inference is based.

Allen's process model also included two control heuristics related to recognizing user intentions. The first assigned ratings to partial plans on the basis of how deeply the inferences producing the plans were nested within beliefs, so as to prefer those inferences that attributed intention to the planning agent. The second was concerned with the ambiguity of multiple possible inferences from a single partial plan. If two or more mutually exclusive inferences could be made from a nested belief about a planning agent's wants, the planning agent could not realistically expect an observer to be able to decide which inference the planning agent intended to be made. Therefore, each of the n new partial plans resulting from application of one of n mutually exclusive inferences was assigned a rating that was $1/n$ of the rating of the original partial plan.

To identify the meaning or illocutionary force of an utterance, a plan recognition system must work with speech acts. Cohen [CP79] represented speech acts as operators in a planning system. Many of Searle's conditions on speech acts were formalized as preconditions on the operators. Others, such as the condition of being not obvious, which Searle included as a general preparatory condition of speech acts, are features of actions in general and are naturally satisfied as part of the planning process. For example, since a rule of rational planning is that one does not plan to perform an action of no consequence, one would not incorporate into a plan a request for someone to perform an action if it is obvious that the person will perform the action in the absence of the request (if the request action is of no consequence).

Allen distinguished between two kinds of speech acts. Surface speech acts were associated with the mood of the sentence and represented the starting point for the plan deduction process. He defined two surface speech acts:

S.Inform(_speaker, _hearer, _prop)
Effects: Believes(_hearer, Wants[_speaker, Know(_hearer, _prop)])

S.Request(_speaker, _hearer, _action)
Effects: Believes(_hearer, Wants[_speaker, _action])

Indicative mood utterances were translated into inform speech acts. Imperative and interrogative utterances were translated into request speech acts; for interrogatives, the requested action was an inform.

Illocutionary acts comprised the second kind of speech acts. These included the following:

Inform(_speaker, _hearer, _prop)
Preconditions: _prop ∧ Believes(_speaker, _prop)
Plan body: Believes(_hearer, Wants[_speaker, Know(_hearer, _prop)])
Effects: Know(_hearer, _prop)

Request(_speaker, _hearer, _action)
Plan body: Believes(_hearer, Wants[_speaker, _action])
Effects: Wants(_hearer, _action)

Inform and Request were inadequate for modeling requests for information. A request for the referent of a description must be modeled as a request that the hearer perform an inform action. But when the request is made, the speaker does not know the referent that the hearer will provide and therefore cannot define the requisite inform act. Similarly, when a speaker requests that a hearer inform him about whether a proposition is true, the speaker does not know which of the propositions P or $\neg P$ is the one whose truth will be conveyed. Consequently, two other versions of informing, Informref and Informif, were included and used for modeling requests for information.

Informif(_speaker, _hearer, _prop)
Preconditions: Knowif(_speaker, _prop)
Plan body: Believes(_hearer, Wants[_speaker, Knowif(_hearer, _prop)])
Effects: Knowif(_hearer, _prop)

Informref(_speaker, _hearer, _term)
Preconditions: Knowref(_speaker, _term)
Plan body: Believes(_hearer, Wants[_speaker, Knowref(_hearer, _term)])
Effects: Knowref(_hearer, _term)

In these speech act definitions, "Knowref(_speaker, _term)" means that the speaker knows the referent of the term and "Knowif(_speaker, _prop)" means that the speaker knows if the proposition _prop is satisfied.

As an example of how a surface request is modeled using these speech act definitions, consider the utterance "Can you teach CS180?" It is a request that the hearer inform the speaker whether the hearer can do the specified teaching and is translated into the following surface speech act:

S.Request(SPEAKER, HEARER, Informif[HEARER, SPEAKER,
        Cando(HEARER, Teach[HEARER, CS180])])

In this representation scheme, surface requests and surface informings have no preconditions or bodies, since they are primitive actions that are realized with utterances. Note the correspondence between the body of an illocutionary act of requesting or informing and the effect of a surface request or a surface informing. Since the body of the illocutionary act matches the effect of the surface act, Allen's representation captures the notion that the simplest way of performing the former is to execute the latter.

Allen's formulation of an illocutionary request relies on the cooperative nature of the dialogues he was modeling: it assumes that if the hearer believes that the speaker wants an action for which the hearer is the agent, the hearer will adopt that action as one of his own wants. Note also that the effect of Allen's illocutionary inform depends on the hearer deciding to believe the communicated proposition—a condition that the speaker can try and bring about but does not control. Although Allen argued that the intent being conveyed is that the hearer believe the proposition, this use of a perlocutionary effect in the representation of an illocutionary act is problematic.

In Allen's scheme, understanding the meaning of an utterance consists of identifying the surface speech act that the speaker intends to be recognized from his utterance and identifying, by making the inferences intended by the speaker, the illocutionary act(s) whose effects the speaker intended the listener to recognize as effects he wanted to achieve. Thus Allen's model was a computational strategy that captured both Grice's theory of meaning by equating understanding with recognition of speaker intent and Searle's view of how the illocutionary force of an indirect speech act could be identified by making inferences based on shared knowledge. It also incorporated Searle's view of language as rule-governed behavior in two ways. First, it used syntactic analysis of the utterance to identify the communicated surface speech act. Second, it captured Searle's conditions for speech acts either in its representation of speech act operators or as conditions satisfied during the planning process.

Hire-band(_agent, _band, _event)
Plan body: Sign-contract(_agent, booking-agent(_band), _band, _event)
Effects: Band-hired(_agent, _band, _event)

Figure 2.4
Domain operator for hiring a band for an event

As an example of how Allen's system recognizes intention, consider
the action of hiring a band, whose operator is given in figure 2.4, and
the utterance "Can you tell me if you know who is the booking agent
for the Sixties Band?" Several interpretations are possible. The most
direct takes the utterance at face value and results in an answer of yes
or no according to whether the hearer is capable of telling the speaker
about his knowledge. The most indirect interpretation interprets the
utterance as an actual request for the identity of the booking agent.
Midway between the two is an interpretation as a yes-no question about
whether the hearer knows who the booking agent is.

Let us examine the details of how these interpretations are derived.
Analysis of the utterance translates it into a surface request speech act
and produces the following hearer belief:

Believes(HEARER, Wants[SPEAKER,
  S.Request(SPEAKER, HEARER, Informif[HEARER, SPEAKER,
    Cando(HEARER, Informif[HEARER, SPEAKER,
      Knowref(HEARER, the booking agent for the Sixties Band)])])])

Here Knowref(HEARER, the booking agent for the Sixties Band) means
that the hearer knows the referent whose description is "the booking agent for the Sixties Band" and will be abbreviated "Knowref(H,
booking-agent)," with hearer and speaker abbreviated H and S respectively. If we assume that the domain is very constrained so that all
queries will be motivated by a desire to hire a band for an event, then
the domain goal of hiring a band forms the expectation in each partial
plan. Figure 2.5 illustrates an inference path from the surface speech act
shown at the bottom of the figure to the domain goal of hiring a band
shown at the top. This sequence of inferences leads to the most indirect
interpretation of the utterance. Much of the inferencing in this example
is done within such nested beliefs as the following:

Believes(H, Wants[S, Believes(H, Wants[S, ...])])

This attributes to S the intention that H recognize the indicated wants. In particular, the line preceded by a single asterisk in figure 2.5 was deduced by making inferences within nested beliefs. Consequently, it is identified as a want that S intended H to recognize from the utterance: that H identify for S the booking agent for the Sixties Band. Therefore, the utterance is recognized as a request that H tell S who the booking agent is for the Sixties Band, as indicated by the line preceded by two asterisks, which produces an indirect interpretation of the utterance.

On the other hand, taking a different line of inferencing from branch point 1 in figure 2.5 produces only a direct interpretation of the utterance, as shown in Figure 2.6. In this case the inferences within nested beliefs lead to a recognition that S intends H to believe that S wants H to tell S whether H is able to inform S about whether H knows the identity of the booking agent for the Sixties Band. This produces a direct interpretation of the utterance as a request that the hearer inform the speaker whether the hearer is able to tell the speaker whether the hearer knows who the booking agent is for the Sixties Band, which is indicated by the line preceded by two asterisks.

The middle interpretation, as a yes-no question about whether the hearer knows the identity of the booking agent for the Sixties Band, results from following the inference path leading to the indirect interpretation from branch point 1 in figure 2.5 but taking a different inference path from branch point 2. From the belief

Believes(H, Wants[S, Believes(H, Wants[S,
        Informif(H, S, Knowref[H, booking-agent])])])

one can infer

Believes(H, Wants[S,
        Request(S, H, Informif[H, S, Knowref(H, booking-agent)])]).

This produces an interpretation as a request that the hearer inform the speaker as to whether she knows the identity of the booking agent for the Sixties Band. The same top-level goal of hiring a band is eventually inferred in all three cases, but since the inferencing is not done within nested beliefs, the intention that the hearer recognize this goal is not attributed to the speaker.

Allen uses helpful behavior to account for the fact that the hearer may tell the speaker who the booking agent is even if the hearer interprets the utterance literally. Having inferred the speaker's goal of hiring a band, the cooperative hearer notes any obstacles that may hamper the speaker from achieving his goals and adopts for himself the goal of helping the

Believes(H, Wants[S, Hire-band(S, SIXTIESBAND, _event)])
     ↑ Infer that S may want an action whose body contains an
     | action that he wants.
Believes(H, Wants[S, Sign-contract(S, booking-agent(SIXTIESBAND), SIXTIESBAND, _event)])
     ↑ Infer that S may want a proposition containing a term
     | whose referent he wants to know.
Believes(H, Wants[S, Knowref(S, booking-agent)])
     ↑ Infer that S may want the effect of an action that he wants.
Believes(H, Wants[S, Informref(H, S, booking-agent)])
     ↑ Infer that S may want the action that he wants the agent
     | H of the action to want.
Believes(H, Wants[S, Wants(H, Informref[H, S, booking-agent])])
     ↑ Infer that S may want the effect of an action he wants.
**   Believes(H, Wants[S, Request(S, H, Informref[H, S, booking-agent])])
     ↑ Infer that S may want the action whose body contains a
     | proposition that he wants.
*   Believes(H, Wants[S, Believes(H, Wants[S, Informref(H, S, booking-agent)])])
     ↑ Within the nested beliefs, infer that S may want the action
     | whose precondition he wants satisfied.
Believes(H, Wants[S, Believes(H, Wants[S, Knowref(H, booking-agent)])])
     ↑ Within the nested beliefs, infer that S may want the propo-
     | sition whose truth value he is querying to be satisfied.
Believes(H, Wants[S, Believes(H, Wants[S, Knowif(S, Knowref[H, booking-agent])])])
     ↑ Within the nested beliefs, infer that S may want the effect
     | of an action that he wants.
Branch point 2
Believes(H, Wants[S, Believes(H, Wants[S, Informif(H, S, Knowref[H, booking-agent])])])
     ↑ Within the nested beliefs, infer that S may want an action
     | whose precondition he wants satisfied --- the cando precon-
     | dition is a general precondition on every action.
Believes(H, Wants[S, Believes(H, Wants[S, Cando(H, Informif[H, S, Knowref(H, booking-agent)])])])
     ↑ Within the nested beliefs, infer that S may want the
     | proposition whose truth value he is querying to be
     | satisfied.
Believes(H, Wants[S, Believes(H, Wants[S, Knowif(S, Cando[H, Informif(H, S, Knowref[H, booking-agent])])])])
     ↑ Within the nested beliefs, infer that S may want the effect
     | of the Informif action.
Branch point 1
Believes(H, Wants[S, Believes(H, Wants[S, Informif(H, S, Cando[H, Informif(H, S, Knowref[H, booking-agent])])])])
     ↑ Infer that S may want the effect of the surface request
     | speech act.
Believes(H, Wants[S, S.Request(S, H, Informif[H, S, Cando(H, Informif[H, S, Knowref(H, booking-agent)])])])

Figure 2.5
Inferences leading to an indirect interpretation of an utterance

speaker overcome these obstacles. In the case of obstacles arising from
lack of knowledge, such as not knowing the identity of the band's booking
agent, the cooperative, helpful hearer will provide this information to
the speaker. So in all three interpretations of the utterance, the hearer's
response may include the identity of the booking agent, but for different
reasons. Helpful behavior also explains why information providers often

Believes(H, Wants[S, Hire-band(S, SIXTIESBAND, _event)])
  Infer that S may want an action whose body contains an
  action that he wants.
Believes(H, Wants[S, Sign-contract(S, booking-agent(SIXTIESBAND), SIXTIESBAND, _event)])
  Infer that S may want a proposition containing a term
  whose referent he wants to know.
Believes(H, Wants[S, Knowref(S, booking-agent)])
  Infer that S may want the effect of an action that he wants.
Believes(H, Wants[S, Informref(H, S, booking-agent)])
  Infer that S may want an action whose precondition he
  wants satisfied.
Believes(H, Wants[S, Knowref(H, booking-agent)])
  Infer that S may want the proposition whose truth value
  he is querying to be satisfied.
Believes(H, Wants[S, Knowif(S, Knowref[H, booking-agent])])
  Infer that S may want the effect of an action that he wants.
Believes(H, Wants[S, Informif(H, S, Knowref[H, booking-agent])])
  Infer that S may want an action whose precondition he
  wants satisfied --- the cando precondition is a general
  precondition on all actions
Believes(H, Wants[S, Cando(H, Informif[H, S, Knowref(H, booking-agent)])])
  Infer that S may want the proposition whose truth value
  he is querying to be satisfied.
Believes(H, Wants[S, Knowif(S, Cando[H, Informif(H, S, Knowref[H, booking-agent)])])])
  Infer that S may want the effect of an action that he wants.
Believes(H, Wants[S, Informif(H, S, Cando[H, Informif(H, S, Knowref[H, booking-agent])])])
  Infer that S may want the action that he wants the agent
  H of the action to want.
Believes(H, Wants[S, Wants(H, Informif[H, S, Cando(H, Informif[H, S, Knowref(H, booking-agent)])])])
  Infer that S may want the effect of an action that he wants.
** Believes(H, Wants[S, Request(S, H, Informif[H, S, Cando(H, Informif(H, S, Knowref[H, booking-agent)])])])
  Infer that S may want the action whose body contains a
  proposition that he wants.
* Believes(H, Wants[S, Believes(H, Wants[S, Informif(H, S, Cando[H, Informif(H, S, Knowref[H, booking-agent])])])])
  Infer that S may want the effect of the surface request
  speech act.
Believes(H, Wants[S, S.Request(H, H, Informif[H, S, Cando(H, Informif(H, S, Knowref(H, booking-agent)])])])

Figure 2.6
Inferences leading to a literal interpretation of an utterance

produce more information than even an indirect interpretation of the
utterance would suggest.

Sidner [SI81,Sid83b,Sid85] contended that a system must differentiate
between the response intended by a speaker and extra helpful information that might be included in the response. According to Sidner,
the intended response should always be produced unless contradicted
by other factors (such as that the requested information is privileged
or that the system lacks the ability to respond as intended), whereas

extra helpful information may or may not be included, according to how appropriate it is to the speaker's current goal.

Sidner proposed a model for recognizing the response intended by a user, and she experimented with this model in a natural language interface to a graphics display system [SI81,Sid83b]. Her model included rules for interpreting indirect speech acts that were compilations of Allen's plan recognition strategies. These rules short cut the full inference chains constructed in Allen's system [CPA81] and mapped utterances to speaker beliefs and wants on the basis of how language is typically used in task-oriented situations. In addition, Sidner's rules took into account the user's beliefs about the system's capabilities. Since a rational agent will not request information about whether another agent can do something that it is mutually believed he is able to do and will not expect the agent to do something that it is mutually believed he is not able to do, certain interpretations can be eliminated from consideration. For example, consider the following two utterances: "I want to reserve tickets for the concert" and "I want to have dinner nearby before the concert." If the hearer is a ticket agent for a concert hall, he can be expected to handle ticket reservations for patrons and perhaps offer suggestions about local restaurants, but not to provide or arrange for preconcert dinners. Therefore, under these mutual beliefs about the hearer's capabilities, the first utterance can be understood as an indirect request that the ticket agent do whatever is necessary to reserve the tickets, whereas the second utterance might be interpreted as an indirect request for restaurant suggestions but not as a request that the ticket agent begin organizing the dinner. Although compiled rules were sufficient to identify intended meaning in the large majority of cases in Sidner's graphics domain, Allen contended that the full plan recognition strategy must be available for use when the default rules fail to produce an interpretation [CPA81].

2.6   Plan Recognition in Dialogue

Although Allen's plan inference system modeled recognition of an agent's plan from an agent's utterance and differentiated between keyhole and intended recognition, it was limited by its reliance on a very restricted domain of trains and its inability to handle dialogue. The train domain had only two domain goals (meeting a train and boarding a train), each of which could be accomplished by a few primitive steps, and Allen's system was primarily concerned with utterances that might occur at the outset of a dialogue. In more complex domains the information seeker's complete plan will consist of a hierarchy of domain subplans and subgoals that accomplish his overall domain goal. Such a complete plan is not immediately evident from a single utterance, and individual utterances must be related to one another to build the user's plan incrementally as the dialogue progresses.

Early work in dialogue understanding concentrated on apprentice-expert dialogues, during which an expert guided an apprentice in performing a task. Grosz [Gro77b,Gro81] formulated heuristics for recognizing shifts in focus of attention in the task structure and devised a strategy that used the knowledge currently focused on by the dialogue participants to identify the referents of definite noun phrases appearing in an utterance. This work, together with subsequent research on focusing [Rob81,Sid81,McK83,Car87a], provided the basis for extending Allen's work to incremental recognition of an agent's plan during a dialogue.

2.6.1 Focusing

Focusing is the process of concentrating one's attention to varying degrees on subsets of one's knowledge base [Gro81]. Since the knowledge bases of dialogue participants are huge, it is impossible for them to consider all of their knowledge when formulating or interpreting an utterance. For example, the speaker must be able to consider only a limited subset of knowledge in attempting to construct a description that he believes will be correctly understood by the listener. The listener must be able to reason on a limited subset of his knowledge in identifying the intended referents of descriptions used by the speaker. Thus focusing is essential for effective communication. However, focusing is dynamic in that the knowledge focused on by the participants changes during the course of the dialogue. Only if the participants follow one another's *focus shifts*, so that equivalent subsets of their knowledge bases are highlighted, can miscommunication be avoided [Gro81].

Grosz claimed that focus shifts could be suggested by linguistic clues, such as clue words and phrases (*but, incidentally, as I was saying*), and by nonlinguistic clues derived from how the entities under discussion are related to one another. Her focusing mechanism captured focus shifts indicated by nonlinguistic clues during apprentice-expert task dialogues. She noted that the structure of apprentice-expert dialogues closely resembles the structure of the task being performed. Grosz used the task structure to partition the knowledge base into focus spaces containing groups of entities and relationships and to relate focus spaces to one another.

One focus space was always *active* and contained those entities most relevant to the subtask that was the current focus of attention in the dialogue. Previously active focus spaces were designated as either *closed*, meaning that they were associated with subtasks that were now completed and that the entities in the focus spaces were no longer highlighted, or *open*, meaning that they were associated with a task whose performance included the subtask that was the current focus of attention in the dialogue. Open focus spaces formed a stack of focused entities to which attention might return when the subtask associated with the active focus space was completed. Since these focus spaces were associated with progressively more general tasks, they represented subsets of knowledge highlighted to lesser and lesser degrees as one moved deeper into the stack.

When an utterance indicated that a new subtask was being started, Grosz's focusing mechanism pushed the current active focus space onto the stack of open focus spaces and introduced a new active focus space associated with the new subtask. When a subtask was completed, its focus space was closed; at this point, either the top element of the stack of open focus spaces became active (modeling a move back to the more general task that the completed subtask was a part of) or a new active focus space was introduced (modeling a move to a subtask parallel to the completed subtask). For example, if the apprentice said that he was starting a new subtask, perhaps loosening screws as part of removing a wheel, then a new focus space, one associated with loosening screws, might be activated. The previous active focus space associated with removing the wheel became open but not active. Once the screws had been loosened and were being taken off, the focus space associated with loosening the screws was closed, and a new focus space associated with removing screws was activated.

Entities not explicitly mentioned in the dialogue could also be in focus because of their relationship to other currently focused items. These were said to be *implicitly focused*. For example, the screws holding a wheel onto its base were implicitly focused when the task of removing the wheel was in focus. Grosz differentiated between *explicitly* and *implicitly focused knowledge* because explicitly referring to implicitly focused entities could suggest a change in the active focus space, whereas referring to entities already explicitly focused would not.

Grosz's process model was the basis for a new strategy that emphasized relevance rather than recency in identifying the referents of descriptions by searching for the most relevant entity matching a given description instead of the most recently mentioned entity matching it. The amount of computation was limited by using the concept of focusing to identify a limited subset of the entities in the knowledge base as possible referents of the description and to order them for consideration. This was accomplished in two steps. In a network structure representing the description, those items that were constrained to be in focus, such as items referenced by definite noun phrases, were selected for matching first, since a smaller subset of the knowledge base needed to be considered and their successful match would limit the portion of the knowledge base analyzed in matching the remainder of the description. In the matching of the selected item, the active, open, and implicit focus spaces provided an ordering of the entities considered from the knowledge base.

Grosz's work provided the basis for tracking the focus of attention in a dialogue and for identifying the relationship of individual utterances to the task structure. Besides this global focusing that causes some subsets of entities in the knowledge base to be more relevant than others, the linguistic structure of an utterance can cause one focused item to be more salient than others. This more local kind of focusing has been called immediate focus [Gro81,Sid81]. In her work on resolving anaphoric references, Sidner formulated rules for identifying and tracking immediate focus [Sid81]. Robinson [Rob81] extended the focusing work of Grosz and Sidner in order to develop a process model for determining the referents of verb phrases in apprentice-expert dialogues, such as variants of *do* in the utterance "I've done it."

McKeown [McK83,McK85b,McK85a] extended the concept of focusing to the generation of coherent natural language text. She expanded on Sidner's focus rules to explain how speakers should choose among several potential topics of discussion. McKeown claimed that when faced with a choice of topic, a speaker should choose to move to a recently introduced topic if he has something further to say about it; otherwise the speaker must reintroduce the topic at a later time. Similarly, the speaker should choose to finish discussion of the current topic before switching back to a previous one.

2.6.2 Incremental Plan Inference

My research built on the plan recognition work of Allen and the focusing work of Grosz and McKeown to develop a strategy for incrementally building the underlying task-related plan motivating an informa-

tion seeker's queries in task dialogues more general than apprentice-
expert dialogues. I was interested in a class of information-seeking dialogues in which the information seeker is attempting to construct a plan
for a task that will be executed after the dialogue terminates. These
dialogues are representative of a large percentage of interactions with
database management systems, decision support systems, and expert
systems. Typical tasks include marketing a new product, purchasing a
home, or pursuing a degree at a university.

In apprentice-expert dialogues the overall task that the apprentice
is attempting to perform is known at the outset of the dialogue, and
the ordering of actions and subtasks in the plan being executed strongly
influences the dialogue between expert and apprentice. This differs from
the kind of information-seeking dialogue that I have investigated, in
which the information seeker is attempting to construct a plan for a task
that will be executed after the dialogue terminates. In such dialogues
the information seeker's utterances are not tightly constrained by the
order in which actions in the task will eventually be executed.

Two factors appear to provide a solution to the problem of identifying
how an utterance fits into an information seeker's domain plan. The
first is the organized nature of naturally occurring information-seeking
dialogues. Dialogue transcripts indicate that humans generally ask all
their questions that are relevant to a plan for one subgoal before moving
on to ask questions about a plan for another subgoal of the overall task.
One possible explanation for this behavior is that it may require less
mental effort than switching back and forth among partially constructed
plans for different subgoals.

The second factor producing structure in information-seeking dialogues is their cooperative nature. Since the dialogues are cooperative
and miscommunication can occur if both dialogue participants are not
focused on the same subset of knowledge [Gro81], the information seeker
is expected to shift topics slowly between consecutive utterances and to
adhere to the focusing constraints espoused by McKeown. On the basis of these expectations about possible shifts in focus of attention, I
formulated focusing heuristics that rank the possible relationships between (1) an utterance and (2) the existing dialogue context represented
by the plan inferred for the information seeker and his current focus of
attention in that plan. These focusing heuristics are the basis for my
strategy that assimilates individual utterances of an ongoing dialogue
and incrementally expands the system's model of the user's underlying
task-related plan. This plan recognition framework is presented in detail
in chapter 3.

Sidner also was concerned with incremental plan inference. She contended that a discourse consists of several discourse units, each of which conveys a single intended response and may consist of multiple utterances [Sid85]. She studied the role of clue words (words and phrases such as *now* and *by the way* that contain information about the structure of a discourse [Rei78a]) in helping a listener segment the discourse and identify the relationship of individual units to one another. Clue words have also been studied by Reichman [Rei78a] and Polanyi and Scha [PS83] in structuring conversations and Cohen [Coh84,Coh87] in argument understanding. Clearly, clue words are an important aid in understanding discourse, particularly when they suggest transitions or relationships different from those predicted by focusing heuristics. As we will see in the next section, Litman incorporated clue word processing into her system for plan recognition.

2.7   Recognizing Plan-Construction Plans

In addition to his domain goals, a planning agent involved in an information-seeking dialogue has two other kinds of goals: *plan-construction* or *problem-solving goals* that he is pursuing to further instantiate and construct his task-related plan, such as comparing the cost of alternative ways of achieving a subgoal, and *discourse* or *communicative goals*, such as answering a question or seeking clarification. The plan inference systems described so far do not adequately capture these different levels of planning activity. For example, in my own system, described in detail in chapter 3, the inferred plan consists only of domain goals inferred from user statements or requests for information. In Allen's model, speech acts and knowledge goals were entered into the inferred plan, so that it became a combination of domain goals, knowledge goals, and linguistic actions, with little distinction among them.

Wilensky [Wil78,Wil80,Wil81] argued that a plan inference system must reason not only about how actions achieve domain goals but also about how the selection and ordering of actions is influenced by such planning goals as minimizing the expenditure of resources. This requires recognizing the agent's plan for constructing his domain plan. Litman [LA84,Lit85,Lit86a,LA87] extended this concept of reasoning about higher-order goals to speech acts and communication. She developed a model of plan recognition that differentiated between a domain plan and an agent's currently executing plan for constructing it and captured the possible relationships between utterances and plan segments [LA87]. As a result her model was able to handle clarification and correction subdialogues. Ramshaw [Ram89a,Ram89b] subsequently extended Litman's work and developed an extensive model of the plan construction process. The next sections describe these efforts to recognize and model metalevel planning and reasoning.

Thus far I have used the term *plan* to refer to the overall plan constructed by the planning agent or information seeker and have used the term *operator* to refer to domain knowledge about how an action is performed. Since an operator describes what must be done to perform the action with which it is associated and therefore represents a possible abstract plan for performing that action, the term *plan* has often been used to refer both to the plan that the system has inferred and is attributing to an agent and to the operators in the system's plan library. This has some advantages, such as being able to use the common terminology of *metaplan* as opposed to *metaoperator* and being able to refer to the potential immediate motivation for an action as a *candidate plan* (chapter 3) instead of as a *candidate operator*. In the remainder of this book I will use *plan* to refer to either one as long as the intended meaning is clear from the context.

2.7.1   The Notion of Metaplans

Whereas first-level domain knowledge represents facts about a domain or rules for reasoning in the domain, *metaknowledge* represents similar knowledge about knowledge. Metaknowledge can take many different forms. Davis [Dav80] employed metarules that ordered applicable inference rules in a problem solver so that the rules most likely to produce decisive results were applied first. Stefik [Ste81] organized the MOLGEN system's planning knowledge into three distinct layers: a domain layer containing knowledge about actions that could be executed in a genetics laboratory, a design layer containing knowledge about how to develop a genetics experiment, and a strategy layer containing knowledge about strategies for constructing plans. The plan developed at the domain level contained the actions to be executed in the laboratory and was the result of performing the planning actions contained in the design-level plan. Similarly, the design-level plan was constructed by the strategy level using knowledge about planning strategies, such as the strategy of deferring decisions as long as possible or the strategy of invoking heuristics to make educated but imperfect guesses. Thus the two top layers, the design and strategy levels, contained planning and metaplanning knowledge respectively. The advantage of such a multilayer architecture is that it allows the full power of the system's reasoning mechanisms to be applied at each level of decision making [Ste81].

Wilensky [Wil80,Wil81] showed that it is necessary to represent and reason about *metaplans*, or plans about how to plan, in plan recognition as well as in planning. He argued that knowledge about the planning process should be encoded declaratively rather than being embedded in special problem-solving procedures such as the NOAH critics. Since plan recognition is the inverse of planning, the same kinds of knowledge are needed by both processes. If knowledge about the planning process is represented declaratively, as is knowledge about particular domain plans, the knowledge can be shared by both the planning and plan understanding mechanisms, and the system's extendibility will be enhanced [Wil81].

Wilensky was primarily interested in goal interactions, cases in which two or more of an agent's goals affect one another either positively or negatively [Wil78,Wil83]. One example of goal interaction is goal conflict, where actions to achieve one of the agent's goals will have a negative effect that thwarts another goal. Wilensky pointed out that an agent's observed action in such a case might be motivated by the goal of resolving conflicts between the domain goals. Recognizing the agent's plan would require recognizing not only the competing domain goals but also the metalevel goal of resolving conflicts between them and the plan for achieving this metagoal. Thus in such cases the plan recognition system would need access to planning knowledge. That is, not only would the system need domain knowledge such as the knowledge that taking a train is one way of getting to a desired destination but also planning knowledge such as the knowledge that performing an action that eliminates a negative effect of an action may resolve conflicts between the goal achieved by that action and another goal. Wilensky contended that if this planning knowledge were expressed declaratively, the same mechanism used to infer domain plans could be used to recognize the more complex plans motivating actions taken to achieve planning goals.

In Wilensky's planner and understander, general metathemes such as "Don't waste resources" and "Achieve as many goals as possible" were always present. In the case of planning, these metathemes detected particular situations that resulted in the creation of metagoals. For example, the metatheme of not wasting resources detected situations in which two goals overlapped and created the metagoal of combining the plans for the goals. This metagoal could be advanced by several metaplans, such as achieving the common subgoals first, integrating the two plans, or constructing a new plan that achieved both goals. The planner used the normal planning process to apply these metaplans and construct a detailed domain plan.

Wilensky proposed that in understanding or plan recognition, meta-goals and metathemes be used to explain an agent's observed actions. For example, if a planning agent were observed integrating the actions of two plans, this could be explained with the metagoal of combining the plans in order to avoid wasting resources, from which one could infer that the agent believed that the combined plan would be more efficient than the sequence of two individual plans. Similarly, if a planning agent did not appear to be integrating the actions of two apparently overlapping plans, one might infer that he did not believe that they overlapped or that he did not know how to combine them. For example, consider the following variation of one of Wilensky's example stories:[4]

> John wanted to buy himself a watch and get a present for Mary. Since the store was having a sale of two similar items for only $5 more than the price of one, it was crowded. John purchased a watch for himself and a purse for Mary.

The metatheme of not wasting resources would lead one to think that the character might want to purchase a watch as Mary's gift. To explain the character's actions in the story, one has to postulate either that Mary would not have liked a watch or that the character did not recognize his opportunity. Thus metagoals and metaplans contribute to understanding both situations in which characters pursue metagoals and situations in which they fail to pursue them.

One of the main advantages of representing metagoals and meta-plans declaratively is that the full power of the planning and plan-understanding processes can be used in constructing and recognizing complex plans. Wilensky's metagoals and metaplans were concerned with adjusting plans that had been constructed; Litman expanded on this notion to represent knowledge about constructing plans.

2.7.2   Recognizing Plan Construction Metaplans

To model the plans and goals of dialogue participants, Litman [Lit85, LA87] proposed using not only a library of domain-dependent task-related plans but also a set of domain-independent metaplans, which she referred to as *discourse plans*. Instead of representing how one might

---

[4]In Wilensky's story the character purchases a watch for Mary, thereby efficiently achieving both his goal of owning a watch and his goal of getting a gift for Mary.

achieve domain goals, such as boarding a train, these discourse metaplans represented how one might achieve goals pursued during a dialogue, such as correcting another plan. However, since her discourse
plans modeled how an agent could extend, continue, or modify the
plan being constructed during the dialogue, they were in many respects
metaplans for developing and executing the underlying task-related plan
rather than communicative plans with such goals as expressing surprise.
Therefore, to avoid confusion, I will refer to Litman's discourse plans as
plan-construction metaplans.

Litman's plan-construction metaplans fell into three categories: introduction (called topic shift by Litman), continuation, and modification
(called clarification by Litman).

Introduction
   Introduce-plan   Introduce a new plan for discussion.
   Modify-plan   Change the current plan to a similar one on a new topic.
Continuation
   Continue-plan   Execute next action in overall plan.
   Track-plan   Discuss next action in overall plan.
Modification
   Identify-parameter Identify a parameter in a plan.
   Correct-plan   Revise an incorrect plan.

The introduction category consisted of metaplans for introducing a new
plan as the topic of discussion (Introduce-plan) or changing the current
plan to a similar one (Modify-plan). Agents might pursue these plans
to initiate a dialogue, to begin a subdialogue, or to change to a totally
new topic of discussion. For example, an agent might introduce the
domain plan for taking a train trip by stating that he is going to buy
a ticket, then initiate a subdialogue by introducing a new domain plan
for purchasing a snack (which will be stacked above the plan for taking
a train trip), and then later resume discussion and construction of the
plan for taking a train trip (by popping the stack). Although Litman
characterized this class of plans as topic shifts, the example at the end of
this section, similar to one in [LA87], will use Introduce-plan to introduce
a metaplan to clarify the referent of a description. However, in this case
the introduced metaplan links by chaining to a plan that is already on
the stack rather than inserts a new domain plan onto the stack.

The second category of plan-construction metaplans, continuation,
consisted of plans for executing (Continue-plan) or discussing (Track-
plan) the next action in the agent's overall plan. Litman contended that

this class contained the plans that an agent was most expected to pursue at any point in a dialogue, since they represented an absence of problems and corresponded with the agent's pursuing the next actions in his plan. I will question the validity of this claim later.

The third category, modification, consisted of metaplans for either instantiating details in the plan (Identify-parameter) or revising an incorrect plan (Correct-plan). For example, an agent whose goal is to board a train might identify a parameter in his intended plan, such as the type of accommodation (reserved versus open seating), or might ask the information provider to identify a parameter, such as the departure gate of a train.

Except that they took plans as arguments, Litman's plan-construction metaplans had the same structure as domain plans. She divided preconditions into two classes. The first contained propositions that had to be satisfied before the plan could be executed but that could themselves be planned for. The second contained propositions called constraints that would be satisfied if the plan was reasonable in the given context. For example, suppose that an agent wants to vacation on a particular island. If the island has an airport and the agent has money for a ticket, then the agent can plan to fly there. But the requirements that the island have an airport and that the agent have money for a ticket are intuitively different. If the agent does not have enough money for a ticket, he can plan to satisfy this requirement, but if the island does not have an airport, it is unreasonable for the agent to arrange for an airport to be built on the island so that he can fly there for a vacation. Litman's constraints are similar to the applicability conditions that were independently added to the plans in my system's plan library (chapter 3), but she included constraints in both metaplans and domain plans and made greater use of them in plan recognition.

To illustrate the structure of plan-construction metaplans and the use of constraints in them, consider the second metaplan shown in figure 2.7. Its body and constraints indicate how the speaker can identify a parameter in an action in a plan, namely by giving a descriptive term satisfying a proposition (see the body of the plan), where the proposition specifies both the term and the parameter in the action in the plan (see the constraints in the plan).[5] The effects are that the hearer then has an adequate description of the parameter and that the action whose

---

[5]Note that Litman represents an inform action as Informref(_speaker, _hearer, _term, _prop), which says that the speaker informs the hearer of the identity of the term _term satisfying proposition _prop.

Introduce-plan(_speaker, _hearer, _action, _plan)
Constraints:
    Step(_action, _plan)
    Agent(_action, _hearer)
Plan body:
    Request(_speaker, _hearer, _action)
Effects:
    Want(_hearer, _plan)
    Next(_action, _plan)

Identify-parameter(_speaker, _hearer, _parameter, _action, _plan)
Constraints:
    Parameter(_parameter, _action)
    Step(_action, _plan)
    Parameter(_parameter, _proposition)
    Parameter(_term, _proposition)
    Want(_hearer, _plan)
Plan body:
    Informref(_speaker, _hearer, _term, _proposition)
Effects:
    Next(_action, _plan)
    Know-parameter(_hearer, _parameter, _action, _plan)

Figure 2.7
Two of Litman's plan-construction metaplans

parameter was identified is the next action that the agent is expected to address in subsequent dialogue.

Modeling discourse   Litman modeled discourse with a stack of domain plans and plan-construction metaplans. The stack actually consisted of a set of substacks, each of which contained a domain plan at the bottom and a plan-construction metaplan at the top, with each plan linked to the plan immediately beneath it in the substack (see figure 2.8). Each substack modeled a topic of discussion, with the domain plan at the bottom of the substack providing the domain topic and the chain of plan-construction metaplans at the top representing the plan pursued by the most recent utterance addressing this topic. Since plan-construction plans are metaplans, they took other plans as arguments, and this provided the link between each element of a substack and its immediate successor. The individual substacks were not linked to one another. Therefore, a stack consisting of several substacks represented a

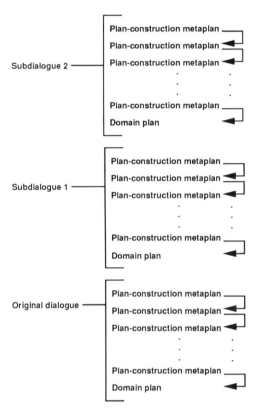

Figure 2.8
Plan stack

dialogue in which several subdïalogues had been initiated, each of which
was modeled by a substack.

Litman adhered to the stack paradigm in modeling discourse [Gro77a,
Rei84, PS83, Pol87a]. When the current topic was suspended and a new
topic introduced, a substack modeling the dialogue on the new topic
was pushed onto the plan stack. Similarly, when a topic was completed
and a previous topic resumed, the stack was popped until the substack
associated with the resumed topic resided at the top of the stack. Consequently, topic resumption in a dialogue had to correspond to the order of
substacks in the stack, and a topic that had been popped from the stack
could not be resumed but had to be reintroduced into the discourse. Although the stack paradigm is an ideal and violations of it can be found

in naturally occurring discourse, it does account for the structure of a large majority of dialogues.

Plan recognition   In Litman's model, plan recognition was influenced by the following:

- Heuristics on rational planning: domain-independent heuristics that eliminated unreasonable plans from consideration, such as plans whose effects were already satisfied

- Traditional plan chaining: recursive recognition of a sequence of plans in which the preconditions or plan body of each newly recognized plan contained an action or goal achieved by the previously recognized plan in the sequence

- Coherence heuristics: an ordering on the plan-construction metaplans according to how coherently each would represent a continuation of the dialogue

- Constraints encoded into plans in the plan library: limitations on domain plans that were reasonable to consider and the links that were allowable between plan-construction metaplans and other plans. These potential links provided a second means of chaining to recognize a sequence of plans.

The first two were adapted from Allen's model of plan recognition and extended so that they would work on both domain plans and metaplans.

Coherence heuristics ordered the plan-construction metaplans according to how coherently each would continue the current dialogue. This order was affected by clue words in the utterance being analyzed. For example, a clue phrase such as *by the way* suggested that plans in the introduction category, which could be used to shift topic, should be considered first. In the absence of clue words, first preference was given to plan-construction metaplans in the continuation category, second preference to those in the modification category, and third preference to those in the introduction category. Within each category, preference was given to the plan most predicted by the stack paradigm.

Litman presented several arguments for this ordering. She claimed that plans in the continuation category should be preferred, since they represented exactly what an agent was most expected to do barring any unforeseen problems, such as not being able to identify a domain plan parameter or not understanding the information provider's response. To some extent Allen's model of cooperative behavior supports Litman's contention. As mentioned in section 2.5, Allen's model accounted for helpful extra information included in a response. In his model the information provider recognized the agent's plan, identified any obstacles to the agent's executing that plan (including lack of knowledge of parameters in the plan), and constructed a response containing information intended to help the agent overcome those obstacles. Thus Allen's model might suggest that in a cooperative dialogue both participants should mutually believe that the information provider's response has removed all obstacles and that the strongest expectation is for the agent to continue with the topmost uncompleted plan on the plan stack. Unfortunately, this rests on the assumption that the information provider will know enough about the agent's actual knowledge to be able both to correctly identify the agent's obstacles in the plan *and* to provide, in a way that will need no further clarification, enough information to remove those obstacles. In many cases this assumption does not hold.

I contend that a speaker's question or response establishes an anticipated discourse goal for the other participant of accepting the question or response or, if it cannot yet be accepted (perhaps because it contains entities that the hearer cannot adequately identify), of working toward being able to accept it. A question or response can be explicitly accepted with a statement such as "I understand" or "Thank you," but most often acceptance is implicitly accomplished by failing to pursue discourse goals directed toward clarifying the utterance so that it could be accepted. Thus metaplans that clarify a question or response should be preferred over those that presume that the question has been understood or that the response has achieved its purpose. This will be further dealt with in the discussion of elliptical fragments in chapter 6.

Litman also used the principle of Occam's razor to argue for her coherence heuristics. Informally, this principle espouses choosing the simplest hypothesis. Litman's heuristics followed this principle by introducing the fewest new plans possible. On the other hand, focusing heuristics, the stack paradigm, and the always present realization that one's question or response may require clarification in order to achieve its goals argue that clarification of a question or response should be given preference over continuation plans.

Constraint satisfaction played several roles in Litman's plan inference system. First, it eliminated some plans from consideration because of context. For example, Litman's domain plan for taking a train trip included the constraint that the train one plans to travel on be the same as the train for which one is purchasing a ticket. Consequently, a request for a ticket for the 2:00 P.M. train to Windsor (train W4) would

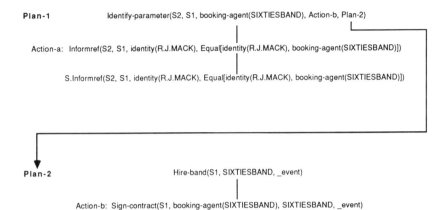

Figure 2.9
Plan stack after second utterance

eliminate from consideration plans to take a trip on any train other than W4. Second, constraint satisfaction introduced plans for consideration during plan recognition and established links between plan-construction metaplans and other plans on the plan stack. For example, once the system recognized that the information seeker wanted it to identify an entity, the constraints that the entity be a parameter of an action, that the action be a step in a plan, and that the information seeker want the plan caused appropriate plans to be introduced as possible objects of the Identify-parameter metaplan.

Clarification subdialogues As an example of how Litman's system handled clarification dialogues, consider the following set of three utterances:[6]

S1: Who is the booking agent for the Sixties Band?

S2: R. J. Mack.

S1: Who's R. J. Mack?

Figure 2.9 shows the plan stack immediately following S2's utterance. It consists of two plans: a plan-construction metaplan (Plan-1) and a domain plan (Plan-2). The Hire-band domain plan, shown in figure 2.4 (on page 44), was inserted into the plan stack as a result of S1's first utterance, since it contains an action whose parameter (the booking agent for the Sixties Band) S1 was requesting identification of. The top element of the plan stack indicates that S2's utterance is an attempt to provide

---

[6]This example is similar to one in [LA87].

the requested identification by means of an illocutionary inform speech act realized as a surface inform, and that the entity being identified is a parameter of an action in the Hire-band domain plan.

S1's second utterance initiates a clarification dialogue. It is translated into the following surface request:

S.Request(S1, S2, Informref[S2, S1, _term2,
      Equal(_term2, identity(R.J.MACK)])

Although coherence heuristics suggest that S1 is most expected to continue the current plan, chaining from the surface speech act does not produce a structure satisfying the required constraints. The second preference is for metaplans in the modification category. Since the body of the metaplan for introducing a plan shown in figure 2.7 contains a Request speech act and since one way to execute a Request speech act is to perform a surface request, chaining from the utterance leads to the inference that S1 might be introducing a plan.[7] The constraints on the Introduce-plan metaplan specify that the requested action be part of the plan being introduced. Since the requested action is an Informref speech act and the body of the Identify-parameter metaplan contains an Informref action, further chaining leads to the inference that the plan being introduced is an Identify-parameter metaplan where the parameter to be identified is identity(R.J.MACK). Finally, the constraints in the Identify-parameter metaplan specify that the entity being identified be a parameter of an action in yet another plan. In this case, chaining from Identify-parameter connects the recognized structure with the top element of the plan stack, Plan-1, representing the inference that S1 wants clarification of the term previously identified by S2. Since chaining from the surface speech act eventually led to an Identify-parameter metaplan that linked to a plan already on the stack, the second preference for metaplans in the modification category is satisfied. Figure 2.10 shows the resulting plan stack, in which the top three plans are plan-construction metaplans, the bottom plan is a domain plan, and each plan in the stack has the plan immediately beneath it as a parameter.

Thus we see that Litman's process model is an elegant strategy that coordinates recognition of two kinds of plans, domain plans and plans for constructing plans via a dialogue, into a unified framework. Since her metaplans can refer to other plans, Litman's system is able to model both clarification subdialogues in which a speaker's plan is to provide or obtain further identification of an entity that was already identified as

---

[7] Additional metaplans would be needed to capture other ways of introducing a plan, such as by stating that one is going to perform an action in the plan.

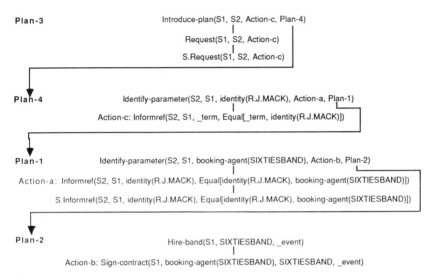

Figure 2.10
Plan stack after third utterance

part of a plan in the plan stack and correction subdialogues in which a speaker attempts to correct an existing plan.

2.7.3 A Rich Model of Problem-Solving Behavior

Expectations about potential speaker utterances play a major role in understanding ill-formed input. These expectations appear to be strongly influenced by beliefs about an information seeker's domain plan and his strategy for constructing it. In investigating the use of pragmatic knowledge in identifying and repairing alias errors (errors that evaded the layers of constraints intended to catch them, such as misspellings that produce lexically correct but unintended words), Ramshaw extended Litman's work to produce a rich model of an agent's plan-construction behavior [Ram89a,Ram89b].

In Litman's metaplan model the agent's domain plan resided at the bottom of the substack modeling a particular subdialogue, and since each metaplan referred to the plan immediately beneath it in the stack, only one metaplan referred to the domain plan. Ramshaw's model had a different structure. Each of the metaplans had a domain plan as argument, and the discourse model was a tree structure of metaplans referring to domain plans, with one path capturing the motivation for the current query. For example, a leaf node might represent a query that checked whether a precondition of a domain plan was satisfied or that explored the constraints on constructing a workable domain plan; the ancestors of the leaf node modeled the problem-solving steps that led to the observed query.

The metaplan tree shown in figure 2.11 models the behavior of an agent S trying to construct a detailed plan for hiring a band. S has investigated hiring the Jazz Band and, having found that plan unsatisfactory for some reason, is now investigating a plan for hiring the Sixties Band. This plan contains the subgoal of signing a contract with the constraint that the agent signing the contract be the booking agent for the Sixties Band. The right path of the metaplan tree indicates that S wants to construct a plan for achieving this subgoal and that the motivation for S's current query, represented by the leaf node, is to identify the fillers for the _agent variable that will satisfy the constraints on the Sign-contract plan.

Ramshaw's two main categories of problem-solving metaplans were plan-building metaplans and query metaplans. Metaplans in the plan-building category captured an agent's consideration and refinement of domain plans. In addition to metaplans (such as Build-subplan) that modeled an agent's selection of one domain plan from a class of plans for achieving the same goal, this category included metaplans (such as Instantiate-var and Add-boolean-constraint) that modeled an agent's refinement of a plan by specifying a particular instantiation of a variable or constraints on that instantiation.

Whereas the plan-building metaplans represented an agent's plan-construction intentions and normally had to be inferred by chaining from his observed actions, query metaplans correlated directly with observed utterances and captured an agent's attempts to obtain information that would help him decide how to further develop and refine his partially specified domain plan. A typical query metaplan was Ask-pred-value; it was executed by requesting the value of a variable that would satisfy a specified proposition (usually one that was a precondition of a domain plan under consideration). For example, the right leaf node in figure 2.11 correlates with a request for the booking agent of the Sixties Band, that is, with a request for the value of the variable _agent that is the same as the value of the function booking-agent(SIXTIESBAND). Other query metaplans correlated with queries that explored the possible instantiation of variables in domain plans under consideration or checked whether preconditions in those plans were satisfied.

To more fully capture the kinds of behavior exhibited in naturally occurring information-seeking dialogues, Ramshaw formulated two

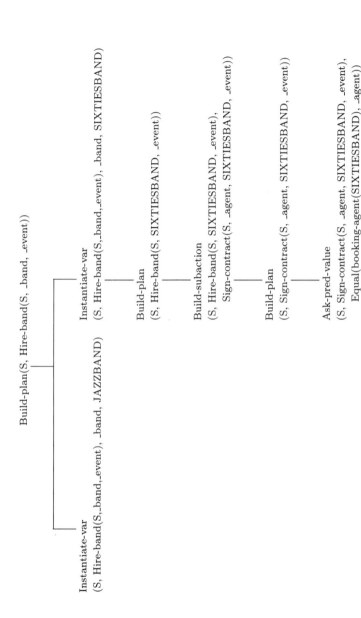

Figure 2.11
A sample metaplan context tree

other categories of metaplans. Inform metaplans were similar to query metaplans in that they correlated directly with utterances by the problem-solving agent. However, instead of capturing a planning agent's problem-solving behavior, inform metaplans captured his attempts to communicate it to the information provider. If one were to include problem-solving goals (such as constraints on how the agent was willing to develop his domain plan) among the goals that might be communicated to the information provider, it would seem that inform metaplans could represent a higher level of metaplans or meta-metaplans that operate on the problem-solving metaplan structure.

Ramshaw's fourth category of metaplans, evaluative metaplans, captured an agent's attempts to evaluate the goodness of a particular domain plan as opposed to its feasibility. In addition to metaplans that evaluate a single domain plan, Ramshaw proposed metaplans that would capture an agent's consideration and evaluation of several plans in parallel. For example, in constructing a plan for hiring a band, an agent might first check whether each of the bands under consideration was available on the date of the event and then compare the cost of each band and the kind of music each would provide before selecting one particular band and developing a complete plan for hiring it. Note that such evaluative metaplans captured a different kind of movement within the metaplan tree: instead of exploring the tree depth-first by finishing consideration and refinement of one subplan before starting to consider an alternative subplan, these evaluative metaplans captured a kind of breadth-first movement in which the planning agent's queries switch back and forth among several alternative plans for achieving a goal.

With each new user query a search was begun for the most coherent expansion of the existing metaplan tree that would include a leaf node for a query metaplan correlated with the new utterance. As in other plan inference systems, heuristics were used to control the search. The heuristics took the form of condition-action rules invoked when a new node was generated during the search process. The conditions specified for executing the action part of a rule encoded particular features of the problem-solving and domain contexts that might justify assigning or altering the rating for a node, and the action part carried out the scoring. These heuristics favored coherence by taking into account both the distance of a node from the focus of attention immediately preceding the new utterance and the pattern of exploration (depth-first exploration of a single plan versus parallel exploration of several plans) suggested by the agent's problem-solving metaplans as recognized from the preceding dialogue. In addition, the heuristics took into account beliefs about the planning agent's domain knowledge, such as whether the agent knew that the preconditions of a domain plan would fail for certain instantiations of variables and whether the agent would therefore be unlikely to consider those alternatives, and knowledge about which domain plans were statistically most likely to be selected by agents trying to achieve a particular goal.

Ramshaw's model of plan recognition captured much of the information about an agent's problem-solving strategy that is implicitly communicated during an information-seeking dialogue. Since the metaplan tree provided a rich model of the agent's domain and plan-construction plans and the control heuristics captured expectations about probable next moves in refining the plan, his framework was well-suited for suggesting and ranking potential matches of ill-formed utterances with queries motivated by the existing dialogue context.

2.8   A Brief Overview of Plan Recognition in Other Domains

Early work in text understanding suggested that world knowledge plays a major role in understanding. In an attempt to capture some of this knowledge, Schank and Abelson designed a representation for stereotypical events called scripts [SA75]. The best known of these was the restaurant script, which encoded knowledge about stereotypical behavior in a restaurant. The notion behind scripts was that actions in a story invoke expectations based on knowledge about the world and that these expectations can be used to assimilate and understand subsequent actions. For example, if one is told that a man has just eaten a meal in a restaurant and has put $2 on the table, one is likely to infer that the $2 is a tip, since leaving a tip on the table after a meal is typical restaurant behavior. Scripts enabled text-understanding systems to invoke the appropriate expectations and perform the reasoning necessary to understand actions in stereotypical situations.

However, scripts captured only stereotypical behavior and stories generally contain unanticipated events and actions. Schank and Abelson suggested that knowledge about goals, plans for accomplishing goals, and actions comprising plans could be used to relate a character's actions in a story and to postulate an explanation for them, which would thereby constitute *understanding* the events in the story [SA75,SA77]. This view led to Wilensky's explanation-based model of story understanding [Wil78]. His domain knowledge included not only operators associated with actions but also *themes*, such as self-preservation, that accounted for certain universally accepted domain goals. For example, the self-preservation theme would account for the domain goal of protecting oneself. Wilensky's system performed a kind of incremental plan recognition in that a character's newly observed action was *understood* and *explained* by chaining from the action to either a previously inferred goal that was now part of the system's model of the story or to a general theme. However, since Wilensky's system relied on a breadth-first search for an inference chain that could serve as an explanation, it could only handle short action sequences. Even in story understanding, focusing heuristics are needed to recognize the role that a character's action plays in achieving his goals.

As described in section 2.7.1, Wilensky extended the notion of explanation-based understanding and contended that to understand a story, one must recognize not only a character's domain plan but also his reasons for constructing this plan in preference to another. This was particularly important in explaining a character's actions when two or more of the character's goals interacted with one another either positively or negatively. Bruce and Newman took this notion of goal interaction even further. They showed how a character's goals and actions might be predicated on the presumed goals and anticipated actions of other agents and argued that story understanding requires the inference of complex interacting plans of multiple agents [BN78].

Plan recognition is also important in tutoring and consultation systems. To effectively tutor a student, one must recognize misconceptions leading to the student's erroneous solutions. This often requires identifying and evaluating the student's plan for solving the problem. Similarly, in order to provide advice to a system user, a consultant must identify the plan that the user constructed for accomplishing his task and analyze it for errors and inefficiencies.

One of the first attempts at plan recognition had as its goal an automated consultant for MACSYMA, an interactive system for computer algebra [Gen79,Gen82]. In finding the root of an equation or the integral of an expression, there are often many ways to solve the problem. Furthermore, an incorrect solution may result from substeps that are individually correct but whose relationship to one another is incorrect; that is, step S_i may not produce the input needed for step S_{i+1} [Gen82]. Thus, reconstructing the user's plan based on his asserted goal, his observed actions, and his unexpected results was essential if the MACSYMA consultant was to provide useful advice.

The MACSYMA Advisor assumed that a known set of planning methods was employed by the user to construct a plan for solving his problem but that incorrect beliefs about expressions (such as whether they were fully expanded) or about MACSYMA actions (such as whether the operator Coeff required that its argument be a fully expanded expression) might lead to a faulty plan. Planning methods were associated with goals and were represented as procedural nets, as in NOAH [Sac75,Sac77], with applicability conditions, effects, and a procedural definition for generating a sequence of actions and subgoals for achieving the goal of the method. Thus Genesereth's planning methods corresponded to operators in other planning systems. Both actions and planning methods had input and output objects representing the data to be operated on by the action or the plan generated by the method and the data that would be produced. For example, input to the Expand action was an expression, and the output produced was another expression in expanded form.

Similar to Allen's expansion of partial plans by making inferences from both the expected goal and the observed utterance (expectation and alternative), plan recognition in the MACSYMA Advisor combined top-down plan prediction from the user's expected goal with bottom-up inferencing from the user's observed actions to construct plausible user plans that accounted for the current situation. The bottom-up inferencing chained from observed actions to possible planning methods that might have proposed those actions, to subgoals suggested by expansion of the expectation. In addition, the input and output for the observed actions was propagated backward through the plan to develop constraints on the input and output variables associated with the planning methods. By comparing the user's inferred plan with the procedural definitions of the planning methods used in the plan, the system could identify some user beliefs that produced the plan. For example, if a planning method generated a subgoal whenever certain conditions were not satisfied and the subgoal's associated planning methods would have generated additional actions that were not executed by the user, the system could infer from the absence of these additional actions that the user believed that all the original conditions were satisfied. Unfortunately, the system generally could not infer what the user believed these conditions to be. As a result, it used somewhat ad hoc methods to propose possible user beliefs about these conditions. In addition, the system used a library of buggy plans to capture common user misconceptions. Nonetheless, Genesereth's was the first plan recognition system to try to account for the fact that the user might have some erroneous beliefs that could affect the plan he constructed. But note that Genesereth assumed that

the user's planning methods were correct and that only his beliefs about
such things as the expressions he was operating on or the MACSYMA
operators he was using might be wrong. In chapter 7 we will see how
Pollack developed a model of plan recognition that separates user beliefs
from system beliefs and provides an elegant mechanism for recognizing
and reasoning about invalid plans.

As research on intelligent tutoring systems and computer consultants
progresses and more complex problem situations are attacked, recognition of the student's problem-solving plan will become more and more
important. An example of recent work in this area is modeling student
problem solving in the domain of algebraic manipulation of rational
numbers [VD87].

With all this emphasis on plan recognition by computer systems, the
question that naturally arises is, Do humans perform plan recognition
when they interact with other humans? As noted in chapter 1, many
examples of humor appear to be based on the failure of one person to
infer the plans and goals of other agents and respond accordingly. This
suggests that in many situations people are expected to perform plan
inference.

Cohen, Allen, and Perrault performed two studies designed to shed
insight on user expectations of system behavior [CPA81]. In the first
study, users interacted with PLANES [Wal78], a natural language system for database access, and in the second study with an ideal version
of PLANES in which a human played the role of the machine and more
intelligent responses could be provided. These experiments showed that
users of question-answering systems "expect the system to infer and respond to their apparent but unstated goals" ([CPA81] page 247). Since
it seems unlikely that users would expect machines to respond more in-
telligently than humans, these studies suggest that humans expect other
humans to infer unstated goals during a conversation.

The most compelling evidence that humans infer the plans and goals
of other agents is a study by Schmidt, Sridharan, and Goodson [SSG78]
of how people interpret action sequences. Subjects were presented with
descriptions of an ordered sequence of actions and were asked to describe
what the agent was trying to do or to predict subsequent actions. Their
summaries organized the events into structures in which actions were
executed to perform other actions or achieve certain goals. In fact,
the subjects generally inferred some overall unstated goal for the agent
and used expectations about how this goal could be achieved to predict
subsequent actions. In addition, subjects not only attributed to an agent
the beliefs, wants, and intentions appropriate to the inferred plan but

also continued to attribute to the agent, as events unfolded, whatever additional beliefs and intentions were necessary to retain the plan as a workable explanation of the agent's behavior.

Schmidt, Sridharan, and Goodson attempted to capture this behavior in a model of plan recognition that contained a world model, a person model, and an expectation structure. The world and person models represented the system's beliefs about the domain and about the beliefs, wants, and intentions of the agent of the actions. The expectation structure represented the system's hypothesis about the agent's plan. It contained actions linked to other actions by enablement and associated with the plan as a whole ReasonFor propositions that captured external motivation for pursuing the goal of a plan. For example, a ReasonFor proposition associated with a plan for eating would be that the agent was hungry. In Schmidt, Sridharan, and Goodson's model, a hypothesis about an agent's plan was viable only if the system could ascribe to the agent appropriate motivation for pursuing the plan—only if the system's beliefs about the agent provided sufficient reasons for the agent to pursue the plan. This notion of ReasonFor propositions corresponds with Wilensky's idea of themes (general explanations for goals) [Wil78,Wil83].

Although Schmidt, Sridharan, and Goodson discussed several methods for identifying an agent's overall goals and thereby hypothesizing an initial plan structure, in their implementation the context determined the agent's overall goal. The plan associated with the goal was expanded as much as possible without making unwarranted assumptions about subactions or parameter bindings. For example, if the agent entered a store, the system might infer that the agent intended to purchase something, but the item to be purchased would be left unbound in the expectation structure, since a decision about the identity of that item would be premature. Thus the model adopted a wait-and-see strategy when the observed actions did not justify adding detail to the plan. If subsequent actions conflicted with the hypothesis, revision critics were activated to revise the plan in order to retain it as a viable hypothesis. For example, if the system believed that the agent wanted to drive his car but found that the car was out of gas, the plan could be revised to include transferring gas from a lawn mower to the car in order to enable the agent to get the car to a gas station. The revision critics were primarily concerned with revising plans affected by unforeseen events and did not deal with revisions necessitated by an incorrect hypothesis on the part of the system. This is not surprising, since the context provided the agent's overall goal and the wait-and-see strategy prevented premature commitment to a particular course of action. However, as we will see in chapter 7, analysis of naturally occurring dialogue indicates that information providers often construct incorrect hypotheses about agents and their goals and that these hypotheses must later be revised to take into account new information provided by the dialogue.

This model of plan recognition accounted for many features of human behavior. The expectation structure captured the structure of human subjects' summaries of action sequences, including their attribution of an overall goal to the agent and a reason or motivation for pursuing the goal. It also accounted for the subjects' ability to predict subsequent actions in a plan and anticipate failure of the plan before it occurred. The combination of the wait-and-see approach and the revision critics captured the subjects' unwillingness to prematurely commit the agent to a particular course of action and their ability to revise plans to account for unexpected actions. Thus Schmidt, Sridharan, and Goodson's research provides experimental evidence supporting the claim that people do infer the plans and goals of other agents.

2.9   Summary

Experimental evidence suggests that people infer the plans and goals of other agents and that they expect other agents to infer their plans and goals and to use them in addressing their needs. If information systems are to play the role of a cooperative assistant in problem solving and decision making, they must exhibit the same kind of behavior. Thus plan recognition must play an important role in understanding natural language dialogue and in generating intelligent, cooperative responses.

In this chapter we have explored the roots of natural language plan recognition in work in other areas, most notably planning, philosophy of meaning and intention, and focusing. I have presented Allen's seminal work on a model of plan recognition for natural language understanding and have shown how other researchers have built on it to handle extended dialogue. In the next several chapters I will examine one such model in detail and show how strategies have been developed that reason on it to interpret several kinds of problematic utterances. Then in chapter 7 I will return to the general issue of plan recognition, discuss the limiting assumptions of the models presented thus far, and explore more robust models of plan inference.

3 Constructing a Context Model

In task-related information-seeking dialogues, one participant is motivated by a task that he wants to perform and is seeking information to construct a plan for accomplishing that task. My research has been concerned with a class of information-seeking dialogues in which the task is not being performed during the system's interaction with the user, as is the case in apprentice-expert dialogues, but instead is being constructed for future execution. In some cases only a partial plan will be constructed, with further details filled in later. For example, a freshman accessing an advisement system may only construct a partial plan for earning a degree, leaving other aspects of the plan to be fleshed out in subsequent years.

This chapter describes my process model for incremental plan inference in task-related information-seeking dialogues. It has been implemented in a system called TRACK, which forms one module of the user-modeling component (UMC) shown in figure 1.1. TRACK assimilates utterances from an ongoing dialogue and incrementally updates and expands the system's beliefs about the underlying task-related plan motivating the information seeker's queries. These plan-related beliefs comprise one segment of an overall user model. The next sections present the details of my process model and illustrate it with several working examples from my implementation. Throughout the rest of the book, information seeker and information provider will often be referred to as IS and IP respectively.

3.1 Overview of the Plan Inference Framework

Figure 3.1 presents an overview of my plan inference framework, which has been implemented in the TRACK system. A new utterance must first be parsed, and a representation of its semantic meaning constructed and passed to TRACK. TRACK then processes it in two stages. The first phase, local analysis, is responsible for hypothesizing a set of subgoals and subplans on which the speaker's attention *might* be currently focused by virtue of this single utterance. It extracts the speaker's immediate goal from the semantic representation of the speaker's utterance and applies a set of plan identification heuristics that relate the speaker's immediate goal to the system's domain-dependent library of goals and plans and produce a set of *candidate focused goals* and associated *candidate focused plans*. The second phase, global analysis, relates the new utterance to the overall plan that the user is believed to be

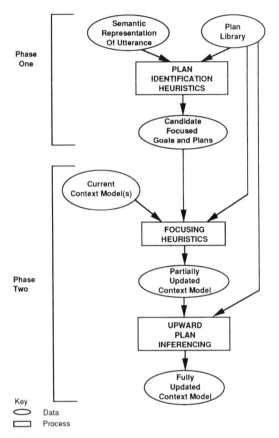

Figure 3.1
Overview of the plan inference framework

constructing. I use a tree structure called a *context model* to represent
the system's beliefs about the speaker's underlying task-related plan as
inferred from the preceding dialogue. Focusing heuristics are used to determine the most expected relationship between one of the hypothesized
subplans and the speaker's focus of attention in the context model, select
the subplan believed most appropriate to the existing plan context, insert it into the context model as the new current focus of attention, and
expand the context model to include this new subplan. If the system's
knowledge of goals and ways of achieving them suggests that this partially updated context model is part of a plan for a unique sequence of
higher-level goals, then the context model is expanded to include them.

This processing is equivalent to a listener asking herself the following questions:

- What task-related subplans might the information seeker be addressing with this single new utterance?

- In light of the preceding dialogue, which of these subplans is most likely to be the one under investigation by the information seeker, and what is its relationship to the overall plan that the information seeker is trying to construct?

For example, if the information seeker says "What is the address of Dr. Smith's office?" then he might want to visit Dr. Smith or send an item to Dr. Smith, since both require knowing the address of Dr. Smith's office. These two subgoals and the subplans for accomplishing them would become candidate focused goals and associated candidate focused plans. At this stage of analysis we do not know which candidate focused plan is the plan under investigation by the information seeker, since we have not yet considered the preceding dialogue. If the context model indicated that the information seeker was formulating a plan for getting advice about courses from Dr. Smith, the candidate focused plan for visiting Dr. Smith would be relevant and would be used in updating the context model.

This chapter describes my strategy for dynamically constructing a model of an information seeker's underlying task-related plan from an ongoing dialogue and for tracking his focus of attention in the plan.

3.2   Domain Knowledge

The heuristics and processing strategies used in TRACK are domain-independent and are based on observed characteristics of naturally occurring information-seeking dialogues. However, for any given domain, TRACK must be provided with the set of domain-dependent goals that a user might pursue and a set of plans for achieving these goals. This domain knowledge is representative of that required by a capable human information provider and is stored in TRACK's plan library.

The notation used to represent goals and plans is based on a typed logic. Constants will be represented as uppercase strings, and variables as lowercase strings preceded by the underline character "_" and followed by the characters ":&" and an uppercase string giving the variable's type. The examples presented in this book are extracted from several different domains. The semantics of individual propositions will not be formally defined but should be assumed to have their intuitive meaning. For example, Course-offered(CS180, NEXTSEM) is the proposition that CS180 is offered next semester.[1]

A primitive goal is one that can be achieved by executing a primitive action in the domain. I view a plan as the means by which an agent can accomplish a nonprimitive task-related goal. Using an extension of the STRIPS [FN71] and NOAH [Sac75,Sac77] formalisms described in chapter 2, I represent a plan as a structure containing applicability conditions, preconditions, a plan body, and effects.

Applicability conditions are conditions that must be satisfied before the plan can even be considered, whereas preconditions are conditions that must be satisfied before the plan can be executed. The plan body contains a set of simpler subgoals, each of which can be accomplished by a primitive action or has an associated domain plan. Effects are goal propositions describing the results of successfully executing a plan. Effects may be classified as primary or secondary. A goal proposition is a primary effect of a plan if the plan is a reasonable choice for achieving that goal; a goal proposition is a secondary effect of a plan if satisfying the proposition is merely a side effect of executing the plan.

It is important to maintain a distinction between the plan body, the preconditions, and the applicability conditions. The plan body describes the execution of the plan, whereas preconditions describe the world state that must exist *before* the plan can be executed. For example, obtaining a degree entails satisfying a number of requirements such as earning credit in the courses specified for a major field of study and maintaining a minimum grade point average. These comprise the plan body of a plan for obtaining a degree. However, obtaining a degree also requires that one be enrolled at the university; this is a precondition for execution of the plan.

Applicability conditions indicate whether a plan is relevant in the existing world state. Although one can plan to accomplish unsatisfied preconditions, it is anomalous to attempt to satisfy applicability conditions. For example, consider the following two goals:

Admit-as-major(AGENT, CS)
Change-major(AGENT, _major:&MAJOR, CS)

---

[1]To avoid specifying times that will eventually appear outdated, I will use the constant NEXTSEM in many examples. However, the semantic representations analyzed by the machine would include such constants as FALL1991 or SPRING1992. Similarly, I will use a constant ending in "NS," such as CS105-10-NS, to designate a specific section of a course for next semester.

Change-major(_agent:&STUDENT, _major:&MAJOR, CS)
Applicability conditions:
    Admitted-university(_agent:&STUDENT)
    Declared-major(_agent:&STUDENT, _major:&MAJOR)
Preconditions:
    Have-GPA(_agent:&STUDENT, _ave:&GPA-AVERAGE)
        where Greater-than(_ave:&GPA-AVERAGE, 3.0)
Plan body:
    Obtain-acceptance(_agent:&STUDENT, CS)
    Submit-change-major-form(_agent:&STUDENT, CS)
Primary effects:
    Change-major(_agent:&STUDENT, _major:&MAJOR, CS)
    Declared-major(_agent:&STUDENT, CS)
  ¬ Declared-major(_agent:&STUDENT, _major:&MAJOR)

Figure 3.2
Plan for changing one's major to computer science

The plans for both goals have the effect that the agent's major becomes
computer science. However, the first is applicable only if the agent is
a prospective student applying for admission to the university, whereas
the second (figure 3.2) is applicable if the agent is already matriculated.
If the agent is a current student, it is unreasonable for him to *plan* to
be dismissed so that he can reapply for admission to the university as a
computer science major.

    Wilkins used preconditions similar to my applicability conditions in
representing operators in the SIPE system [Wil84]. What I call a precondition Wilkins incorporated into the set of actions and goals comprising
an operator. His reasons for having *unplannable* preconditions in his representation scheme were both to capture the appropriateness of applying
an operator in a given situation and to connect different levels of detail in
a hierarchical planner. A proposition that at one level of abstraction was
part of the specification of how an operator was to be performed might
appear at a lower level of abstraction as a precondition of an operator,
which would indicate that further planning for the lower-level operator
is inappropriate unless the proposition is already satisfied. But mixing
standard preconditions (conditions that must exist before an operator
can be performed but that can be planned for) with the set of goals
and actions that constitute performing an operator fails to capture the
intuitive difference between the two. For this reason my representation

scheme distinguishes among applicability conditions, preconditions that can be planned for, and how one goes about performing an action. My applicability conditions are similar to Litman's constraints [LA87] but different from Allen's applicability conditions [All79].

The preconditions and the plan body consist of a set of restricted goals, or R-goals. An R-goal is a goal proposition with an optional set of attached propositions constraining how the arguments in the goal may be instantiated. For example, the goal of earning credit in a section of CS180 is specified as follows:

Earn-credit-section(_agent:&STUDENT, _sec:&SECTION)
where
Is-section-of(_sec:&SECTION, CS180)
Section-offered(_sec:&SECTION, _sem:&SEMESTER)

An R-goal may have a repetition part specifying repetition of the R-goal with different parameter instantiations. For example, one might specify earning 12 credits in Group 1 courses (courses designated as satisfying humanities requirements) as follows:

Until Have-credits(_agent:&STUDENT, GROUP1, 12)
Repeat
Earn-credit(_agent:&STUDENT, _crse:&GROUP1-COURSE,
        _sem:&SEMESTER, _cr:&CREDITS, CREDIT)
where
Credits-of(_crse:&GROUP1-COURSE, _cr:&CREDITS)
Course-offered(_crse:&GROUP1-COURSE, _sem:&SEMESTER)

A better representation might use a temporal logic to indicate that the goal proposition is to be satisfied at some time in the future whereas the proposition restrictions need only be satisfied at the time the goal is initiated; in this case the proposition restrictions could be used to specify that only courses in which the agent did not already have credit could be used to instantiate the goal proposition. Repetition parts are included here only to allow a more complete description of goals and plans in the domain but play no role in the theory being developed.

Figure 3.2 illustrated a sample plan used by TRACK. TRACK's plans are hierarchical, since many of the subgoals in the bodies of plans and many preconditions are nonprimitive and therefore have associated plans that may be substituted for them. For example, the subgoal Obtain-acceptance(_agent:&STUDENT, CS) has an associated plan with constituent subgoals such as File-application, Submit-transcript, and Have-interview. Thus a plan can be expanded to any desired degree of detail by replacing nonprimitive preconditions and subgoals with their associated plans.

In chapter 2 we saw the importance of hierarchical abstraction and hierarchical planning and how these were captured in ABSTRIPS and NOAH. Hierarchical abstraction is also important during dynamic plan recognition. Not only must the plan recognizer build the user's plan incrementally during the dialogue; it must also track the user's focus of attention in the plan. This entails recognizing the level of detail at which the user is currently formulating his plan and is considering alternative courses of action. As we will see in section 3.4, TRACK accomplishes this by modeling the information seeker's overall plan as a hierarchical structure of goals and associated plans and by representing the information seeker's current focus of attention as a subgoal and an associated subplan in this structure.

3.3   Local Analysis

In the TRACK system, local analysis infers the speaker's immediate goal from an utterance, relates this goal to the system's domain-dependent knowledge of goals and plans, and constructs a set of candidate focused goals and associated candidate focused plans. These candidate focused goals and associated plans represent those subtasks on which the speaker's attention might be centered in light of this single utterance.

3.3.1   The Immediate Goal

The speaker's immediate goal is extracted from the semantic representation of his utterance. Using a variation of Cohen and Allen's representation of surface speech acts described in chapter 2, the semantic representation of a declarative utterance is the following:

S.Inform[SPEAKER, HEARER, P]

And the semantic representation of an interrogative utterance is either of these two representations:

S.Request[SPEAKER, HEARER, Informif(HEARER, SPEAKER, P)]
S.Request[SPEAKER, HEARER, Informref(HEARER, SPEAKER,
       _x:&XTYPE | P)]

Here _x is a variable of type XTYPE, appearing in proposition P and whose values satisfying P are requested. The speaker's immediate goal is then one of the following (which correspond to the above three semantic representations):

Want[SPEAKER, Know(HEARER, P)]
Want[SPEAKER, Knowif(SPEAKER, P)]
Want[SPEAKER, Knowref(SPEAKER, _x:&XTYPE | P)]

For example, the query "Is French 112 a three credit-hour course?" has the following semantic representation:

Request[SPEAKER, HEARER, Informif(HEARER, SPEAKER,
        Credits-of[FRENCH112, 3])]

The speaker's immediate goal, extracted from this representation, is this:

Want[SPEAKER, Knowif(SPEAKER, Credits-of[FRENCH112, 3])]

The system as implemented does not concern itself with the mechanics of parsing and constructing semantic representations of utterances. These semantic representations are the input to the system from which the immediate goal is extracted. The system handles indirect speech acts by using default interpretation rules similar to Sidner and Israel's shortcut plan-recognition rules described in chapter 2. However, the primary objective of my research was not the interpretation of indirect speech acts, so these rules will not be discussed.

3.3.2   Candidate Focused Goals and Plans

The information seeker's *current focused goal* is the task-related goal on which his attention is centered at the time of the current utterance. IS can achieve this goal by executing a plan whose effect list contains the goal. The plan selected by IS is called the *current focused plan* because it represents IS's plan for accomplishing the subtask on which his attention is centered.

Local analysis must relate an individual utterance to the system's knowledge of goals and plans and identify a set of *candidate focused goals* and associated *candidate focused plans*. Each hypothesized candidate focused goal and plan pair represents a domain plan on which the system believes the information seeker's attention might be focused at that time along with the goal that the system believes might be motivating consideration of this plan. IS's actual current focused goal and plan cannot be selected from this set until global analysis relates the isolated utterance to the context established by the preceding dialogue.

I use a set of eight plan identification heuristics to hypothesize domain-dependent goals and associated plans that IS might be addressing with his utterance. These heuristics are based on Allen's inference rules [AP80], described in chapter 2, and handle utterances of the following types:

- A statement that the information seeker wants a proposition to be true: "I want to have a Bachelor of Arts Degree."

- A statement that a proposition is true: "I am a CS major."

- A request for information about how one can achieve a goal: "How do I become a CS major?"

- A request to know if a proposition is true: "Do I have credit for CS105?"

- A request to know the instantiations of a term that satisfy a proposition: "Who is teaching section 10 of CS105 this spring?"

- A request to know the allowable choices for a parameter appearing in a specified goal within a particular plan: "What courses must I take in order to satisfy the foreign language requirement?"

The plan identification heuristics If IS states that he wants some proposition P to be true and P is currently not satisfied, then IS may be considering ways of making P true. Thus it is reasonable to believe that IS might be focused on plans that achieve P, namely those plans whose primary effect list contains P. For example, the immediate goal obtained from the utterance "I want to have a Bachelor of Arts degree" is the following':

Want[IS, Know(IP, Want[IS, Have-degree(IS, BA)])]

From this IP can infer Want[IS, Have-Degree(IS, BA)].[2] The proposition Have-degree(IS, BA) is a primary effect of the plan Obtain-degree(IS, BA), and this plan is therefore identified as a candidate focused plan. This reasoning leads to the following plan identification heuristic:

> *Rule P1:* If IS wants proposition P to be true and P is not currently satisfied, P becomes a candidate focused goal, and those plans that contain P on their primary effect list become associated candidate focused plans.

---

[2]I am assuming that IS's statements are true. Thus I am not dealing with misconceptions or deception. This limitation will be discussed in chapter 7.

If IS states that he wants a situation described by proposition P, which he knows is already satisfied, he must be considering plans in which proposition P plays a role, namely plans in which P is part of the preconditions or plan body. For example, the immediate goal obtained from the utterance "I want my major to be CS" is the following:

Want[IS, Know(IP, Want[IS, Declared-major(IS, CS)])]

From this IP can infer Want[IS, Declared-major(IS, CS)]. If the information seeker is already a computer science major, he will be looking not at plans for declaring a computer science major but instead at plans of which this goal is a component, such as Satisfy-major(IS, BA, CS) or Satisfy-major(IS, BS, CS). This reasoning leads to the following heuristic:

> *Rule P2:* If IS wants proposition P to be true and P is satisfied, those plans that contain P as part of their preconditions or plan body become candidate focused plans, and the propositions in the primary effect list of each plan become the associated candidate focused goals.

If IS states that a proposition is true, IP is justified in believing that IS believes that the proposition is relevant to the plan under consideration, that is, that the proposition is part of the preconditions, applicability conditions, or plan body of the plan or that the negation of the proposition is part of the desired state. For example, the immediate goal obtained from the utterance "I am a CS major" is this:

Want[IS, Know(IP, Declared-major[IS, CS])]

Since the participants in an information-seeking dialogue are assumed to be working cooperatively, IP can infer that IS believes that being a CS major is relevant to the plan under consideration by IS. Thus the candidate focused plans will include Satisfy-major(IS, BA, CS) and Satisfy-major(IS, BS, CS), in which the proposition is a component, as well as the plan Change-major(IS, CS, _major:&MAJOR), whose effect is to change the student's major. Such reasoning leads to this heuristic:

> *Rule P3:* If IS wants IP to know that proposition P is true, those plans that contain P as part of their applicability conditions, preconditions, or plan body become candidate focused plans, and the propositions in the primary effect list of each plan become the associated candidate focused goals. In addition, those plans that contain $\neg P$ in their primary effect list become candidate focused plans with $\neg P$ as their associated candidate focused goal.

If IS asks about how to achieve a goal or whether he can achieve a goal, he is requesting knowledge of plans that accomplish the goal, namely those plans whose primary effect lists contain the goal. This reasoning leads to the following heuristic:

> *Rule P4:* If IS wants to know how to achieve a goal or whether he can achieve a goal, that goal becomes a candidate focused goal and those plans that contain the goal on their primary effect list become associated candidate focused plans.

If IS wants to know whether a proposition P is true, he may want P to be true as part of accomplishing a plan. Or as noted by Allen [AP80] and discussed in chapter 2, he may in fact be asking about P because he wants $\neg P$ to be true. Therefore, the candidate focused plans must include those plans that contain P or $\neg P$ as a satisfied applicability condition or as part of the preconditions or plan body. This reasoning leads to the following heuristic:

> *Rule P5:* If IS wants to know whether a proposition P is true, those plans that contain P or $\neg P$ as part of their preconditions, plan body, or satisfied applicability conditions become candidate focused plans, and the propositions in the primary effect list of each plan become the associated candidate focused goals.

If IS's utterance requests the values of a term that make a particular proposition satisfied, that proposition must be relevant to the plan under consideration. Therefore, any goals whose plans might prompt such a request should become candidate focused goals, and the plans should become candidate focused plans. For example, the utterance "Who is teaching section 10 of CS105 next semester?" requests the value of the term _fac:&FACULTY such that the proposition Teaches(_fac:&FACULTY, CS105-10-NS) is satisfied. Consider the plan for learning the material of a section of a course, shown in figure 3.3. This plan contains the proposition Teaches(_fac:&FACULTY, _sect:&SECTION) as a constraint on a subgoal in its body. Substituting CS105-10-NS for _sect:&SECTION produces the proposition Teaches(_fac:&FACULTY, CS105-10-NS) addressed by IS's utterance. Making this substitution throughout the plan produces a plan for learning the material of section 10 of CS105 next semester. Therefore, the goal Learn-material(IS, CS105-10-NS, _syl:&SYLLABUS) becomes a candidate focused goal, and the plan produced by substituting CS105-10-NS for _sect:&SECTION becomes a candidate focused plan. Similarly, IS can ask for the values of a term that make a proposition true in order to know the complementary values that make the proposition false. Thus

---

Learn-material(_agent:&STUDENT, _sect:&SECTION, _syl:&SYLLABUS)
Plan body:
   Learn-from-person(_agent:&STUDENT, _sect:&SECTION, _fac:&FACULTY)
      where Teaches(_fac:&FACULTY, _sect:&SECTION)
   Learn-from-text(_agent:&STUDENT, _txt:&TEXT)
      where Uses(_sect:&SECTION, _txt:&TEXT)
Primary effects:
   Learn-material(_agent:&STUDENT, _sect:&SECTION, _syl:&SYLLABUS)

Figure 3.3
Plan for learning course material

plans containing either P or $\neg P$ must be included as candidate focused plans. This reasoning leads to the following heuristic:

> *Rule P6:* If IS wants to know the values of a term x that result in a proposition P being satisfied, those plans that contain P or $\neg P$ as part of their applicability conditions, preconditions, or plan body become candidate focused plans, and the propositions in the primary effect list of the plan become the associated candidate focused goals.

If IS wants to know the elements that comprise the possible choices for an argument in a subgoal (an R-goal in the preconditions or plan body) specified by the speaker, IS is requesting information about how an R-goal can be instantiated in a plan. Since we are assuming a cooperative dialogue, the R-goal must be relevant to the plan that IS is considering. Therefore, candidate focused plans are those plans in which the R-goal appears as part of the preconditions or plan body. For example, the immediate goal obtained from the utterance "What science courses must I take?" is the following:

Want[IS,Knowref(IS, _x:&SCIENCE-CRSE |
    In-Plan[Earn-Credit(IS, _x:&SCIENCE-CRSE, _s:&SEMESTER,
      _c:&CREDITS, _st:&CREDITSTATUS), _y:&PLAN])]

Since the information seeker wants to know the science courses that he must take as part of some unspecified plan under consideration, any such plans must be candidate focused plans. The plan under consideration will often be specified in the utterance, as in the following query: "What courses must I take in order to satisfy the foreign language requirement?" This reasoning leads to the following heuristic:

> *Rule P7:* If IS wants to know the elements that comprise the possible choices for an argument in a subgoal specified by IS, those plans containing that subgoal become candidate focused plans, and the propositions

in the primary effect list of each plan become the associated candidate focused goals.

If IS asks if an element is a member of a certain class, that class must be relevant to the plan under consideration. Therefore, candidate focused plans should include any plans that might prompt such a request, namely those plans that contain a subgoal with an argument restricted to elements in that class. For example, the immediate goal obtained from the utterance "Is CS355 a second writing course?" is the following:

Want[IS, Knowif(IS, Isa(CS355, SEC-WRITING-CRSE))]

The goal

Earn-credit(IS, _crse:&SEC-WRITING-CRSE, _ss:&SEMESTER,
        _cr:&CREDITS, CREDIT)

appears in a plan for satisfying a university requirement that a student take a second writing course during his junior or senior year. In formulating his underlying plan, IS may be investigating possible courses that can be used to fulfill this requirement. Such reasoning leads to this heuristic:

> *Rule P8:* If IS wants to know if an element is of type X, then those plans containing a subgoal with an argument that is restricted to elements of type X become candidate focused plans, and the propositions in the primary effect list of each plan become its associated candidate focused goals.

3.4   Global Analysis

The output from the first phase of processing is a set of goal-plan pairs. These represent plans that the user might be focused on and the goals that might motivate the user's consideration of these plans. These candidate focused goals and plans were selected without regard to any contextual information. The second processing phase, global analysis, must relate them to any existing inferred plan context and appropriately expand the system's beliefs about what the user is trying to do. First, the most appropriate candidate focused goal-plan pair is identified and integrated into the current context model. This requires two different kinds of context processing. The first constructs a context model at the start of a dialogue or when the speaker terminates the current dialogue and pursues an entirely new task. The second type of context processing updates the existing model to account for new utterances in an ongoing

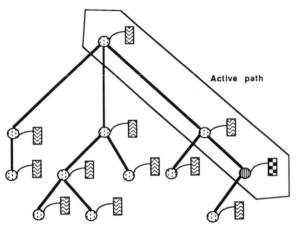

Figure 3.4
Structure of a typical context model

dialogue. In both cases the context model is then expanded to include any further inferences that can be made about the user's plan.

3.4.1   The Context Model

The context model is a tree structure representing the system's beliefs about the information seeker's underlying task-related plan and current focus of attention in this plan. A node in the tree represents a goal that the information seeker has investigated achieving and that has an associated plan. Each node, except for the root, is a descendant of a higher-level goal whose associated plan contains the child node as a precondition or subgoal. The root of the tree is the most general goal inferred for the information seeker, and the entire dialogue thus far has been directed toward formulating a plan for achieving this goal. Figure 3.4 illustrates the structure of a typical context model.

The context model represents the overall plan considered by the speaker. Within each context model, one node is marked as the *current focused goal*, or particular aspect of the task on which the information seeker's attention is currently focused. Associated with this goal is a *current focused plan*. The path from the root of the context model to the current focused goal is called the *active path*. The nodes along the active path represent the global context, or sequence of progressively lower-level goals and associated plans that led to the subplan on which the information seeker's attention is currently centered.

Figure 3.5 presents a context model. The nodes along the active path are preceded by an asterisk; the current focused goal is the last node on the active path. This context model indicates that the speaker has investigated taking CS470 and CS360, both in order to satisfy the requirements of the computer science department for a Bachelor of Arts degree, since both are descendants of the root node Satisfy-major(IS, BA, CS). The active path is the path from the root to the current focused goal:

Learn-from-person(IS, CS360-10-NS, _fac:&FACULTY)
where
Teaches(_fac:&FACULTY, CS360-10-NS)

The nodes along this active path represent the global context, or the sequence of progressively more specific tasks that led to the current focus of attention. For example, as part of the plan associated with the goal of learning the material of a section of CS360, the information seeker is investigating a plan for the following R-goal:

Learn-from-person(IS, CS360-10-NS, _fac:&FACULTY)
where
Teaches(_fac:&FACULTY, CS360-10-NS)

Thus this goal and its associated plan comprise a child node of the following higher-level goal:

Learn-material(IS, CS360-10-NS, _syl:&SYLLABUS)
where
Is-syllabus-of(CS360-10-NS, _syl:&SYLLABUS)

3.4.2   Building the Initial Context Model

At the start of a dialogue the current context model is empty. When the first utterance occurs, the user's immediate goal is extracted from its semantic representation and then the candidate focused goals and plans are computed from the heuristics described in section 3.3.2. Since there is no established context, there is no basis on which to choose from among the candidate focused plans, and multiple context models

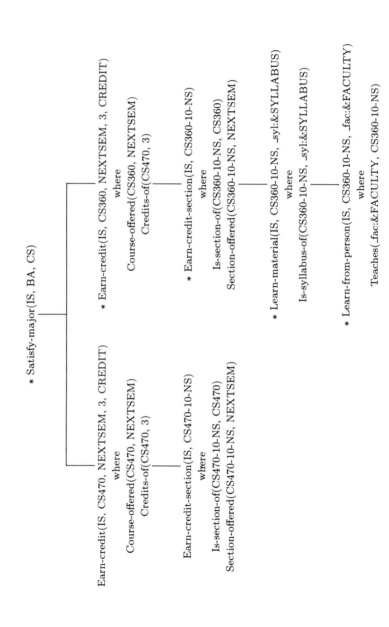

Figure 3.5
A sample context model

may need to be constructed. If the dialogue is cooperative and coherent, then subsequent utterances will eventually reduce the number of context models to one. Therefore, each candidate focused goal and associated plan becomes a current focused goal-plan pair at the root of a context model. Recall that the current focused goal and plan represent that aspect of the overall task on which the system believes the information seeker's attention is currently centered. If the user's utterance addressed a subgoal in the current focused plan (as would be the case when plan identification heuristic rule P7 is used), this subgoal is noted. As we will see in the next section, if there is a most recently considered subgoal in the current focused plan, it provides very strong expectations about the next utterance.

To illustrate how an initial context model is constructed at the start of a new dialogue, consider the utterance "Who is teaching section 10 of Political Science 110 next semester?" The immediate goal extracted from the semantic representation of this utterance will be the following:

Want(IS, Knowref[IS, _fac:&FACULTY |
    Teaches(_fac:&FACULTY, PLSC110-10-NS)])

Rule P6 hypothesizes that the plan for the goal Learn-material(IS, PLSC110-10-NS, _syl:&SYLLABUS) is a candidate focused plan, since it contains the subgoal

Learn-from-person(IS, PLSC110-10-NS, _fac:&FACULTY)
where
Teaches(_fac:&FACULTY, PLSC110-10-NS)

and IS wants to know the constants of type FACULTY that will satisfy the proposition Teaches(_fac:&FACULTY, PLSC110-10-NS). Initially the context model contains only this goal-plan pair. However, as will be described in section 3.4.4, further inferences about IS's task-related plan can now be made, and the context model should be expanded upward to include these additional goals and plans, all of which will be part of the active path. Figure 3.6 presents the enlarged context model, with the nodes along the active path preceded by an asterisk.

If the plan identification heuristics hypothesize only one candidate focused goal-plan pair, only one context model is built and the system has definite expectations for future utterances. If more than one context model is constructed, the system is uncertain about IS's goals. It might request clarification if this ambiguity prevented a response to IS's query or if it believed an obstacle existed to IS's pursuing the current focused goal in one of the context models. This relates to the general

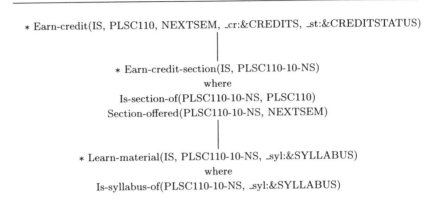

* Earn-credit(IS, PLSC110, NEXTSEM, _cr:&CREDITS, _st:&CREDITSTATUS)

|

* Earn-credit-section(IS, PLSC110-10-NS)
where
Is-section-of(PLSC110-10-NS, PLSC110)
Section-offered(PLSC110-10-NS, NEXTSEM)

|

* Learn-material(IS, PLSC110-10-NS, _syl:&SYLLABUS)
where
Is-syllabus-of(PLSC110-10-NS, _syl:&SYLLABUS)

Figure 3.6
Initial context model

maxim of human behavior that one notify another of obstacles to anticipated courses of action but not request information about another's plans unless necessary for a response (that is, don't be nosy).

3.4.3   Updating the Context Model

As each new utterance occurs, the context model must be expanded to reflect an updated hypothesis about the information seeker's plans and goals. I use focusing heuristics to evaluate the possible relationships between the candidate focused goal-plan pairs and the context model, select the candidate focused goal-plan pair that is most appropriate to the existing plan context, insert it as the new focus of attention, and expand the context model to incorporate it into the tree structure.

In the kind of information-seeking dialogues that I am studying, IS is formulating a plan for a task that will generally be executed at some time in the future. Therefore, the dialogue is not constrained by the order of execution of the steps of the underlying task, as in apprentice-expert dialogues [Gro77a,Rob81]. However, information-seeking dialogues do exhibit structure, and this appears to be caused by two factors.

The first is the organized nature of naturally occurring information-seeking dialogues. Analysis of naturally occurring dialogues indicates that once IS's attention is focused on achieving a particular subgoal, he will generally finish investigating a partial plan for it before starting to develop plans for achieving other subgoals. One possible explanation for this observed behavior is that it may require less mental effort than switching back and forth among partially constructed plans for different subgoals.

The second factor producing structure in these dialogues is their cooperative nature. Since IP is helping IS construct a plan for IS's underlying task, both participants are expected to maintain a meaningful exchange during which the relationship of individual utterances is explicitly or implicitly conveyed. Thus one expects the participants to maintain approximately the same focus of attention in consecutive utterances and to adhere to the focusing constraints espoused by McKeown [McK83,McK85b] (see chapter 2).

These intuitive notions have led me to develop a set of focusing heuristics that are used to track IS's focus of attention and relate utterances to the existing dialogue context. The focusing heuristics represent an ordered set of expectations about how IS might move within his underlying task-related plan and select parts of it for discussion during the course of a cooperative and coherent information-seeking dialogue. The focusing heuristics are tried in order until one of them succeeds in hypothesizing a relationship between a candidate focused plan and the current context model.

Focusing heuristics The focusing heuristics are described in this section. Figure 3.7 illustrates each heuristic's expectation about the relationship between a candidate focused goal-plan pair and the context model on the assumption that the tree shown in figure 3.7a is the context model immediately preceding the utterance. Node R represents the root of the initial context model, node CF (marked with an asterisk) represents the current focused goal and plan, and node SG represents the most recently considered subgoal in the current focused plan.

Since the current focused plan is the plan on which IS's attention is currently centered, he is expected to continue investigating aspects of this plan until he is satisfied with its formulation. Once IS begins considering a particular subgoal in the current focused plan, our strongest expectation is that he will investigate plans for achieving the subgoal. IS must have had a reason for introducing the subgoal; if he does not consider it further at this time, he must make the effort of reintroducing it and reestablishing its context in order to investigate it at a later time. Furthermore, IS is expected to maintain approximately the same focus of attention in consecutive utterances. Therefore, the subtask most closely related to this newly introduced subgoal and addressed by the utterance is likely to be the aspect of the overall task now being considered by IS. This leads to the first focusing heuristic:

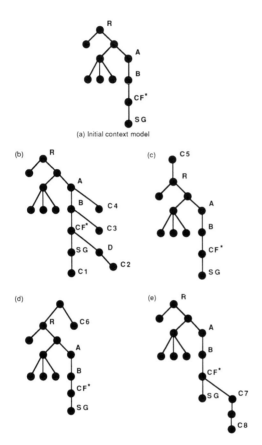

(a) Initial context model

Figure 3.7
Examples of relationships between candidate plans and the context model

> *Rule F1:* If a breadth-first expansion of a plan for the most recently
> considered subgoal in the current focused plan includes a candidate
> focused goal-plan pair, select the candidate focused goal-plan pair that
> occurs earliest, and expand the context model to include it.

For example, if figure 3.7b is an expansion of the context model shown in
figure 3.7a, node C1 might represent such a candidate focused goal-plan
pair.

As mentioned above, IS is expected to finish investigating the current
focused plan before considering other aspects of his overall task. Therefore, if IS does not investigate a subplan for the most recently considered
subgoal in the current focused plan, our next strongest expectation is

that he will investigate some other aspect of the current focused plan. Since he is expected to maintain approximately the same focus of attention in consecutive utterances, the subtask most closely related to the current focused plan and addressed by his utterance is likely to be the aspect of the overall task now being considered by IS. This leads to the second focusing heuristic:

> *Rule F2:* If a breadth-first expansion of the current focused plan includes a candidate focused goal-plan pair, select the candidate focused goal-plan pair that occurs earliest, and expand the context model to include it.

For example, if figure 3.7b is an expansion of the context model shown in figure 3.7a, node C2 might represent such a candidate focused goal-plan pair (C2 is a part of a plan for the goal at node D, which in turn is part of a plan for the goal at node CF).

The active path in the context model forms a stack of potential focused tasks to which IS may return. As one moves deeper into this stack, from the current focused goal-plan pair back toward the root of the context model, one encounters progressively more general goals and associated plans, each of which contains its predecessor goal in the stack as part of its plan. Thus each step backward along the active path constitutes a termination of the investigation of a subtask and movement back up to consider other aspects of a higher-level task. IS is expected to finish investigating a plan for a subgoal before leaving it, and consecutive utterances are expected to maintain approximately the same focus of attention. Therefore, if the previous heuristics do not indicate that the utterance addresses an aspect of the current focused plan, our next expectation is that the utterance is relevant to a plan associated with a goal on the active path, and goals furthest down on the active path (goals closest to the top of the stack and therefore to the existing focus of attention) are preferred. This leads to the following focusing heuristic:

> *Rule F3:* If expansion of a plan for a goal on the active path includes a candidate focused goal-plan pair, select the candidate focused goal-plan pair whose first ancestor goal on the active path is closest to the current focused goal.

For example, if figure 3.7b is an expansion of the context model shown in figure 3.7a, nodes C3 and C4 are both part of the expansion of a plan for a goal along the active path, but if nodes C3 and C4 both represent candidate focused goal-plan pairs, node C3 is preferred, since it appears in an expansion of the plan associated with node B, which is closer to the current focused goal (represented by node CF) than is node A.

Rules F1 through F3 assume that the user is working in a top-down fashion by introducing a task and then proceeding to consider aspects of that task in greater detail. It is the most common method of communication. In such interactions IP learns at the outset the top-level goal that will be addressed during the dialogue and anticipates that the subgoals of plans for achieving this overall goal will be topics of subsequent utterances. However, IS can also pursue a bottom-up dialogue by investigating a subtask and then relating it to a higher-level plan of which it is a component. This leads to the following focusing heuristic:

> *Rule F4:* If the goal at the root of the context model appears in an expansion of a candidate focused plan, insert that candidate focused goal-plan pair as the root of a new context model, and expand it to include the old context model as a subtree.

Figure 3.7c illustrates a case in which an expansion of the candidate focused plan, represented by node C5, contains the goal associated with the root of the context model.

In a bottom-up dialogue IS can investigate several subtasks of a higher-level task without explicitly stating his overall goal. In such a situation IP may be able to infer how the subtasks relate to one another as components of a higher-level task; if the relationship is not obvious, IS is expected to disambiguate the relationship in subsequent utterances. IP's attempt to infer the correct relationship is captured in the following focusing heuristic:

> *Rule F5:* If an expansion of a plan for another domain goal includes both a context model and a candidate focused goal-plan pair, insert the domain goal and its domain plan as the root of a new context model and expand it to include the old context model and the candidate focused goal-plan pair as subtrees.

Figure 3.7d illustrates a case in which both the candidate focused goal-plan pair, node C6, and the context model are part of the expansion of a higher-level plan.

Each focusing heuristic uses a breadth-first expansion of plans so that the resulting shift in focus of attention will be as small as possible. For example, if nodes C7 and C8 in figure 3.7e both represent candidate focused goal-plan pairs, rule F2 gives preference to C7 over C8, since C7 is closer to the existing focus of attention in the dialogue.

Unfortunately, these heuristics may fail to identify a relationship between an utterance and the existing plan context. In such a case either

IS has incorrect or novel beliefs about how to achieve his goals, the system's existing context model does not accurately represent the plan that IS has in mind, or IS has begun planning for an entirely new and unrelated goal. These issues will be addressed in chapter 7.

3.4.4 Expanding the Context Model with Further Inferences

If the information seeker believes that IS's queries are addressing a subtask that can be part of only one higher-level task, she can infer this higher-level task as part of IS's overall plan. So if there is only one context model and the goal associated with the root of the context model is part of only one higher-level plan, this higher-level plan and its goal are added as the new root of the context model with the old root node as its child. This process is repeated until the context model can no longer be expanded upward by adding inferred higher-level goal-plan pairs.

For example, in figure 3.6 the only candidate focused goal hypothesized by the plan identification heuristics was Learn-material(IS, PLSC110-10-NS, _syl:&SYLLABUS). This goal and its associated candidate focused plan were entered as the root of a context model. This goal appears only in the plan for the goal Earn-credit-section(IS, PLSC110-10-NS), and it in turn appears only in the plan for the goal Earn-Credit(IS, PLSC110, NEXTSEM, _cr:&CREDITS, _st:&CREDITSTATUS). Therefore, the system's beliefs about IS's underlying task-related plan are expanded to include these inferred higher-level goals and plans, and the result is the context model shown in figure 3.6.

3.5 Examples

The following sample dialogues illustrate the plan identification and focusing heuristics. In the illustrations of context models, goals along the active path are preceded by an asterisk; the last such goal always represents the current focused goal-plan pair. The first two examples will be presented in great detail. The third example will omit details that are similar to those included in the first two.

3.5.1 A Top-Down Dialogue

This example is a typical top-down dialogue in which the information seeker expands the current focused plan and then later reverts back to a higher-level plan on the active path.

IS: I want to satisfy the distribution requirements for the Bachelor of Arts degree. How many credits is Political Science 110?

IP: Political Science 110 is 3 credits.

IS: What sections does Dr. Arnold teach?

IP: Dr. Arnold teaches sections 11 and 12.

IS: Is History 101 a Group 1 course?

Some of the world knowledge needed to handle the first two dialogues is shown in Figures 3.3 and 3.8.

The semantic representation of IS's first utterance is the following:

S.Inform(IS, IP, Want[IS, Satisfy-distribution-req(IS, BA)])

And his immediate goal is this:

Want[IS, Know(IP, Want[IS, Satisfy-distribution-req(IS, BA)])]

From this IP can infer Want[IS, Satisfy-distribution-req(IS, BA)]. Rule P1 applies. IS wants to satisfy the distribution requirements for the BA degree; therefore a candidate focused plan is any plan that contains that proposition on its primary effect list. Thus at this stage the context model consists of the single goal Satisfy-distribution-req(IS, BA) and its associated plan.

However, the root of this context model is itself part of the body of only one higher-level plan, the plan for the goal Obtain-degree(IS, BA). Therefore, the context model is expanded upward to include this enlarged global context, as shown below:

IS's second utterance is "How many credits is Political Science 110?" Its semantic representation is the following:

S.Request(IS, IP, Informref[IP, IS, _cr:&CREDITS |
        Credits-of(PLSC110, _cr:&CREDITS)])

And IS's immediate goal, therefore, is this:

Satisfy-distribution-req(_agent:&STUDENT, BA)
Plan body:
   Satisfy-group-req(_agent:&STUDENT, GROUP1)
   Satisfy-group-req(_agent:&STUDENT, GROUP2)
   Satisfy-group-req(_agent:&STUDENT, GROUP3)
   Satisfy-group-req(_agent:&STUDENT, GROUP4)
Primary effects:
   Satisfy-distribution-req(_agent:&STUDENT, BA)

Satisfy-group-req(_agent:&STUDENT, GROUP1)
Plan body:
   Until Have-credits(_agent:&STUDENT, GROUP1, 12)
   Repeat
   Earn-credit(_agent:&STUDENT, _crse:&GROUP1-COURSE, _sem:&SEMESTER,
         _cred:&CREDITS, CREDIT)
     where
     Course-offered(_crse:&GROUP1-COURSE, _sem:&SEMESTER)
     Credits-of(_crse:&GROUP1-COURSE, _cred:&CREDITS)
Primary effects:
   Satisfy-group-req(_agent:&STUDENT, GROUP1)

Learn-from-person(_agent:&STUDENT, _sect:&SECTION, _fac:&FACULTY)
Plan body:
   Attend-class(_agent:&STUDENT, _plc:&MTG-PLACE,
         _day:&MTG-DAYS, _time:&MTG-TIME)
     where
     Is-meeting-place(_sect:&SECTION, _plc:&MTG-PLACE)
     Is-meeting-day(_sect:&SECTION, _day:&MTG-DAYS)
     Is-meeting-time(_sect:&SECTION, _time:&MTG-TIME)
Primary effects:
   Learn-from-person(_agent:&STUDENT, _sect:&SECTION, _fac:&FACULTY)

Figure 3.8
Some world knowledge about plans

Want(IS, Knowref[IS, _cr:&CREDITS |
   Credits-of(PLSC110, _cr:&CREDITS)]])

Rule P6 applies. IS wants to know the constants of type CREDITS that satisfy the proposition Credits-of(PLSC110, _cr:&CREDITS). Thus the candidate focused plans are those plans in which this proposition or its negation appears. Two such candidate focused plans are produced, one for each of the following goals:

Satisfy-group-req(IS, GROUP1)
Earn-credit-all-courses(IS, _numb:&TOTALCREDITS)

The first is a plan for satisfying the Group 1 distribution requirements for the Bachelor of Arts degree; its body contains the following R-goal:

Earn-credit(IS, _crse:&GROUP1-COURSE, _sem:&SEMESTER,
   _cred:&CREDITS, CREDIT)
where
Course-offered(_crse:&GROUP1-COURSE, _sem:&SEMESTER)
Credits-of(_crse:&GROUP1-COURSE, _cred:&CREDITS)

The proposition Credits-Of(PLSC110, _cr:&CREDITS) from IS's query unifies with the proposition Credits-of(_crse:&GROUP1-COURSE, _cred:&CREDITS), since PLSC110 is a member of the subtype GROUP1-COURSE, the set of Group 1 courses.

   The second candidate focused plan is a plan for accumulating at least _numb credits in an unrestricted set of courses; its body contains the following R-goal:

Earn-credit(IS, _crse:&COURSE, _sem:&SEMESTER,
   _cred:&CREDITS, CREDIT)
where
Course-offered(_crse:&COURSE, _sem:&SEMESTER)
Credits-of(_crse:&COURSE, _cred:CREDITS)

The proposition Credits-of(PLSC110, _cr:&CREDITS) from IS's query unifies with the proposition Credits-of(_crse:&COURSE, _cred:CREDITS) in this plan, since PLSC110 is a member of the type COURSE, the set of all courses.

   Since a context model already exists, global analysis must relate these candidate focused goal-plan pairs to the existing plan context. Rule F2 applies, since the body of the current focused plan Satisfy-distribution-req(IS, BA) contains the candidate focused goal Satisfy-group-req(IS, GROUP1). Therefore, the current focused plan is expanded to include this candidate focused goal-plan pair, and the candidate focused goal-plan pair is marked as the new current focus of attention, that aspect of the task on which IS's attention is now believed to be centered. In addition, Earn-credit(IS, PLSC110, _sem:&SEMESTER, _cr:&CREDITS, CREDIT) is noted as the most recently considered subgoal within the current focused plan, thus making it the most likely candidate for future expansion. The resulting context model is shown below:

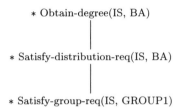

* Obtain-degree(IS, BA)

* Satisfy-distribution-req(IS, BA)

* Satisfy-group-req(IS, GROUP1)

IS's third utterance is "What sections does Dr. Arnold teach?" Its semantic representation is the following:

S.Request(IS, IP, Informref[IP, IS, _ss:&SECTION |
    Teaches(ARNOLD, _ss:&SECTION)])

And IS's immediate goal is this:

Want(IS, Knowref[IS, _ss:&SECTION |
    Teaches(ARNOLD, _ss:&SECTION)])

Once again rule P6 applies: the candidate focused plans are those plans containing the proposition Teaches(ARNOLD, _ss:&SECTION) or its negation. Only one candidate focused goal-plan pair is produced: the goal Learn-Material(IS, _ss:&SECTION, _syl:&SYLLABUS) and its associated domain plan whose body contains the following R-goal:

Learn-from-person(IS, _ss:&SECTION, ARNOLD)
where
Teaches(ARNOLD, _ss:&SECTION)

Once again global analysis must relate this candidate focused goal-plan pair to the existing context model. Rule F1 applies, since the candidate focused goal appears within the body of the plan for Earn-credit-section(IS, _ss:&SECTION), which in turn appears in the body of the plan for Earn-credit(IS, PLSC110, _sem:&SEMESTER, _cr:&CREDITS, CREDIT), which is a plan for achieving the most recently considered subgoal in the current focused plan of the existing

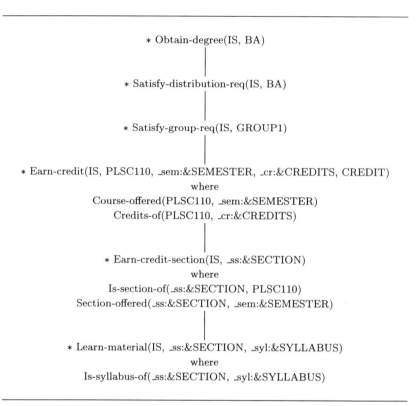

Figure 3.9
Further updating of the context model

context model. The context model is expanded along this path to include the candidate focused goal-plan pair and it becomes the current focused goal-plan pair in the updated context model shown in figure 3.9.

IS's last utterance is "Is History 101 a Group 1 course?" Its semantic representation is this:

S.Request[IS, IP, Informif(IP, IS,
          Isa[HISTORY101, GROUP1-COURSE])]

And IS's immediate goal is the following:

Want(IS, Knowif(IS, Isa[HISTORY101, GROUP1-COURSE])

Since IS was previously investigating learning the material of Political Science 110 in order to satisfy the Group 1 distribution requirement, the system can hypothesize that IS is now examining other courses that might fulfill this requirement. In detail, the plan for Satisfy-group-req(IS, GROUP1) contains the following subgoal:

Earn-credit(IS, _crse:&GROUP1-COURSE, _sem:&SEMESTER,
        _cred:&CREDITS, CREDIT)
where
Course-offered(_crse:&GROUP1-COURSE, _sem:&SEMESTER)
Credits-of(_crse:&GROUP1-COURSE, _cred:&CREDITS)

Since IS's last utterance asks if the proposition Isa(HISTORY101, GROUP1-COURSE) is true, IS may want to know if History 101 is a valid instantiation of the term _crse:&GROUP1-COURSE in this plan. Therefore, plan identification heuristic P8 hypothesizes the plan for Satisfy-group-req(IS, GROUP1) as a candidate focused plan.

Since this goal does not appear in an expansion of the current focused plan, focusing heuristics F1 and F2 fail. Yet the candidate focused goal-plan pair does occur within an expansion of a plan for a goal on the active path in the context model, namely Satisfy-group-req(IS,GROUP1). In fact, it is precisely this goal and associated plan. Therefore, heuristic F3 applies. The focus of attention reverts back to this active plan, its previous descendants are marked as inactive but retained in the context model, and the candidate focused goal-plan pair becomes the new current focus of attention. The resulting context model is the same as before, except that the active path now contains only the first three nodes in figure 3.9.

3.5.2   A Bottom-Up Dialogue

This example illustrates a dialogue in which the information seeker considers a subtask and then relates it to one of several possible higher-level plans. Some of the world knowledge needed to handle this dialogue is shown in figures 3.3 and 3.8 (on pages 86 and 99).

IS: Who is teaching section 10 of Political Science 110 next semester?

IP: Dr. Kane.

IS: What days does it meet?

IP: It meets on Tuesday.

IS: Is History 101 a Group 1 course?

From the first utterance, the system can recognize that IS is considering what he must do to learn the material covered in section 10 of Political

Science 110 next semester. From this it can infer that IS is considering taking Political Science 110. Figure 3.6 presents the context model established by IS's first utterance.

IS's next utterance indicates that he is further considering what is involved in learning the material covered in this section: he is considering when he must attend class in order to learn from the person teaching the course. In detail, the semantic representation of IS's second utterance is the following:

S.Request(IS, IP, Informref[IP, IS, _day:&MTG-DAYS |
        Is-meeting-day(PLSC110-10-NS, _day:&MTG-DAYS)])

Thus IS's immediate goal is this:

Want(IS, Knowref[IS, _day:&MTG-DAYS |
        Is-meeting-day(PLSC110-10-NS, _day:&MTG-DAYS)])

Rule P6 hypothesizes that the plan for the goal Learn-from-person(IS, PLSC110-10-NS, _fac:&FACULTY) is a candidate focused plan, since it contains the following subgoal:

Attend-class(IS, _plc:&MTG-PLACE, _day:&MTG-DAYS,
        _time:&MTG-TIME)
where
Is-meeting-place(PLSC110-10-NS, _plc:&MTG-PLACE)
Is-meeting-day(PLSC110-10-NS, _day:&MTG-DAYS)
Is-meeting-time(PLSC110-10-NS, _time:&MTG-TIME)

This is the only candidate focused plan. In the plan for the current focused goal Learn-material(IS, PLSC110-10-NS, _syl:&SYLLABUS), the most recently considered subgoal prior to this new utterance was Learn-from-person(IS, PLSC110-10-NS, _fac:&FACULTY). Focusing heuristic F1 identifies the relationship between the current utterance and the existing context model, namely, that the current utterance is investigating a subplan for the most recently considered subgoal in the current focused plan of the context model. As a result the current focused plan in the context model is expanded to include the new candidate focused goal-plan pair as the new focus of attention; the updated context model is shown in figure 3.10.

IS's last utterance, "Is History 101 a Group 1 course?", has the following semantic representation:

S.Request(IS, IP, Informif[IP, IS,
        Isa(HISTORY101, GROUP1-COURSE)])

Therefore IS's immediate goal is this:

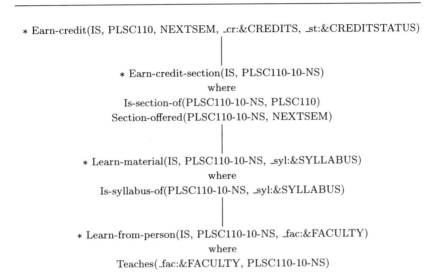

* Earn-credit(IS, PLSC110, NEXTSEM, _cr:&CREDITS, _st:&CREDITSTATUS)

* Earn-credit-section(IS, PLSC110-10-NS)
where
Is-section-of(PLSC110-10-NS, PLSC110)
Section-offered(PLSC110-10-NS, NEXTSEM)

* Learn-material(IS, PLSC110-10-NS, _syl:&SYLLABUS)
where
Is-syllabus-of(PLSC110-10-NS, _syl:&SYLLABUS)

* Learn-from-person(IS, PLSC110-10-NS, _fac:&FACULTY)
where
Teaches(_fac:&FACULTY, PLSC110-10-NS)

Figure 3.10
An updated context model

Want(IS, Knowif[IS, Isa(HISTORY101, GROUP1-COURSE)])

Using the same reasoning that was used on the last utterance of the previous example, plan identification heuristic P8 hypothesizes Satisfy-group-req(IS, GROUP1) as a candidate focused goal and its associated domain plan as a candidate focused plan.

Since this goal does not appear in an expansion of the current focused plan or any plans on the active path, focusing heuristics F1 through F3 fail. The goal at the root of the existing context model in figure 3.10 unifies with a subgoal in the candidate focused plan, so heuristic F4 succeeds in identifying a relationship between the new utterance and the existing plan context. A new tree is formed with the candidate focused goal-plan pair as its root, the plan associated with the root is expanded to generate the root of the old context model, and the old context model is entered as a subtree of the new tree. The root of this new context model is now the current focused goal-plan pair, since it represents the aspect of the task on which IS's attention is now believed to be centered. The elements of the old context model are no longer on the active path. Figure 3.11 shows the updated context model.

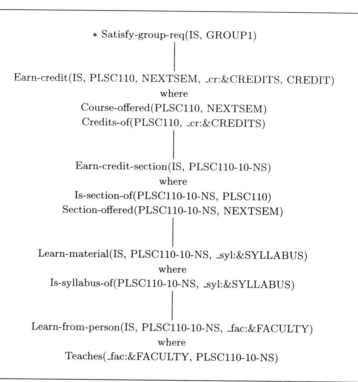

Figure 3.11
The final updated context model

3.5.3   Another Bottom-Up Dialogue

This example illustrates a dialogue in which the speaker considers sub-tasks of an overall task without directly relating them for the listener. This type of dialogue is the most difficult to assimilate correctly.

IS: I want to earn a computer science major. Who is teaching section 10 of CS180 next semester?

IP: Dr. Noyes is teaching section 10 of CS180 next semester.

IS: What courses must I take in order to satisfy the foreign language requirement?

IP: You must pass an intermediate level foreign language course.

From IS's first utterance, plan identification heuristic P1 hypothesizes Satisfy-major(IS, BA, CS) and Satisfy-major(IS, BS, CS) as candidate focused goals and their associated plans as candidate focused plans. Since there is no way of choosing between these, two context models are built, each with one of the candidate focused goal-plan pairs as its root.

From IS's second utterance, "Who is teaching section 10 of CS180 next semester?" plan identification heuristic P6 hypothesizes Learn-material(IS, CS180-10-NS, _syl:&SYLLABUS) and its associated plan as the candidate focused goal-plan pair. The focusing heuristics must determine how this relates to the preceding dialogue as represented by the context model. The strongest expectation is that IS is continuing with some aspect of the current focused plan. Since the preceding utterance did not address any particular goal in this plan, there is no most recently considered subgoal. Because learning the material of a section of CS180 appears in an expansion of the plans for majoring in computer science, heuristic F2 applies, and TRACK expands the context models as shown in figure 3.12.

IS's next query is "What courses must I take in order to satisfy the foreign language requirement?" Since IS is asking about the argument (courses) of a subgoal (taking courses) that is part of a plan for achieving a second goal, plan identification heuristic P7 hypothesizes the second goal, Satisfy-language-req(IS), and its associated plan as the candidate focused goal-plan pair. The focusing heuristics must now determine how this relates to the preceding dialogue as represented in the context model.

The strongest expectation is that IS will continue with some aspect of the current focused plan. However, the candidate focused goal-plan pair does not appear in an expansion of the current focused plan, which suggests that IS has shifted focus to another aspect of the overall task. In fact, none of the first four focusing heuristics find a relationship between the candidate focused goal-plan pair and the existing context model.

However, heuristic F5 finds that the goal Obtain-degree(IS, BA) has an associated plan that can be expanded to include both the candidate focused goal-plan pair and the context model whose root is Satisfy-major(IS, BA, CS). This suggests that IS has shifted his attention to another subtask (satisfying the foreign language requirement) of a higher-level plan (obtaining a Bachelor of Arts degree), of which the old current focused plan (obtaining a computer science major) is also a part.

Therefore, this goal and its associated plan become the root of a new context model, as shown in figure 3.13, and Satisfy-language-req(IS)

* Satisfy-major(IS, BA, CS)
|
* Earn-credit(IS, CS180, NEXTSEM, _cr1:&CREDITS, CREDIT)
where
Course-offered(CS180, NEXTSEM)
Credits-of(CS180, _cr:&CREDITS)
|
* Earn-credit-section(IS, CS180-10-NS)
where
Is-section-of(CS180-10-NS, CS180)
Section-offered(CS180-10-NS, NEXTSEM)
|
* Learn-material(IS, CS180-10-NS, _syl:&SYLLABUS)
where
Is-syllabus-of(CS180-10-NS, _syl:&SYLLABUS)

* Satisfy-major(IS, BS, CS)
|
* Earn-credit(IS, CS180, NEXTSEM, _cr1:&CREDITS, CREDIT)
where
Course-offered(CS180, NEXTSEM)
Credits-of(CS180, _cr:&CREDITS)
|
* Earn-credit-section(IS, CS180-10-NS)
where
Is-section-of(CS180-10-NS, CS180)
Section-offered(CS180-10-NS, NEXTSEM)
|
* Learn-material(IS,CS180-10-NS, _syl:&SYLLABUS)
where
Is-syllabus-of(CS180-10-NS, _syl:&SYLLABUS)

Figure 3.12
The context models after two utterances

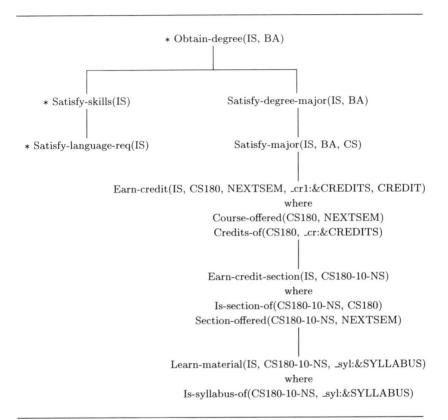

* Obtain-degree(IS, BA)

* Satisfy-skills(IS)   Satisfy-degree-major(IS, BA)

* Satisfy-language-req(IS)   Satisfy-major(IS, BA, CS)

Earn-credit(IS, CS180, NEXTSEM, _cr1:&CREDITS, CREDIT)
where
Course-offered(CS180, NEXTSEM)
Credits-of(CS180, _cr:&CREDITS)

Earn-credit-section(IS, CS180-10-NS)
where
Is-section-of(CS180-10-NS, CS180)
Section-offered(CS180-10-NS, NEXTSEM)

Learn-material(IS, CS180-10-NS, _syl:&SYLLABUS)
where
Is-syllabus-of(CS180-10-NS, _syl:&SYLLABUS)

Figure 3.13
The context model after three utterances

becomes the new current focus of attention. The other previous context
model, whose root was Satisfy-major(IS, BS, CS), is discarded.

So IS's third utterance has led TRACK to deduce that he wants to
pursue a Bachelor of Arts degree. Note that our plan inference process makes what Pollack [Pol87b] terms the "appropriate query assumption," namely, that IS does not ask queries that are inappropriate to
his intended goal. This assumption and its ramifications will be further
discussed in chapter 7.

3.6   Summary

This chapter has presented a model for hypothesizing and tracking the changing task-level goals of an information seeker during the course of a dialogue. It allows a complex set of domain-dependent plans that form a hierarchical structure of component goals and actions.

Analysis of an utterance consists of two stages. During local analysis, candidate focused goals and plans are hypothesized from individual utterances. Global analysis uses focusing heuristics to select the goal-plan pair that is most appropriate to the current dialogue context and integrate it into the existing plan structure, which thereby incrementally expands the system's model of the user's plan as the dialogue progresses.

Thus this model addresses one aspect of dialogue assimilation, that of incrementally inferring the underlying task-related plan motivating an information seeker's queries. Chapters 4, 5, and 6 apply this accumulated knowledge to understanding two classes of problematic utterances: pragmatically ill-formed queries and intersentential elliptical fragments. Chapter 7 then discusses restrictive assumptions underlying most current models of plan inference and describes work directed toward relaxing them.

4 Understanding Pragmatically Ill-Formed Input

In a cooperative information-seeking dialogue the information provider is engaged in helping the information seeker construct a plan for his underlying task. However, naturally occurring communication is both incomplete and imperfect. Not only does the information seeker fail to explicitly communicate all aspects of his goals and partially constructed plan for achieving these goals, but also his utterances are often imperfectly formulated. They may be ill-formed in the strict syntactic or semantic sense, or they may present pragmatic problems in understanding. However, analysis of naturally occurring dialogue suggests that the information seeker expects the information provider to facilitate better and more helpful communication by assimilating the dialogue, inferring from it much of what the information seeker wants to accomplish, and using these inferences to remedy many of the information seeker's faulty utterances.

This chapter presents a strategy for understanding one class of pragmatically ill-formed utterances. My approach relies on the system's beliefs about the information seeker's underlying task-related plan as the primary mechanism for suggesting potential interpretations and so considers only interpretations that are relevant to what the system believes the information seeker is trying to accomplish. This strategy is superior to previous approaches because it uses a model of the established dialogue context to identify and address the information seeker's perceived intentions and needs. This framework for understanding pragmatically ill-formed utterances has been implemented for a university world model. Once again, the information seeker will be referred to as IS and the information provider as IP; the information seeker is assumed to be the speaker, and the information provider the listener and respondent.

4.1 Pragmatically Ill-Formed Queries

4.1.1 Terminology

An *entity* is a uniquely identifiable element in the world. An *entity set* or *class* is a collection of entities of the same type; for example, the class FACULTY is the set of all faculty members. An *attribute* or *property* is a characteristic of members of a class. For example, members of the class FACULTY have such attributes as Rank, Status, and SS# (Social Security Number). An *entity relationship model* [Che76] is a collection of attributes, classes, and relationships in which the members of classes can participate. Two types of relations occur: an attribute relation

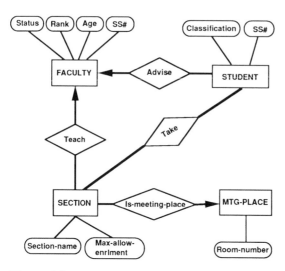

Figure 4.1
An entity relationship model

between the members of a class and a set of attribute values and an entity relation between members of two or more classes.

Figure 4.1 presents a typical entity relationship model. Attributes are enclosed in ovals and classes in rectangles. Attribute relations are represented by lines connecting an attribute and a class; entity relations are represented by diamonds containing the relation name and connected by solid lines to the classes participating in the relation. In figure 4.1 members of the class FACULTY have the attributes of Status, Rank, Age, and SS#. They also participate in several relations: faculty teach sections and advise students.

Attributes generally have at most one value for a given entity, and therefore attribute relations are functions. Entity relations may be many-many, and so such functionality does not exist. A relation R between members of CLASS1 and CLASS2 will be represented as R(_x1:&CLASS1, _x2:&CLASS2). Although an attribute Att of members of entity set CLASS1 is usually represented in functional notation as Att(_x:&CLASS1), I will use the notation Att(_x:&CLASS1, _attval:&ATT-DOMAIN), where ATT-DOMAIN is the set of values that attribute Att can assume. This provides a consistent terminology between the two kinds of relations and also with the representation of plans as presented in chapter 3.

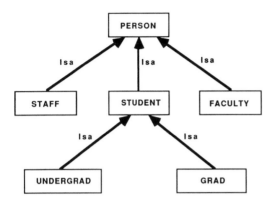

Figure 4.2
A generalization hierarchy

However, a distinction remains between attribute relations and entity relations. An attribute relation is essentially a function that operates on an entity and produces a constant having no conceptual representation as an element with constituent properties. Entity relations are many-many, many-one, or one-one relations between members of classes, each of which has attributes and may participate in other relations. For example, in the model illustrated in figure 4.1, the Teach relation associates members of the class FACULTY with members of the class SECTION, but the latter are also associated with members of the class MTG-PLACE via the Is-meeting-place relation.

In the following sections I will refer to attribute relations simply as attributes and reserve the term relation for entity relations. Although the rules for attributes and relations are similar, they will be presented separately for the sake of clarity.

A *generalization hierarchy* uses Isa relations to generalize classes. Figure 4.2 depicts a generalization hierarchy in which UNDERGRAD and GRAD are subclasses of STUDENT, and STUDENT, FACULTY, and STAFF are subclasses of PERSON. A generalization hierarchy differs from an entity relationship model in two ways. First, a generalization hierarchy specifies that every member of a subclass actually *is* a member of the indicated more general class, whereas an entity relationship model specifies relations in which members of classes *may* participate. Second, a generalization hierarchy relates similar classes via Isa relations, whereas in an entity relationship model members of dissimilar classes participate in entity relations.

4.1.2   Types of Pragmatic Ill-Formedness

A world model is a representation of knowledge about the world, such as entities and their attributes, relations that can hold among entities, and constraints on these relations. To understand an utterance, a listener must relate it to what she believes is the world model used by the speaker in formulating the utterance [Jos82]. As long as the listener does not have evidence to the contrary, she will generally assume that many of her beliefs about the world are also those of the speaker and interpret utterances with respect to these beliefs.

However, the speaker's view of the world may differ from that of the listener, or the speaker may be careless in formulating the language for his intended statement or query. As a result, the speaker's utterance may be syntactically and semantically correct yet violate the pragmatic rules of the listener's world model. This phenomenon has been termed *pragmatic overshoot* [SW80]. Upon detecting such discrepancies, human listeners often formulate cooperative responses addressing the speaker's perceived needs either by answering a modified utterance believed to represent the speaker's intent or by correcting mistaken assumptions.

Discrepancies of this type may be classified as extensional or intensional failures. An *extensional failure* occurs when the information seeker's utterance presumes the existence of data items that, although theoretically possible, do not currently exist in the world model. Thus extensional failure represents a discrepancy in the beliefs of speaker and listener about the contents of the existing database. Consider an example in which the University of Delaware has a wrestling team with no membership restrictions: the information seeker asks, "How many women on the University of Delaware wrestling team are computer science majors?" A proposition entailed by all but at most one direct answer to a question is called a *presumption* of the question [Kap79]. The above query presumes the existence of women on the University of Delaware wrestling team, since the only direct answer to the query that does not entail this proposition is "None." If the University of Delaware wrestling team consists only of men, IS's query contains a presumption that results in an extensional failure. IP is justified in believing that IS is unaware of this failure, since otherwise the answer to the question would be obvious and IS would not have asked the question. If IP limits her response to the direct answer "None," IS will falsely assume that the presumption that women are members of the wrestling team is correct, for a cooperative respondent would have corrected this presumed discrepancy in IS's knowledge. Kaplan [Kap79,Kap82] formulated a strategy for detecting and responding to utterances containing such extensional failures.

An *intensional failure* occurs when the information seeker's utterance makes erroneous presumptions about the structure of the underlying world model. Such pragmatic ill-formedness can be divided into four classes:

- Attributes and relations specified by IS that do not exist in the world model. An example is "Which apartments are for sale?" This query presumes that objects of type APARTMENT have a Sale-status attribute. However, in a world model for real estate, single apartments are rented, and apartment buildings, condominiums, houses, shopping centers, and movie theaters are sold. Even if the system's world knowledge is expanded to encompass a larger domain, the erroneously presumed attribute will still fail to exist.

- IS-specified restrictions on attributes and relations that can never be satisfied, even with the addition to the world model of new data. The query "Which lower-level English courses have an enrollment limit that is lower than 25 students?" is an example. In a university world model it may be that the enrollment limits on lower-level English courses are not allowed to be lower than 25. However, such constraints may not apply to the current enrollments of English courses, the enrollment limits on upper-level English courses, and the enrollment limits on lower-level courses in other departments. The sample utterance is pragmatically ill-formed, since world model constraints prohibit attributes that satisfy the restrictions specified by the information seeker.

- IS-specified attributes and relations that exceed the world knowledge of the existing model. An example is "What advanced-placement courses did Bob take in high school?" A university world model may be limited to knowledge of courses pursued by a student since matriculation at the university. Although the above query is well-formed with respect to an expanded world model, the system will view the query as pragmatically ill-formed, since the query exceeds the system's existing knowledge of the world.

- IS-specified attributes and relations resulting in a query that is irrelevant to the information seeker's underlying task. For example, suppose the information seeker asks "What is Dr. Smith's home address?" In a university world model the home address of faculty may be available. However, if a student wants to obtain special permission to take a course, a query requesting the instructor's home address is inappropriate; IS should request the instructor's office address or phone number. Such utterances do not violate the underlying world model, but they are a variation of pragmatic ill-formedness in that they violate the information provider's model of the information seeker's underlying task and appropriate plans for accomplishing this task. Joshi, Webber, and Weischedel [JWW84] argue that a cooperative respondent must prevent false inferences; if the information provider fails to notify the information seeker that the information seeker's queries are irrelevant to his underlying task, the information seeker is justified in inferring by default that the information provider has detected no such discrepancy. Thus although queries of this type can be answered, a cooperative information provider will inform the information seeker when queries appear irrelevant to his motivating task and will suggest alternative information that may be useful in constructing a plan for accomplishing that task.

This chapter is concerned with the first class of intensional failures, utterances presuming attributes or relations that do not exist in the underlying world model. Such intensional failures can result from different beliefs about the properties of objects and the relationships among objects, or from how language is used to refer to objects, properties, and relationships. For example, consider the intensional failure resulting from the query "Which apartments are for sale?" If the speaker believes that single apartments are sold, failure is due to incorrect beliefs about attributes of members of the APARTMENT class or about relations in which members of the class can participate. On the other hand, if the speaker knows that single apartments are not sold, then the error is caused by improper formulation of the intended query. Perhaps the context will show that the speaker really wants to know which condominiums are for sale, which apartment buildings are for sale, or even which apartments are for rent.

Analysis of naturally occurring dialogue suggests that when such failures occur, a human listener often responds to a modified query that is well-formed with respect to the listener's world model and that is believed to represent the speaker's intent in making the utterance or at least to satisfy his perceived needs. A robust natural language interface should have the ability to handle pragmatically ill-formed utterances much as people do. This requires that they not merely inform the speaker that the query is incorrect but that they attempt to deduce what the speaker meant to say and respond accordingly. Otherwise, the communication could not be called *natural*, because whenever the speaker's utterance violated the system's view of the world, the system would be unable to understand utterances to which human listeners respond with relative ease. Alternative ways of responding, discussed in chapter 1, depend on whether the listener believes that there is a discrepancy between his beliefs and those of the speaker, on the seriousness with which the listener views any discrepancies, and on how much faith the listener has in the correctness of his own beliefs.

4.1.3   Review of Related Work

Previous researchers have attempted to treat pragmatically ill-formed utterances in isolation without recourse to the preceding dialogue context.

Mays [May80b] proposed a mechanism for detecting the occurrence of an intensional violation by using a robust data model that incorporated a generalization dimension into an entity-relationship model (see also [Web83]). Generalization arcs could be marked as mutually exclusive: thus the classes FACULTY and STUDENT would be mutually exclusive subclasses of PERSON, whereas MAN and FACULTY would be nonmutually exclusive. This allowed Mays to differentiate between an intensionally valid presupposition such as "a faculty member who is male" and the intensional failure "a faculty member who is a student."

Mays discussed the detection of several cases of intensional failure:

- The presupposition of a nonexistent relation between members of classes

- The presupposition that a function can be applied to a domain over which the function is inapplicable

- The presupposition that an element of a class can be a member of two subclasses at the same time, though the two subclasses are mutually exclusive in the domain model.

In each case he suggested providing the information seeker with related knowledge about the underlying data model that would indicate the cause of the failure. For example, if failure was due to the presupposition of a nonexistent relation R between members of classes X and Y, Mays would have a system's response contain information about each relation R between members of some class Z1 and X, each relation R between members of some class Z2 and Y, and each possible relation S between members of classes X and Y. However, he does not use a model of whether these possibilities are applicable to the information seeker's underlying task. In a large world model, such responses will be too lengthy and include too many irrelevant alternatives.

Kaplan [Kap79,Kap82], Chang [Cha78], and Sowa [Sow76] investigated pragmatic ill-formedness caused by a missing join in the logical representation of the information seeker's query. Two relations R and S are said to have a natural join if they have a common argument, called the join element. For example, the relations

Member-of(_x1:&FACULTY, _x2:&COLLEGE)
Dean-of(_y1:&DEAN, _y2:&COLLEGE)

share a common argument, a variable referring to objects of type COL-LEGE, over which they can be joined. The relation produced by the join,

Faculty-college(_x:&FACULTY, _y:&DEAN, _z:&COLLEGE),

contains an entry for each faculty member and dean related to the same member of the class COLLEGE by relations Member-of and Dean-of. Computing joins of relations is necessary to answer such queries as "Who is the dean of the college in which Dr. Smith is a faculty member?" In this example the two relations Member-of and Dean-of are joined using members of the class COLLEGE to produce the relation Faculty-college described above. The desired answer is then computed by extracting the instance of the relation Faculty-college in which the first argument is Dr. Smith and projecting over the second argument.

Problems arise, however, when the query fails to specify the relations to be joined, as in the abbreviated version of the above query: "Who is Dr. Smith's dean?" This is called the *missing joins problem*. Let us assume that Dr. Smith is identified as a member of the class FACULTY. Objects of type FACULTY and DEAN may be indirectly related in several ways, and a choice must be made regarding the relations to be joined. For example, there may be relations relating faculty and the offices they occupy, offices and the buildings in which they are located, and deans and the buildings for which they have responsibility. The first two relations can be joined over an argument of type OFFICE, and the result joined with the third relation over an argument of type BUILDING. If this join is constructed to answer the above query, the result after extracting entries in which the faculty term is Dr. Smith and projecting over the argument of type DEAN will be "the deans with responsibility for the buildings in which Dr. Smith has an office."

Kaplan [Kap79,Kap82] proposed using the shortest relational path connecting the classes. Chang [Cha78] proposed an algorithm based on minimal spanning trees, using an a priori weighting of the arcs to indicate the likelihood of their intended join. Sowa [Sow76] defined a formalism called conceptual graphs for describing the semantics of stored data and their interrelationships and suggested using these structures to construct the expanded relation when the speaker's query incompletely specified the necessary relations and join elements. However, each of these strategies was deficient in that it considered the queries in isolation without using a model of the preceding dialogue to address the speaker's intentions.

4.1.4   Plan-Based Responses to Pragmatically Ill-Formed Queries

The context established by the preceding dialogue provides information that is useful in interpreting utterances and formulating cooperative responses. Consider, for example, the query "What is the area of the special weapons magazine of the *Alamo*?" which appears in the transcript of a dialogue in which the information seeker is attempting to load cargo onto ships using the REL natural language interface [Tho80]. The system was unable to understand this query, since the query erroneously presumed that storage locations had an Area attribute in the associated database. If a human information provider had similar difficulty in interpreting the query, then according to what she believed the information seeker was trying to accomplish, she might respond with the remaining capacity, the total capacity, or perhaps even the location of the *Alamo*'s special weapons magazine. I claim that the information provider's acquired beliefs about the information seeker's plans and goals are crucial in determining which of these the information seeker wants or needs. That is, I claim that beliefs about what IS is trying to do, as inferred from the preceding dialogue, should play a major role in the system's handling of pragmatically ill-formed utterances.

This claim is further supported by considering a single pragmatically ill-formed query preceded by two different dialogue sequences in a world model for real estate: "I'd like to own my own residence, but I don't like a lot of maintenance. Which apartments are for sale?" "We'd like to invest between $30 and $50 million. Which apartments are for sale?" In both of these dialogues the semantic representation of the information seeker's last utterance contains the erroneous proposition that objects of type APARTMENT have an attribute giving their Sale-status. However, single apartments are not sold, whereas condominiums, apartment buildings, apartments complexes, townhouses, houses, shopping centers, movie theaters, and so forth are sold.

In the first dialogue a human listener would probably infer from the information seeker's first utterance that he was interested in purchasing a condominium and she would reply accordingly. However, in the second dialogue a human listener would probably infer that the information seeker is a member of a real estate group that wants to significantly expand its holdings and therefore that he is interested in purchasing an apartment complex or perhaps a luxury apartment building. In each case a cooperative participant would use the preceding dialogue and her knowledge of the speaker to formulate a response that might provide the desired information.

4.2   Overview of the Interpretation Framework

If a natural language system's communication is to be regarded as natural, the system must be able to handle the full spectrum of utterances that humans understand with relative ease. Our approach to handling pragmatically ill-formed utterances is motivated by Grice's theory of meaning [Gri57,Gri69] and his maxim of relation [Gri75a]. According to Grice, the meaning of an utterance is the effect that the speaker intended to produce in his listener by virtue of the listener's recognition of that intent. Furthermore, the speaker would not have made the utterance if he did not believe that his listener could recognize this intention.

Now consider a pragmatically ill-formed utterance. According to Grice's theory, a listener should believe that the speaker thinks the listener can infer the intended meaning of the utterance; otherwise the speaker would not have made it. Furthermore, Grice's maxim of relation suggests that in the absence of clue words indicating a topic shift, the listener should believe that the speaker's ill-formed utterance is relevant to the established dialogue context. A cooperative participant will therefore use this context and the focus of attention immediately prior to the problematic utterance to attempt to deduce the speaker's intended meaning and to enable the dialogue to continue without interruption. I contend that a natural language system should act in the same way. Otherwise the dialogue cannot be called *natural*, since the user would be required to refrain from making many utterances that a human would understand.

The information seeker's inferred task-related plan captures much of the dialogue context, and I contend that it should be used as the basis for understanding pragmatically ill-formed utterances. If the system considers only queries relevant to instantiating and expanding the partial plan represented in its inferred context model, it will limit itself to interpretations that might represent the information seeker's intent or at least satisfy his perceived needs.

My hypothesis is that the context model suggests substitutions for the erroneous proposition appearing in the semantic representation of the information seeker's query. Each of these substitutions produces the semantic representation for a revised query that is relevant to the information seeker's underlying task-related plan and therefore meaningful to the overall dialogue context. If more than one revised query is suggested, the system must select the interpretation that is most likely to represent the speaker's intent. I believe that this choice should be made by evaluating each suggested revised query on the basis of its relevance to the current focus of attention in the dialogue and its semantic similarity to the ill-formed query.

Figure 4.3 presents an overview of my interpretation framework. The processes in this diagram form one module of the utterance interpreter in the architecture for a robust natural language interface shown in figure 1.1. I assume that the erroneous proposition causing the pragmatic ill-formedness is identified with techniques suggested by other researchers [May80b]. The suggestion mechanism analyzes an expansion of the context model to suggest substitutions for the erroneous proposition appearing in the semantic representation of the user's query. If multiple suggestions are made, the selection mechanism selects the substitution deemed most likely to produce a revised query that captures the information seeker's intended meaning or that satisfies his needs.

4.3   The Suggestion Mechanism

The suggestion mechanism examines the current context model and possible expansions of plans for its constituent goals and proposes substitutions for the proposition causing the pragmatic ill-formedness. This erroneous proposition represents either a nonexistent attribute or a nonexistent entity relation.

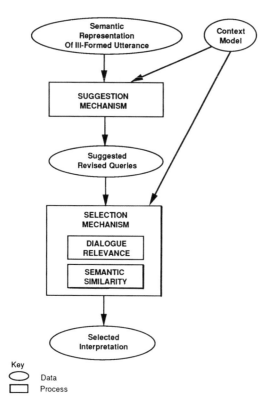

Figure 4.3
Overview of the framework for handling pragmatic ill-formedness

The suggestion mechanism applies two classes of rules. The first is a set of simple substitution rules that reason on the context model to suggest substitutions of attributes, relations, and object classes that might produce a query representing what the speaker really wanted or needed to ask. The second class of rules suggests an expanded relation path (one that fills in the missing joins) that might represent the speaker's intended query. Since the context model is the source of these suggestions, only expanded paths that represent queries relevant to the speaker's underlying task-related plan will be proposed. These two classes of rules may be used together to propose a replacement for the erroneous proposition consisting of both an expanded relation path and a substitution of an attribute, relation, or object class.

4.3.1   Simple Substitutions

Suppose a student wants to pursue an independent study project. Such projects can be directed by full-time or part-time faculty but not by faculty who are in the extension program, visitors, or on sabbatical. In checking on Dr. Smith as a possible faculty sponsor, the student might erroneously enter the query "What is the classification of Dr. Smith?" Only students have a Classification attribute; this attribute can have such values as ARTS&SCIENCE-1992, ENGINEERING-1993, and BUSINESS-1991. Faculty have attributes such as Rank, Status, Age, and Title. Pursuing an independent study project under the direction of Dr. Smith requires that Dr. Smith's status be FULL-TIME or PART-TIME. If the information provider knows that the student wants to pursue independent study, he might infer that the student needs the value of the Status attribute and answer the revised query "What is the status of Dr. Smith?"

Ill-formed queries can occur if the speaker's beliefs about how to refer to an attribute, relation, or object differ from those of the system. Such errors occur even more often in spoken dialogues when the speaker is distracted and inadvertently uses incorrect terminology. In both cases the underlying task-related plan inferred from the preceding dialogue appears to provide the primary clues as to the speaker's intentions, with relevance and semantic criteria differentiating among multiple possibilities.

The context model represents the system's beliefs about the speaker's plan for accomplishing the task motivating his queries. This plan can be expanded by substituting a subplan for each constituent subgoal and by instantiating variables with constants. Since substituted plans also contain goals, this expansion process can be continued to any desired degree of detail until eventually the plan contains only goals that can be achieved by primitive actions. The substitution mechanism contains four *simple substitution rules* that analyze an expansion of the context model and suggest revisions of IS's query. The first two rules handle errors in which an attribute or relation is incorrectly specified in the information seeker's query, and the third and fourth rules handle cases in which an object class is incorrectly specified.

Incorrectly specified attributes   Since the system believes that IS is trying to expand his partially constructed plan, it should anticipate that IS might want to know about propositions appearing in the plan. Thus IS might want to know the value of some attribute of an object specified in a plan proposition. Suppose, for example, that IS erroneously requests

the value of attribute Att1 for an object OBJA in CLASS when in fact
such objects do not have this attribute. The query will contain the
erroneous proposition that the object has an attribute Att1, namely

Att1(OBJA, _att-value:&ATT1-DOMAIN).

Suppose further that the plan inferred for IS contains an attribute Att2
for the object, namely

Att2(OBJA, _att-value:&ATT2-DOMAIN).

A cooperative listener might infer that IS really wants the value of attribute Att2, especially if Att1 and Att2 are semantically similar. This
reasoning motivates the following simple substitution rule:

> *Substitution rule 1:* If IS's proposition erroneously presumes that a
> member x of CLASS has attribute Att1 but does not specify the value
> of the attribute, then replace attribute Att1 with attribute Att2 if the
> following conditions hold: A proposition specifying attribute Att2 for a
> member y of CLASS appears in an expansion of the context model, and
> x and y unify. (Two arguments are said to unify if they are identical
> constants, variables of the same type, or a constant and a variable of
> the same type.)

The substitution mechanism searches an expansion of IS's inferred
plan for propositions satisfying the above conditions. Substitution rule 1
then suggests substituting the attribute from this proposition for the attribute specified in the erroneous proposition contained in IS's query.
This substitution produces the semantic representation for a revised
query that is relevant to the current dialogue and may capture the
speaker's intent or at least satisfy his needs.

For example, consider again the query "What is the area of the special
weapons magazine of the *Alamo*?" Since the special weapons magazine
is a member of the class STORAGE-AREA and members of this class
have such attributes as Remaining-capacity and Total-capacity, but no
Area attribute, the semantic representation of the above query contains
the following erroneous proposition:

Area(SPECIAL-WEAPONS-MAG, _areaval:&SQ-FT)

Suppose that the dialogue preceding the query indicates that IS wants
to allocate cargo of the appropriate type to the various cargo holds. A
subgoal in a plan associated with this goal would be the following:

Assign-cargo(IS, _item:&CARGO, _hold:&STORAGE-AREA)
where
Is-type(_item:&CARGO, _ctype:&CARGO-TYPE)
Cargo-type(_hold:&STORAGE-AREA, _ctype:&CARGO-TYPE)

And a plan for this subgoal would contain a precondition specifying that the storage area must have room for the cargo item:

Greater-than(_rem:&CUBIC-FT, _itemsize:&CUBIC-FT)
where
Volume(_item:&CARGO, _itemsize:&CUBIC-FT)
Remaining-capacity(_hold:&STORAGE-AREA, _rem:&CUBIC-FT)

Substitution rule 1 would examine this plan and suggest substituting either of the propositions

Cargo-type(SPECIAL-WEAPONS-MAG, _ctype:&CARGO-TYPE)
Remaining-capacity(SPECIAL-WEAPONS-MAG, _rem:&CUBIC-FT)

for the erroneous proposition

Area(SPECIAL-WEAPONS-MAG, _areaval:&SQ-FT)

appearing in the semantic representation of IS's query. These substitutions produce suggested semantic representations equivalent to the two revised queries "What is the cargo type of the special weapons magazine of the *Alamo?*" and "What is the remaining capacity of the special weapons magazine of the *Alamo?*"

Incorrectly specified relations In constructing a task-related plan, IS enters objects into the plan partly because of their relationship to other objects. Since the system believes that IS is attempting to instantiate and expand his partially constructed plan, it should anticipate that IS might want to know which objects participate in a relation specified in a particular plan proposition. For example, the subgoal

Learn-from-text(_agent:&STUDENT, _txt:&TEXT)
where
Uses(_sect:&SECTION, _txt:&TEXT)

appears in the plan for learning the material in a section of a course, shown in figure 3.3 of chapter 3 (on page 86). If IS is considering taking a section of CS105, he might want to know what text is being used and might therefore ask, "What text will be used in section 10 of CS105 next semester?"

However, IS might not know how to refer to certain relations or might inadvertently use the wrong reference. Suppose that IS erroneously requests the objects in CLASS1 that are related by R to some object in CLASS2 when in fact objects in CLASS1 and CLASS2 are not related by R. The query will contain the erroneous proposition that objects in CLASS1 are related by R to objects in CLASS2, namely R(_x1:&CLASS1, _x2:&CLASS2). Suppose further that the plan inferred for IS contains a relation S between members of CLASS1 and CLASS2, such as S(_y1:&CLASS1, _y2:&CLASS2). If the arguments in IS's erroneous proposition unify with the arguments in this plan proposition, a cooperative listener might infer that the information seeker really wants the members of CLASS1 that are related by S to a member of CLASS2, especially if relations R and S are semantically similar.

This reasoning motivates the following simple substitution heuristic:

> *Substitution rule 2:* If IS's proposition erroneously presumes a relation R between members of CLASS1 and CLASS2, then replace relation R with relation S if a proposition specifying relation S between a member of CLASS1 and a member of CLASS2 appears in an expansion of the context model and the arguments in the erroneous proposition unify with the corresponding arguments in the plan proposition.

The substitution mechanism searches an expansion of IS's inferred plan for propositions whose arguments unify with the arguments in the erroneous proposition causing the pragmatic ill-formedness. Substitution rule 2 then suggests substituting the relation from the proposition in the plan for the relation specified in IS's query. This substitution produces the semantic representation for a revised query that is relevant to the overall task that the information seeker is pursuing and that may capture his intent in making the ill-formed utterance.

For example, suppose that our world model indicates that faculty teach both courses and seminars and that faculty may participate in seminars, but that faculty do not *take* (in the sense of *earn credit in*) courses or seminars. Then the semantic representation of the query "What seminars is Dr. Smith taking?" contains the erroneous proposition Take(DR-SMITH, _seminar:&SEMINAR). A plan for learning the material in a seminar includes the following subgoal:

Learn-from(IS, _seminar1:&SEMINAR, _fac:&FACULTY)
where
Teaches(_fac:&FACULTY, _seminar1:&SEMINAR)

If the preceding dialogue indicates that IS wants to earn credit in a particular seminar course, the substitution mechanism will find this subgoal as part of IS's expanded plan. Substitution rule 2 will suggest substituting the relation Teaches for the relation Take in the erroneous proposition in IS's query, and this will result in a revised semantic representation equivalent to the query "What seminars is Dr. Smith teaching?" In this case IS may have been using *take* in the sense of handling or teaching.

On the other hand, a plan for evaluating the professional development of departmental faculty might include the following subgoal:

Evaluate(IS, _content:&CONTENT)
where
Content-of(_seminar1:&SEMINAR, _content:&CONTENT)
Participate-in(_fac:&FACULTY, _seminar1:&SEMINAR)

If the preceding dialogue indicates that IS is constructing a plan for evaluating Dr. Smith's professional development, the substitution mechanism will find this subgoal as part of IS's expanded plan. Substitution rule 2 will then suggest substituting the relation Participate-in for the relation Take in the erroneous proposition in IS's query, and this will result in a revised semantic representation equivalent to the query "What seminars is Dr. Smith participating in?" In this case IS may have been using *take* in the sense of learning the material of a given seminar.

Incorrectly specified classes IS might not know how to refer to some domain objects or might inadvertently use the wrong references. This was the case when IS erroneously used the term *apartment* instead of *condominium* in the query "Which apartments are for sale?" If IS erroneously requests the objects in CLASS1 with a given value of attribute Att when in fact such objects do not have this attribute, the query will contain the erroneous proposition that objects in CLASS1 have attribute Att. If the plan inferred for IS contains an attribute Att of members of CLASS2, a cooperative listener might infer that IS really wants the members of CLASS2 with the stated attribute value, especially if the two classes are semantically similar.

This reasoning motivates the following simple substitution rule:

> *Substitution rule 3:* If IS's proposition erroneously presumes that a member of CLASS1 has an attribute Att, then replace CLASS1 with CLASS2 if the following conditions hold: A proposition specifying attribute Att of a member of CLASS2 appears in an expansion of the context model, IS's utterance referred to a general member of CLASS1 rather than to a specific member, and the other arguments in IS's erroneous proposition unify with the corresponding arguments in the plan proposition.

The substitution mechanism searches an expansion of IS's inferred plan for propositions satisfying the above conditions. Substitution rule 3

Purchase(IS, _res:&CONDOMINIUM)
Preconditions:
    Sale-status(_res:&CONDOMINIUM, FOR-SALE)
Plan body:
    Negotiate-price(IS, _res:&CONDOMINIUM)
    Close-sale(IS, _res:&CONDOMINIUM)
Primary effects:
    Purchase(IS, _res:&CONDOMINIUM)

Figure 4.4
Plan for purchasing a condominium

then suggests substituting the class from a plan proposition for the class specified in the erroneous proposition in IS's query.

For example, consider again the dialogue "I'd like to own my own residence but I don't like a lot of maintenance. Which apartments are for sale?" From the context established by the first utterance, the system should expect that IS will be inquiring about dwellings with little owner maintenance and therefore suspect that the second utterance might be asking about condominiums. From the first utterance the TRACK system would infer that IS wants to purchase a residence with little owner maintenance. Such a plan would include the potential subgoal Purchase(IS, _res:&CONDOMINIUM), whose associated plan is shown in figure 4.4. The system would expect that IS will want to complete instantiation and expansion of his partially constructed plan, and therefore might want to know which elements satisfy the plan propositions. Suppose that Sale-status is an attribute of objects that can be sold and that possible values of this attribute include FOR-SALE, OPTIONED, SOLD, and NOT-FOR-SALE. Since single apartments cannot be sold, the semantic representation of IS's second utterance contains the erroneous proposition Sale-status(_x:&APARTMENT, FOR-SALE). But since an expansion of the plan inferred for IS contains the proposition Sale-status(_res:&CONDOMINIUM, FOR-SALE) found in the subplan Purchase(IS, _res:&CONDOMINIUM), substitution rule 3 suggests substituting the class CONDOMINIUM for the class APARTMENT in the erroneous proposition in IS's query and this results in a revised semantic representation equivalent to the query "Which condominiums are for sale?"

Substitution rule 3 requires that IS's erroneous proposition contain a variable whose type is the class for which the substitution is made. If IS's erroneous proposition specifies a particular member of a class, it is much less likely that the class is the cause of the pragmatic ill-formedness. Consider, for example, the query "What is Dr. Smith's classification?" Since IS has identified a particular faculty member, Dr. Smith, IS has implicitly made reference to the class FACULTY, but not explicitly. Therefore, inclusion of this class in the erroneous proposition is unlikely to be the cause of the pragmatic ill-formedness.

However, a pragmatically ill-formed query could result if IS erroneously believes that Dr. Smith is a student or if IS incorrectly identified the constant, perhaps by misspelling, so that the erroneous proposition actually contained a particular constant and class different from that intended by the information seeker. The former requires correction of IS's object-related misconceptions [McC88], but it appears that the latter could be handled by an extension of the rules presented here. This would require measuring the typographical or phonological similarity of a constant specified by IS and constants identifying members of a class suggested as a substitution for the class appearing in the erroneous proposition. For example, if Al Smith is faculty and Al Smyth is a student, then a cooperative listener might infer in the following dialogue that IS intended to ask about Al Smyth, not Al Smith: "I want to determine the distribution of double majors in our department. What is Al Smith's classification?" Although this is an interesting extension of the problem under discussion, I will not consider it further.

A variation of substitution rule 3 suggests an object class substitution when the erroneous proposition in IS's query asserts a nonexistent relation between two classes. Suppose that IS erroneously requests the objects in CLASS2 that are related by R to an object in CLASS1 when in fact objects in CLASS2 and CLASS1 are not related by R. Suppose further that the plan inferred for IS contains a proposition in which members of CLASS3 and CLASS1 are related by relation R. Then, similar to the reasoning captured in substitution rule 3, a cooperative listener might infer that IS really wants the members of CLASS3 that are related by R to a member of CLASS1, especially if CLASS2 and CLASS3 are semantically similar. This reasoning motivates the following simple substitution rule:

> *Substitution rule 4:* If IS's proposition erroneously presumes a relation
> R between members of CLASS1 and CLASS2, replace CLASS2 with
> CLASS3 if the following conditions hold: A proposition specifying rela-
> tion R between a member of CLASS1 and a member of CLASS3 appears

in an expansion of the context model, IS's utterance referred to a general member of CLASS2 rather than to a specific member, and the other arguments in IS's erroneous proposition unify with the corresponding arguments in the plan proposition.

For example, consider the query "What stocks does General Investments sell?" Suppose that General Investments is a mutual fund company; such companies sell mutual funds but not stocks. Therefore, the above query contains the following erroneous proposition:

Sells(GENERAL-INVESTMENTS, _stock:&STOCK).

A plan for diversifying one's investments, particularly if the amount is relatively small, will contain the potential subgoal of investing in a mutual fund, namely Invest(IS, _fund:&MUTUAL-FUND). A plan for this will include the following subgoal:

Consult(IS, _comp:&MUTUAL-FUND-CMPY)
where
Sells(_comp:&MUTUAL-FUND-CMPY, _fund:&MUTUAL-FUND)

Suppose that the preceding dialogue indicates that IS has a small amount of money to invest and wants to spread his investment to several areas for decreased risk. Then the substitution mechanism will find the above subgoal in an expansion of IS's inferred plan and suggest substituting the class MUTUAL-FUND for the class STOCK in IS's erroneous proposition, resulting in a revised semantic representation equivalent to the query "What mutual funds does General Investments sell?"

4.3.2 Expanded Paths

Suppose a student wants to contact Dr. Smith to discuss participating in the undergraduate research program. Then the student might utter the query "What is Dr. Smith's phone number?" Phone numbers are associated with homes, faculty offices, and department offices. Discussions with professors may be handled in person or by phone; contacting a professor by phone requires that the student dial the phone number of Dr. Smith's office. Thus the listener might infer that the student needs the phone number of the office occupied by Dr. Smith.

Although the above query appears quite natural, it incompletely specifies the desired path between objects in the world model; this was referred to earlier as the missing joins problem. One cause of such incompleteness appears to be a desire on the part of the information seeker to use abbreviated, terse queries under the assumption that the existing context will ensure proper interpretation. A second cause of missing joins in the semantic representation of natural language queries is a difference in the world model structures presumed by information seeker and information provider.

Analysis of transcripts of naturally occurring dialogues indicates that utterances with missing joins occur frequently and are generally interpreted correctly by human listeners. The underlying task-related plan inferred from the preceding dialogue appears to provide significant clues as to the speaker's intentions by indicating those paths in the world model that are relevant to the current context.

Hypothesizing missing joins   The substitution mechanism contains two expanded path rules for handling missing joins in the semantic representation of the information seeker's query. These rules apply when the attributes and object classes are not directly related by the attribute or entity relation specified by IS but when there is a path in the world model between the attribute and object class or between the object classes. I call this *path expansion*, since in finding the missing joins, the system constructs an expanded relational path.

Once again, since the system believes that IS is trying to expand his partially constructed plan, it should anticipate that IS may need to know about the objects that play a role in the plan. To request this information, IS may formulate a query that requires joining two propositions over a common element. For example, one plan for contacting a professor about the undergraduate research program will contain the following subgoal:

```
Call-office(IS, _office:&OFFICE)
where
Office-of(_fac:&FACULTY, _office:&OFFICE)
```

and its plan will in turn contain the following subgoal:

```
Dial(IS, _number:&PHONE-NUMBER)
where
Phone-number(_office:&OFFICE, _number:&PHONE-NUMBER)
```

IS might want to know the phone number of the professor's office and ask, "What is the phone number of Dr. Smith's office?" Answering this query requires that the propositions

```
Office-of(SMITH, _office:&OFFICE)
Phone-number(_office:&OFFICE, _number:&PHONE-NUMBER)
```

be joined over the common element _office:&OFFICE.

More generally, suppose that IS wants to know which elements in CLASS3 stand in relation R2 to the elements in CLASS2 that stand in relation R1 to elements in CLASS1. A request for this information requires that the speaker specify a join between the following relations:

R1(_x:&CLASS1, _y:&CLASS2)
R2(_y:&CLASS2, _z:&CLASS3)

But the speaker may decide to shortcut the complete formulation of his intended query and rely on the established context to fill in the missing components. This would be the case if, instead of the previous query, IS had asked, "What's Dr. Smith's phone number?" As a result, the semantic representation of IS's actual utterance may contain one of the following two erroneous propositions:

R1(_x:&CLASS1, _z:&CLASS3)
R2(_x:&CLASS1, _z:&CLASS3)

However, if relation R1 between objects in CLASS1 and CLASS2 and relation R2 between objects in CLASS2 and CLASS3 both appear on a path in the underlying task-related plan inferred for IS, a cooperative listener might infer that IS wants the members of CLASS3 that appear in the join of the relations R1 and R2, which is referred to as the composite relation R1 * R2.

This reasoning leads to the following two path expansion heuristics. The first suggests substituting an expanded relational path for an erroneously presumed relation between two object classes, and the second suggests substituting an expanded path when an object lacks a presumed attribute.

> *Substitution rule 5:* If the semantic representation of IS's query contains the erroneous proposition R(u:&CLASSA, v:&CLASSB), replace it with the expanded path
>
> R0(u:&CLASSA, y1:&CLASS1)
> R1(y1:&CLASS1, y2:&CLASS2)
> R2(y2:&CLASS2, y3:&CLASS3)
> $\vdots$
> Rn(yn:&CLASSn, v:&CLASSB)
>
> if the following conditions are satisfied:
> (1) A path in an expansion of the context model contains the propositions

R0(x:&CLASSA, y1:&CLASS1)
R1(y1:&CLASS1, y2:&CLASS2)
R2(y2:&CLASS2, y3:&CLASS3)

$$\vdots$$

Rn(yn:&CLASSn, z:&CLASSB).

(2) R is one of the relations R0, ..., Rn.
(3) The terms u and v from IS's proposition unify with the terms x and z from the plan propositions.

Substitution rule 6: If the semantic representation of IS's query contains the erroneous proposition Att(u:&CLASSA, att-value1:&ATT-DOMAIN), replace it with the expanded path

Att(y1:&CLASS1, att-value1:&ATT-DOMAIN)
R1(y1:&CLASS1, y2:&CLASS2)
R2(y2:&CLASS2, y3:&CLASS3)

$$\vdots$$

Rn(yn:&CLASSn, u:&CLASSA)

if the following conditions are satisfied:
(1) A path in an expansion of the context model contains the propositions

Att(y1:&CLASS1, att-value:&ATT-DOMAIN)
R1(y1:&CLASS1, y2:&CLASS2)
R2(y2:&CLASS2, y3:&CLASS3)

$$\vdots$$

Rn(yn:&CLASSn, z:&CLASSA)

(2) The terms att-value1 and u from IS's proposition unify with the terms att-value and z from the plan propositions.

As an example of the path expansion heuristics, consider the query "Which faculty does DATA-LOGIC give money to?" In a university world model, faculty are not given money by industries; faculty consult for industries and earn consulting fees, and research projects have government or industrial money supporting them. Therefore, the above query contains the following erroneous proposition:

Gives-funds(DATA-LOGIC, _fac1:&FACULTY)

Suppose that the preceding dialogue indicates that the information
seeker is evaluating individual faculty contributions to the university.
Figure 4.5 presents part of an expansion of the resulting context model.
Upon analyzing this plan, the substitution mechanism finds that the
propositions

Gives-funds(_c1:&CORP, _p:&PROJECT)
Principle-investigator(_p:&PROJECT, _fac:&FACULTY)

appear along a single path and that the terms DATA-LOGIC and
_fac1:&FACULTY from IS's erroneous proposition unify with the terms
_c1:&CORP and _fac:&FACULTY from the above propositions. Thus
substitution rule 5 suggests replacing the erroneous proposition appearing in IS's query with the expanded path represented by the conjunction
of the propositions

Gives-funds(DATA-LOGIC, _p:&PROJECT)
Principle-investigator(_p:&PROJECT, _fac1:&FACULTY).

The resulting revised query is semantically equivalent to a request for
the faculty who are the principal investigators of projects supported by
DATA-LOGIC.

As another example of the path expansion heuristics, consider the
following dialogue:

IS: Who is in charge of the undergraduate research program?

IP: Dr. Smith is in charge of the undergraduate research program.

IS: What is Dr. Smith's phone number?

In a university data model, phone numbers are attributes of homes,
faculty offices, department offices, etc. Although the last query in the
above dialogue appears quite natural, it contains the erroneous proposition Phone-number(SMITH, _numb:&PHONE-NUMBER). From the
first query in the above dialogue, the TRACK system described in chapter 3 would infer that IS is considering taking part in the undergraduate
research program. One potential subgoal in such a plan is to satisfy
the prerequisites, which involve getting permission from the supervisor
of the program. Figure 4.6 illustrates a part of an expansion of the
resulting context model.

The substitution mechanism analyzes the context model and finds
that the propositions

Office-of(_fac:&FACULTY, _office:&OFFICE)
Phone-number(_office:&OFFICE, _number:&PHONE-NUMBER)

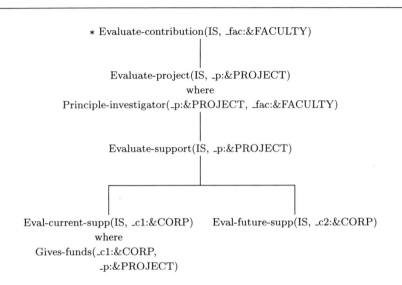

Figure 4.5
A portion of a plan for evaluating faculty

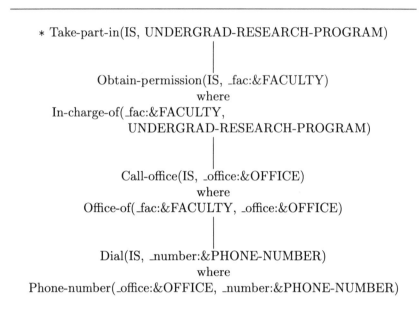

* Take-part-in(IS, UNDERGRAD-RESEARCH-PROGRAM)
|
Obtain-permission(IS, _fac:&FACULTY)
where
In-charge-of(_fac:&FACULTY,
          UNDERGRAD-RESEARCH-PROGRAM)
|
Call-office(IS, _office:&OFFICE)
where
Office-of(_fac:&FACULTY, _office:&OFFICE)
|
Dial(IS, _number:&PHONE-NUMBER)
where
Phone-number(_office:&OFFICE, _number:&PHONE-NUMBER)

Figure 4.6
A partial plan for participating in undergraduate research

appear on the same path. Substitution rule 6 suggests replacing the erroneous proposition with the expanded path represented by the conjunction of the propositions

Office-of(SMITH, _office:&OFFICE)
Phone-number(_office:&OFFICE, _numb:&PHONE-NUMBER).

This substitution produces a semantic representation equivalent to the revised query "What is the phone number of Dr. Smith's office?"

To limit the components of path expressions to those relations that can be meaningfully combined in a given context, substitution rules 5 and 6 make a strong assumption: that the relations comprising the relevant expansion appear on a single path within the context model representing the system's beliefs about the information seeker's inferred plan. For example, suppose that IS's inferred plan is to take CS105 and that one part of an expansion of this plan contains the subgoal

Learn-from-person(IS, _sect:&SECTION, _fac:&FACULTY)
where
Teaches(_fac:&FACULTY, _sect:&SECTION)

and another part of the plan contains the subgoal

Obtain-extra-help(IS, _sect:&SECTION, _ta:&T-ASSISTANT)
where
Assists(_ta:&T-ASSISTANT, _sect:&SECTION).

The plans associated with these subgoals specify respectively that IS attend class at the time the section meets and that IS attend the individual help session held in the computer lab during the section's office hours. Now consider the utterance "When are teaching assistants available?" A direct relationship between teaching assistants and time does not exist. The constraint that all components of a path expression appear on a single path in the inferred task-related plan prohibits combining the proposition

Assists(_ta:&T-ASSISTANT, _sect:&SECTION)

with a proposition such as

Is-meeting-time(_sect:&SECTION, _time:&MTG-TIME)

that appears in the plan for the subgoal Learn-from-person on another path in the context model, to suggest a reply consisting of the times that the CS105 sections meet.

4.4   The Selection Mechanism

The substitution heuristics propose substitutions for the erroneous proposition appearing in the semantic representation of the speaker's query. These substitutions produce a set of revised semantic representations all of which represent queries relevant to the plan that the system believes the information seeker is constructing. If only one revised query is suggested, it is reasonable to believe that it represents the information seeker's intentions, since it is the only suggested variant of his actual query that is relevant to his inferred plan.

On the other hand, if the substitution heuristics propose multiple revised queries, the system must decide if any of these is significantly more likely than the others to represent the speaker's intentions or satisfy his perceived needs. I have identified two criteria that appear important in selecting the most appropriate interpretation. The first is relevance to what the system believes is the information seeker's current focus of attention in his task-related plan. As I argued in chapter 3, the information seeker is expected to finish investigating all aspects of the current focused task and the most recently considered subgoal of this task before considering other subtasks of the overall plan. Thus the more relevant a revised query to that aspect of the task on which the system believes the information seeker's attention is currently focused, the more anticipated is the query at this point in the dialogue. The second criteria is the similarity of the revised query and the information seeker's utterance. The more the information seeker's utterance is altered, the less closely it resembles what he actually said and therefore the less likely it is to represent what he meant to say. The next sections discuss these selection criteria and how they are employed to select among several suggested revised queries.

4.4.1   Relevance

In chapter 3, I contended that some shifts in focus of attention in the plan structure are more likely than others. This leads to the hypothesis that the more expected the shift in the focus of attention that would result from a revised query, the more likely it is that the query represents the speaker's intentions.

Consider again the case in which IS wants to load cargo onto ships and asks, "What is the area of the special weapons magazine of the *Alamo*?" As explained previously, in the ship world model under consideration, storage areas such as the special weapons magazine do not have an

Area attribute, although they may have attributes such as Remaining-capacity and Total-capacity. Thus the semantic representation of the above query contains the erroneous proposition

Area(SPECIAL-WEAPONS-MAG, _areaval:&SQ-FEET)

The suggestion mechanism must analyze the system's beliefs about IS's task-related plan and propose revised queries that might represent his intentions. The overall task of loading cargo might have two subtasks. The first is allocating cargo to the various storage compartments. This necessitates making certain that each load of cargo is assigned to a compartment that has room for it, which leads to such queries as "What is the remaining capacity of the special weapons magazine of the *Alamo*?" The second is assigning workers to fill the storage holds, with perhaps different workers assigned to different sections of the ship. This leads to queries such as "What is the location of the special weapons magazine of the *Alamo*?" Now suppose that the current focus of attention in the dialogue is the subtask of assigning a load of artillery shells to an appropriate storage compartment. The first of the above queries addresses an aspect of the current focused plan, whereas the second requires a major shift in focus of attention. Therefore, the first query is more expected than the second at this point in the dialogue.

To evaluate the relevance of a suggested revised query to the current focus of attention in the dialogue, I measure the focus shift that would occur if the suggested revised query were the speaker's intended utterance. The measure of focus shift is the following:

FocusShift(revquery) = STKLEV + FACTOR * DEPTH
where
STKLEV = the distance in the active stack between the current focused plan
         and the plan whose expansion suggested the revised query (the
         active stack is the stack of goals and plans along the active path in
         the context model)
DEPTH = the depth at which the proposition suggesting the revised query
         appears in the expansion of a plan residing on the active path
FACTOR = 0.2. This value was selected so that the most relevant revised
         queries would be those that address aspects of the current focused
         plan unless this requires expanding the plan in far greater detail
         than represented by the current focus of attention.

Relevance, then, is inversely proportional to focus shift. Revised queries for which FocusShift(revquery) is small are more relevant to the current focus of attention in the dialogue than are those for which it is large.

4.4.2 Semantic Similarity

My second criterion for selecting from among several suggested revised queries is the similarity of a revised query to the speaker's actual utterance. The more the speaker's utterance is altered, the less closely it resembles what he actually said and therefore the less likely it is to represent what he meant to say. To evaluate the similarity of a revised query and the speaker's actual utterance, I measure the difference between the two. Small differences correlate with high semantic similarity.

The substitution heuristics alter the speaker's utterance by substituting a conjunction of propositions for the erroneously presumed proposition or by substituting a new term for a term used by the speaker. Two criteria appear relevant to estimating how much a substitution alters the speaker's query: the number of propositions comprising the substitution and the resemblance between a substituted term and the term used by the speaker. How these individual criteria are combined to estimate the semantic difference between a revised query and the information seeker's utterance depends on the type of revision operation applied to the erroneous proposition.

Path expansion metric Substitutions representing short path expansions are more desirable than those representing longer ones, since they imply fewer shortcuts by the speaker. I use the following metric Dexp(revquery) to compute the change introduced by path expansion:

Dexp(revquery) = twice the number of relations by which the path is extended

Term substitution metric There are a number of reasons why speakers might use incorrect terminology, and these suggest ways for estimating the resemblance between the term used by a speaker and a substituted term. A speaker may use a semantically similar term in place of the correct term, as in the use of *apartment* instead of *condominium* or the use of *area* instead of *remaining capacity*. To capture this, I use a generalization hierarchy to semantically compare substitutions with the items for which they are substituted.

Consider a metric D(A, B) that sums the number of links in a generalization hierarchy from A and B to their closest common ancestor. If A is the item in the erroneous proposition for which a substitution is being made and B is the substituted item, this metric measures the number of generalization steps that must be executed from the primitive classes containing these items until one reaches a semantic category containing both of them. If each step in the hierarchy represents the same amount of generalization, this metric provides an intuitive measure of the semantic difference between the two items.

However, rarely does each step in a hierarchy generalize by the same amount. Therefore, weights are assigned to each step, indicating the relative amount of generalization represented by moving from a particular semantic class to its superclass in the hierarchy. In my implementation these weights are arbitrarily determined according to my estimate of the amount of generalization involved. My measure of semantic difference between two items, D1(A, B), is then the sum of the weighted distances of each item from their closest common ancestor in the generalization hierarchy (this equals infinity if they have no common ancestor).

A speaker may also substitute a part for the whole or the whole for a part, as in the use of *apartment* instead of *apartment building* in the query "We want to invest between \$30 and \$50 million. Which apartments are for sale?" or the use of *apartment building* instead of *apartment* in the query "I need a place to live for next year. Which apartment buildings are for rent?" To capture this part-whole resemblance, I use a Composed-of relation that relates two object classes if the objects in the first class might be viewed as consisting of multiple instances of the objects in the second class. For example, in terms of this relation the class APARTMENT-BLDG is related to the class APARTMENT, since apartment buildings are composed of individual apartments, and the class SUBDIVISION would be related to the class HOUSE, since subdivisions are composed of individual houses. My second measure of semantic difference between two items, D2(A, B), is the length of the path of the Composed-of relations between A and B (which equals infinity if A and B are not related by a sequence of Composed-of relations).

The semantic difference Dsem(A, B) between the term used by the speaker and the substituted term is then measured as the smaller of metrics D1 and D2. Further work is needed to investigate other reasons for improper language, such as similar spelling and similar pronunciation of words.

Revision operations   Since some revisions may represent simple substitutions or path expansions and others may be combinations of these, the kind of revision operation applied to the erroneous proposition will influence the estimate of the semantic difference between the revised query and IS's utterance. Table 4.1 classifies the substitutions of term T for variable V that produce the revised queries into four categories. Categories 3 and 4 represent more significant and therefore less

Table 4.1
Classification of query revision operations

Category	Substitution variable V	Substitution term T
1	IS-specified attribute or relation	Expanded relational path including the attribute or relation specified by IS
2	IS-specified attribute, relation, or class	Attribute, relation, or class semantically similar to that specified by IS
3	IS-specified attribute or relation	Expanded relational path, including an attribute or relation semantically similar to that specified by IS
4	IS-specified class and relation (or attribute)	Double substitution: class and relation (or attribute) semantically similar to an IS-specified class and relation (or attribute)

preferable alterations of the information seeker's query than do categories 1 and 2.

Category 1 contains expanded relational paths R1 * R2 * ... * Rn such that the attribute or relation specified by the information seeker in the erroneous proposition appears in the path expression. For example, the expanded path Treats(DR-BROWN, _p:&PATIENT) * Assigned(_p:&PATIENT, _room:&ROOM) is a category 1 substitution for the erroneous proposition Assigned(DR-BROWN, _room:&ROOM) contained in the semantic representation of the hospital domain query "Which rooms is Dr. Brown assigned?" Since speakers frequently use terse expressions that shortcut specification of the full relational path in the world model, expanded paths often represent their intended utterance.

Category 2 contains simple substitutions that are semantically similar to the attributes, relations, or object classes specified in the information seekers' erroneous propositions. An example of a category 2 substitution is the previously discussed substitution of the attribute Remaining-capacity for the attribute Area in the query "What is the area of the special weapons magazine of the *Alamo*?" If the substituted term bears a close semantic resemblance to the term employed by the speaker, it is reasonable to suspect that he used incorrect terminology in formulating his utterance and that the revised query captures his intent.

Category 3 contains substitutions that are formed by a category 1 path expansion along with a category 2 substitution. For example, suppose that only faculty members teach sections of courses, that graduate students may assist in sections of courses, and that Al Jones is a graduate teaching assistant. Then the conjunction of the propositions

Assists(AL-JONES, _sect:&SECTION)
Is-section-of(_sect:&SECTION, _crse:&COURSE)

is a category 3 substitution for the erroneous proposition

Teaches(AL-JONES, _crse:&COURSE)

contained in the semantic representation of the query "What courses does Al Jones teach?" This sample category 3 substitution not only expands the path between the object class COURSE and the class containing AL-JONES; it also substitutes the relation Assists for the IS-specified relation Teaches. If the substituted attribute or relation bears a close semantic resemblance to the attribute or relation used by the speaker, it is reasonable to believe that he might have used incorrect terminology at the same time that he tried to shortcut specifying the full relational path in the world model.

Category 4 contains substitutions that are the composition of two category 2 substitutions. For example, if the classes FACULTY and STUDENT are mutually exclusive, faculty members may participate in seminars, and students may take courses for credit, then the substitution of Participate-in(DR-SMITH, _seminar:&SEMINAR) is a category 4 substitution for the erroneous proposition contained in the semantic representation of the query "Which courses is Dr. Smith getting credit for?" Instances in which a category 4 substitution represents the information seeker's intended utterance rarely arise, since such instances represent two semantic errors in terminology on the part of the speaker.

Since some revision operations represent more significant alterations than others, the kind of revision operation used to produce the suggested interpretation will influence the metric for computing the semantic difference between the revised query and IS's utterance. Table 4.2 summarizes my metric.

Table 4.2
Semantic difference of revised query

Revision Operation	SemDiff(revquery)
Category 1	Metric Dexp(revquery), which measures the amount by which the relationship path has been expanded
Category 2	Metric Dsem(A, B), which measures the semantic difference between the substituted term and the term for which it is substituted
Category 3	The sum of metric Dexp(revquery), which measures the amount of path expansion, metric Dsem(A, B), which measures the semantic difference between a substituted term and the term for which it is substituted, and a constant C, which estimates the preference for category 1 and 2 revision operations over category 3 and 4 revision operations.
Category 4	The sum of a constant C, which estimates the preference for category 1 and 2 revision operations over category 3 and 4 revision operations, and two applications, one for each term substitution, of metric Dsem(A, B), which measures the semantic difference between a substituted term and the term for which it is substituted.

If the revised query was produced by a category 1 or category 2 revision operation, it differs from the information seeker's utterance in only one way. It contains either an expanded path or a substitution for a term specified by the information seeker. Thus SemDiff(revquery), or the semantic difference between the revised query and the query uttered by the information seeker, is simply the value of the path expansion metric Dexp in the former case or the term substitution metric Dsem in the latter case.

However, a revised query may be the result of a combination of the heuristic rules: either an expanded path and a term substitution or two term substitutions. In this case I measure the semantic difference SemDiff(revquery) either by summing Dexp and Dsem or by summing two applications of Dsem (one for each substituted term). I argued earlier that revised queries produced by revision operations in categories 3 and 4 are less desirable, since they represent two errors on the part of the speaker: either incorrect terminology and a shortcut of the complete specification or two semantic errors. Therefore, I arbitrarily add a constant C to SemDiff(revquery) to enforce a moderate preference for single substitutions.

My studies indicate that C must be large enough that a category 1 or 2 revised query with a semantic difference of S1 will be selected over an equally relevant category 3 or 4 revised query for which S1 is the sum of the semantic measures for each individual revision. But C must not be so large that a category 1 or 2 revised query with a large semantic difference S1 will be selected over an equally relevant category 3 or 4 revised query for which the semantic difference of each individual revision is quite small. If only the revised query with the best evaluation is selected as the appropriate interpretation, a value of C = 3 is satisfactory. However, the next section discusses a tolerance level that allows queries whose evaluations differ by less than this tolerance to be regarded as equally plausible interpretations. In this case a value slightly larger than the tolerance appears to be a good setting for the constant C, since it enforces the above selection considerations.

4.4.3   Metric for Revised Query Evaluation

Relevance to the current focus of attention in the dialogue seems to be more important than semantic difference in selecting the most appropriate revised query, since highly relevant queries are strongly anticipated by the listener and therefore the speaker need not be as careful in his use of language. However, the less similar a suggested revised query is to the speaker's actual utterance, the more likely that a somewhat less relevant but more semantically similar revised query represents his intentions.

For example, once again suppose that IS wants to load cargo on ships and is focused on the task of allocating cargo to the various storage holds. A subgoal in the plan for this task might be the following:

Assign-cargo(IS, _item:&CARGO, _hold:&STORAGE-AREA)
where
Is-type(_item:&CARGO, _ctype:&CARGO-TYPE)
Cargo-type(_hold:&STORAGE-AREA, _ctype:&CARGO-TYPE)

And a plan for this subgoal will in turn contain the following precondition:

Greater-than(_rem:&CUBIC-FT, _itemsize:&CUBIC-FT)
where
Volume(_item:&CARGO, _itemsize:&CUBIC-FT)
Remaining-capacity(_hold:&STORAGE-AREA, _rem:&CUBIC-FT)

Now consider again the query "What is the area of the special weapons magazine?" whose semantic representation contains the erroneous proposition

Area(SPECIAL-WEAPONS-MAG, _areaval:&SQ-FEET).

The substitution mechanism will suggest substituting the proposition

Cargo-type(SPECIAL-WEAPONS-MAG, _ctype:&CARGO-TYPE)

from the current focused plan for the erroneous proposition appearing in IS's utterance; it will also suggest substituting the proposition

Remaining-capacity(SPECIAL-WEAPONS-MAG, _rem:&CUBIC-FT)

appearing in the plan for the subgoal

Assign-cargo(IS, _item:&CARGO, SPECIAL-WEAPONS-MAG)

and therefore slightly less relevant to the current focus of attention in the dialogue. However, the attribute Area has little semantic similarity to the attribute Cargo-type, whereas it is quite similar to the attribute Remaining-capacity, since both can be measurements of space. Therefore, the system is justified in discarding the first suggested revised query, even though it is highly relevant to the current dialogue context, in favor of the somewhat less relevant but far more semantically similar second suggestion. Note, however, that only revised queries relevant to IS's overall task-related plan are even considered.

My selection algorithm attempts to capture this relationship between relevance and semantics. Each suggested revised query is evaluated using the following formula:

$$E(revquery) = w1 * FocusShift(revquery) + w2 * SemDiff(revquery).$$

The relative weights w1 and w2 determine the emphasis on relevance versus semantics; my implementation uses a setting of $w1 = 3$ and $w2 = 1$, to enforce a moderate preference for relevance over semantics. Since this evaluation function is imperfect, two suggested revisions with nearly equal evaluations should be regarded as equally plausible. Therefore, the selection mechanism evaluates each suggested revised query and selects as appropriate interpretations those whose evaluation is within an arbitrarily set tolerance of the suggestion whose evaluation is smallest.

I have also implemented a somewhat different process that I believe provides a plausible model of how human listeners might handle pragmatically ill-formed utterances and that is computationally efficient. Instead of computing and evaluating all revisions suggested by the inferred task-related plan, the system computes those suggestions most relevant to the current focus of attention in the dialogue. If any of these are acceptably close to what the speaker actually said, they are selected and no further revisions are considered. Otherwise, revised queries less relevant to the current focus of attention in the dialogue are constructed and evaluated. The old suggested revised queries are reconsidered along with these new ones, but with the cutoff for acceptable revised queries raised so that the evaluation of a revised query need not be so good for it to be selected as the appropriate interpretation and for further processing to be terminated.

This paradigm appears plausible for several reasons. Since the information seeker's utterance will usually be very relevant to the current focus of attention and semantically similar to the revised query representing his intended request, often only a small portion of the task-related plan will need to be analyzed before an interpretation is selected. Thus the amount of computation is limited. Furthermore, a revised query that was not rated good enough to terminate processing when first suggested may eventually be selected as the appropriate interpretation after revised queries suggested by less relevant aspects of the dialogue have been investigated. (Of course, if all queries have evaluations worse than some preset level, no interpretation should be produced, and the system must request clarification.)

4.5   Examples

The following examples illustrate the suggestion and selection strategies. In computing E(revquery), the evaluation of a suggested revised query, weights of $w1 = 3$ and $w2 = 1$ are used.

4.5.1   Example 1

Consider the following dialogue:

IS: I want to own my own residence, but I don't like a lot of maintenance. Which apartments are for sale?

In a real estate world model, single apartments are rented, not sold. Apartment buildings, condominiums, townhouses, houses, office complexes, shopping centers, and movie theaters are for sale. Thus IS's query contains the erroneous proposition Sale-status(_x:&APARTMENT, FOR-SALE).

The utterance preceding the pragmatically ill-formed query indicates that IS is seeking ownership of a residence for which he will have little maintenance responsibility. Thus the TRACK system described in chapter 3 would infer that IS wants to achieve the following goal:

Own-residence-low-maintenance(IS, _res:&RESIDENCE).

A plan for accomplishing this goal contains the subgoal Purchase(IS, _res:&CONDOMINIUM), whose plan (figure 4.4 on page 128) in turn contains the precondition Sale-status(_res:&CONDOMINIUM, FOR-SALE). The substitution mechanism applies substitution rule 3 and proposes substituting the object class CONDOMINIUM for the class APARTMENT appearing in IS's erroneous proposition, which produces a semantic representation equivalent to the query "Which condominiums are for sale?" The selection mechanism must evaluate this proposed revised query. The relevance metric produces an evaluation of FocusShift(revquery) $= 0 + (.2 * 2) = 0.4$, since this revision was suggested by a component of the current focused plan expanded to a depth of 2. Figure 4.7 illustrates a portion of a semantic generalization hierarchy for a real estate world model; numbers attached to links indicate the relative amount of generalization represented by moving from a particular semantic class to its superclass in the hierarchy. The closest common ancestor of CONDOMINIUM and APARTMENT is the class LOW-MAINTENANCE-RESIDENCE. Therefore, SemDiff(revquery) $= 1 + 2 = 3$. Thus the selection mechanism evaluates this suggested revised query as E(revquery) $= 3 * 0.4 + 3 = 4.2$. This revised query is the only suggestion, and so it is selected as the appropriate interpretation of the information seeker's ill-formed utterance.

4.5.2 Example 2

Consider next the following dialogue:

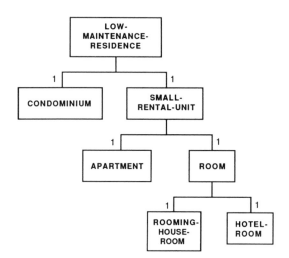

Figure 4.7
Part of a real estate generalization hierarchy

IS: I am the manager of a real estate investment trust. We'd like to invest between $30 and $50 million. Which apartments are for sale?

As in example 1, IS's query contains the erroneous proposition Sale-status(_x:&APARTMENT, FOR-SALE). However, in this case the context established by the first two utterances suggests that IS will be inquiring about high-priced investment property, and therefore the system should suspect that the last utterance might be asking about an instance of such property. Wanting to invest a large sum of money is the applicability condition for one plan for increasing investments, and the TRACK system would infer that IS's attention is focused on this plan. Figure 4.8 presents an expansion of the context model that would be inferred. Substitution rule 3 suggests four substitutions—APARTMENT-BLDG, APARTMENT-COMPLX, SHOP-CENTER, and OFFICE-BLDG—for the class APARTMENT appearing in the erroneous proposition in IS's query. These substitutions produce suggested revised semantic representations equivalent to the following queries:

"Which apartment buildings are for sale?"
"Which apartment complexes are for sale?"
"Which shopping centers are for sale?"
"Which office buildings are for sale?"

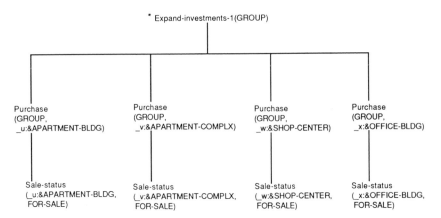

Figure 4.8
Portion of an expanded context model for an investment dialogue

In addition, analysis of portions of the expanded context model not shown in figure 4.8 might suggest other revisions.

The selection mechanism must evaluate these proposed revised queries. As can be seen from figure 4.8, each revision was suggested by a component of the current focused plan expanded to a depth of 2, so FocusShift(revquery) $= 0 + (.2 * 2) = .4$. Metric D1 would analyze the semantic generalization hierarchy and produce a large estimate of the semantic difference between the classes APARTMENT and APARTMENT-BLDG. Figure 4.9 illustrates object classes related by Composed-of. Metric D2 would analyze these relationships and produce a difference measure of 1. The semantic difference between the classes APARTMENT and APARTMENT-BLDG is therefore 1, since it is the smaller of these two measures. Thus the overall evaluation for the revised query resulting from substituting APARTMENT-BLDG for APARTMENT in the semantic representation of IS's query is E(revquery-1) $= 3 * 0.4 + 1 = 2.2$. Similarly, the semantic difference between classes APARTMENT and APARTMENT-COMPLX is 2. Thus the overall evaluation for the revised query resulting from substituting APARTMENT-COMPLX for APARTMENT is E(revquery-2) $= 3 * 0.4 + 2 = 3.2$. Both metrics D1 and D2 will produce very large

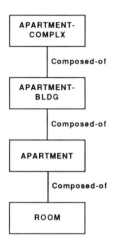

Figure 4.9
Part of a model of subpart relations

estimates of the semantic difference between APARTMENT and the classes OFFICE-BLDG and SHOP-CENTER. The selection mechanism will therefore select the revised query produced by substituting the object class APARTMENT-BLDG for the class APARTMENT as the best interpretation of IS's ill-formed utterance. As a result of the tolerance level for selecting queries whose evaluation is close to that of the query with the best overall evaluation, the revised query produced by substituting the object class APARTMENT-COMPLX for the class APART-MENT may also be selected as a plausible interpretation of IS's utterance.

4.5.3   Example 3

Now consider the following dialogue:

IS: I want to take CS220 next semester. When's Mitchel meet?

In a university world model, faculty members do not have an Is-meeting-time attribute. So IS's utterance contains the following erroneous proposition:

Is-meeting-time(MITCHEL, _tme:&MTG-TIME)

However, faculty present colloquia, chair committees, and teach sections of courses, and colloquia, committees, and sections of courses

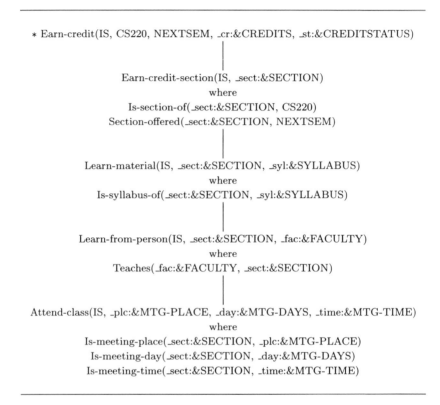

* Earn-credit(IS, CS220, NEXTSEM, _cr:&CREDITS, _st:&CREDITSTATUS)

Earn-credit-section(IS, _sect:&SECTION)
where
Is-section-of(_sect:&SECTION, CS220)
Section-offered(_sect:&SECTION, NEXTSEM)

Learn-material(IS, _sect:&SECTION, _syl:&SYLLABUS)
where
Is-syllabus-of(_sect:&SECTION, _syl:&SYLLABUS)

Learn-from-person(IS, _sect:&SECTION, _fac:&FACULTY)
where
Teaches(_fac:&FACULTY, _sect:&SECTION)

Attend-class(IS, _plc:&MTG-PLACE, _day:&MTG-DAYS, _time:&MTG-TIME)
where
Is-meeting-place(_sect:&SECTION, _plc:&MTG-PLACE)
Is-meeting-day(_sect:&SECTION, _day:&MTG-DAYS)
Is-meeting-time(_sect:&SECTION, _time:&MTG-TIME)

Figure 4.10
Portion of an expanded context model for example 3

meet at scheduled times. From the first utterance in the above dialogue the TRACK system would infer that the speaker is considering
taking CS220. Figure 4.10 presents part of an expansion of the resulting context model. The substitution mechanism analyzes the expanded
context model and finds that the two relations

Teaches(_fac:&FACULTY, _sect:&SECTION)
Is-meeting-time(_sect:&SECTION, _time:&MTG-TIME)

appear on the same path. Substitution rule 6 suggests substituting the
expanded relational path represented by the conjunction of the propositions

Teaches(MITCHEL, _sect:&SECTION)
Is-meeting-time(_sect:&SECTION, _tme:&MTG-TIME)

for the erroneous proposition appearing in IS's query. This substitution produces a semantic representation equivalent to the revised query
"When do sections taught by Mitchel meet?" This revision was suggested by a component of the current focused plan at a depth of 4, so
FocusShift(revquery) = .2 * 4 = .8. The revision expands the path by
one relation, so the semantic difference of the suggested revised query is
2, which produces an overall evaluation of 4.4 for this suggestion. Since
it is the only suggested revised query, it is selected as the appropriate
interpretation of IS's ill-formed utterance.

4.5.4   Example 4

Finally, consider the following dialogue:

IS: Are any sections of CS440 offered next semester?

IP: Yes.

IS: Who is teaching section 10?

IP: Dr. Jones is teaching section 10 of CS440 next semester.

IS: I want to register for it. What is the size of section 10?

In a university world model, sections do not have size attributes. Sections have such attributes as current enrollment, maximum enrollment,
minimum required enrollment, expected enrollment, and optimum enrollment, and rooms have area attributes, given in square footage. Thus
IS's query contains the following erroneous proposition:

Size(CS440-10-NS, _size:&SIZE-DOMAIN)

   The dialogue preceding the pragmatically ill-formed query indicates
that IS wants to earn credit in section 10 of CS440 and is currently focused on the task of registering for that section. A plan for registering
for a section contains the precondition that the maximum enrollment
exceed the current enrollment for the section, that is, that the section
not be filled. The higher-level plan of taking a particular section of a
course contains the precondition that the expected enrollment in the section be acceptable to the student. Figure 4.11 presents a portion of IS's
inferred task-related plan. Substitution rule 1 proposes substituting the
attributes Curr-enrlment, Max-allow-enrlment, and Expected-enrlment
for the attribute Size appearing in IS's erroneous proposition. These

three substitutions produce semantic representations equivalent respectively to the queries

"What is the current enrollment in section 10?"
"What is the maximum enrollment allowed in section 10?"
"What is the expected enrollment in section 10?"

The selection mechanism must evaluate these proposed revised queries. Figure 4.12 presents a portion of a generalization hierarchy for the attributes under consideration; numbers attached to links indicate the relative amount of generalization. The current focused plan prior to the pragmatically ill-formed query was the plan for the goal Register(IS, CS440-10-NS, NEXTSEM). The revised query produced by substituting the attribute Curr-enrlment for the attribute Size has a focus shift measure of FocusShift(revquery-1) $= 0 + (.2 * 1) = .2$ and a semantic difference of 2, which results in an overall evaluation of E(revquery-1) $= 3 * .2 + 2 = 2.6$.

Similarly, the revised query produced by substituting the attribute Max-allow-enrlment for the attribute Size has a focus shift measure of FocusShift(revquery-2) $= 0 + (.2 * 1) = .2$ and a semantic difference of 3, which results in an overall evaluation of E(revquery-2) $= 3 * .2 + 3 = 3.6$.

The revised query produced by substituting the attribute Expected-enrlment for the attribute Size was suggested by expansion of the plan Earn-credit-section(IS, CS440-10-NS), which is immediately beneath the current focused plan in the stack of active plans. Therefore, this revised query has a focus shift measure of FocusShift(revquery-3) $= 1 + (.2 * 1) = 1.2$ and a semantic difference of 2, which results in an overall evaluation of E(revquery-3) $= 3 * 1.2 + 2 = 5.6$.

Such suggestions as substitution of the attributes Min-req-enrlment or Optimum-enrlment for the attribute Size were not considered, since they are irrelevant to IS's inferred plan. (Note, however, that such substitutions might be relevant for other inferred plans.) The selection mechanism will select the revised query produced by substituting the attribute Curr-enrlment for the attribute Size as the best interpretation of IS's utterance. Depending on the tolerance level for selecting queries whose evaluation is close to that of the query with the best overall evaluation, one or both of the revised queries produced by substituting the attribute Max-allow-enrlment and the attribute Expected-enrlment for the attribute Size may also be selected as plausible interpretations of IS's utterance.

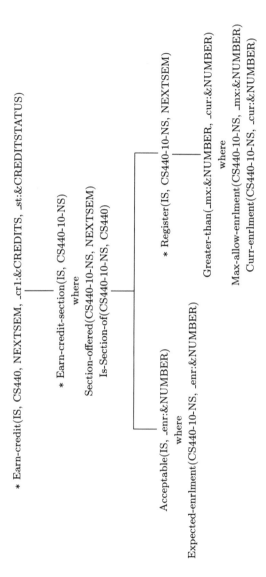

Figure 4.11
Portion of an expanded context model for example 4

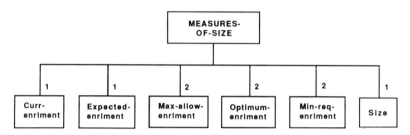

Figure 4.12
Portion of a generalization hierarchy for example 4

4.6 Summary

If we want systems that engage in truly natural dialogue, then they
must be able to understand pragmatically ill-formed queries that are
easily handled by human listeners. Such understanding requires the use
of knowledge gleaned from the preceding dialogue. Previous strategies
for handling pragmatic ill-formedness analyzed the ill-formed utterance
in isolation from the dialogue context and thus were unable to model
whether the proposed response was relevant to the speaker's intentions.

This chapter has presented a strategy for understanding pragmatically ill-formed queries that relies on the information seeker's inferred
task-related plan as the primary mechanism for suggesting potential interpretations. As a result, the system considers only revised utterances
that are relevant to what it believes that the information seeker is trying
to accomplish. These suggested interpretations must then be evaluated
on the basis of relevance and semantic criteria. A response based on
this interpretation will address the information seeker's perceived needs,
inferred both from the preceding dialogue and the ill-formed utterance.

5 Toward Understanding Intersentential Ellipsis

Contextual ellipsis in dialogue is the use of a syntactically incomplete sentence fragment, along with the context in which the fragment occurs, to communicate a complete thought and accomplish a speech act. Such fragments are often referred to as *intersentential ellipsis*, since they appear between sentences in a dialogue. Allen [All79] noted that intersentential ellipsis differs from other forms of ellipsis in that proper interpretation often depends more on pragmatic knowledge, such as beliefs about the speaker's underlying task-related plan, than on the syntactic structure or semantic content of preceding utterances. For instance, in examples [EX1] and [EX2] speaker 1's elliptical fragment can only be properly understood within the context of his communicated goal and the relevant plans for accomplishing it.[1]

[EX1]

Speaker 1: I want to cash this check. Small bills only, please.

[EX2]

Speaker 1: Who are the candidates for programming consultants?

Speaker 2: Mary Smith, Bob Jones, and Ann Doe have applied for the job.

Speaker 1: Tom's recommendation?

Speaker 2: He thinks Bob Jones and Ann Doe have the necessary background and should be invited for an interview.

The elliptical fragment "Small bills only, please." that appears in [EX1] could be used in several ways. It might be a command to one's subordinates to limit the charges on their expense accounts, a stipulation regarding the characteristics of birds ordered for the zoo, or a request that one be given small denominations of paper money. Since speaker 1's first utterance establishes that his goal is to cash a check and since relevant plans for achieving that goal can include a subplan for getting a particular distribution of paper money, the third interpretation is appropriate. In [EX2] speaker 1's goal is hiring programming consultants, perhaps for an introductory programming course, and relevant plans for doing this include a subplan for identifying the best applicant. This leads to the elliptical fragment's being interpreted as a request for Tom's opinion about the job applicants.

These examples show that identifying the aspect of the speaker's task-related plan that an elliptical fragment draws attention to is important in comprehending intersentential ellipsis. It is not enough, however. Every

---

[1] The second example was suggested by Ralph Weischedel.

utterance has an immediate conversational or communicative goal, called
a *discourse goal* in chapters 1 and 2. Such goals include answering a question, seeking clarification, and expressing surprise. As has been shown
by the research of Reichman [Rei78a,Rei84], Mann, Moore, and Levin
[MML77], and Pollack, Hirschberg, and Webber [PHW82], real understanding requires that the listener recognize the discourse goal being
fulfilled by an utterance.

Several previous research efforts have investigated understanding intersentential ellipsis. However, they have emphasized syntactic and semantic strategies and have not sufficiently explored the contributions
of the speaker's plans and goals to the interpretation of ellipsis. Nor
have they addressed recognition of the speaker's discourse goal. I have
developed a pragmatics-based strategy that reasons on a user model,
including a model of the user's underlying task-related plan, beliefs, and
expected discourse goals, to produce a rich interpretation of intersentential elliptical fragments, including recognition of the speaker's discourse
goal.

This chapter reviews previous research on understanding intersentential ellipsis. It then describes the kinds of pragmatic knowledge that
must be part of a successful interpretation strategy and discusses the
importance of each kind. Chapter 6 presents my process model, which
comprehends an elliptical fragment by identifying both the aspect of the
information seeker's task-related plan highlighted by the fragment and
the discourse goal fulfilled by it.

5.1   Strategies for Interpreting Intersentential Ellipsis

As illustrated by the example "I want to cash this check. Small bills only,
please." intersentential elliptical fragments cannot be fully understood in
and of themselves. Therefore, a strategy for interpreting such fragments
must rely on knowledge obtained from sources other than the fragment
itself. Three possibilities exist:

- The syntactic form of preceding utterances

- The semantic representation of preceding utterances

- Expectations gleaned from understanding the preceding discourse

Strategies based on the first two kinds of knowledge have been ex-
tensively investigated, but the contribution of knowledge about the
speaker's plans and goals to the interpretation of ellipsis has hitherto
been inadequately explored.

5.1.1 Syntactic Strategies

The first strategy uses the syntactic form of the preceding sentence as a pattern that can be manipulated to produce a complete grammatical utterance representing what the speaker meant by the elliptical fragment. Such a strategy might perform one or both of the following transformations on the syntactic form of a preceding utterance:

- A substitution/expansion operation in which the elliptical fragment is substituted for a syntactic constituent in the preceding utterance or the syntactic representation of the preceding utterance is expanded to accommodate the fragment

- A transformation operation that maps questions onto answers, statements onto questions, etc.

Hendrix [HSSS78] developed a heuristic for handling simple cases of ellipses that are syntactically and semantically similar to a phrase in the preceding user utterance. Basically, this heuristic substitutes the parse tree of the elliptical fragment for the subtree representing a similar phrase in the parse tree of the previous utterance. For example, consider the following dialogue sequence:

Speaker 1: Who is teaching CS360?

Speaker 2: Dr. Smith

Speaker 1: CS440?

Hendrix's algorithm substitutes the parse tree for *CS440* for the subtree representing *CS360* in the parse tree associated with the first utterance by speaker 1. Since he employed a semantic grammar, some might claim that Hendrix used a semantic strategy. However, I put this heuristic in the syntactic class because it effectively transforms the syntactic representation of a preceding utterance into a representation of what the speaker intended by the elliptical fragment. Hendrix's heuristic was limited to fragments in which the intended utterance was similar to the preceding utterance by that speaker, such as repeated questions.

Weischedel and Sondheimer [WS82] extended Hendrix's heuristic to account for expansion ellipsis and turn-taking dialogues. Furthermore, they removed Hendrix's assumption of a semantic grammar. They represented the grammar using an augmented transition network (ATN) and viewed the pattern for a preceding sentence as the complete ATN path associated with the parse of that sentence. The Weischedel-Sondheimer heuristic first permits transformations that map paths for one class of utterance onto paths associated with other classes of utterances. For example, paths for interrogative utterances may be mapped onto paths associated with declarative responses. It then manipulates this path by allowing insertion of the elliptical fragment into the pattern, including substitutions and expansions, to produce an expanded syntactic unit. For example, consider the following dialogue sequence:

Speaker 1: Did you enjoy your trip?

Speaker 2: Very much.

The Weischedel-Sondheimer strategy would produce an ATN path equivalent to that produced by the complete utterance "I enjoyed my trip very much."

However, many examples of ellipsis cannot be handled by syntactic strategies. Consider again the dialogue presented in [EX1]. No transformation or modification of speaker 1's first statement will produce an utterance that represents the intended meaning of speaker 1's elliptical fragment. Syntactic strategies are limited by their reliance on the precise form of a preceding utterance. Thus they can only handle elliptical fragments that represent utterances syntactically similar to a preceding statement or query.

5.1.2   Semantic Strategies

The second potential strategy uses the semantic representation of the last utterance as a pattern that suggests slots for which an elliptical fragment may provide a filler or a substitution. Waltz [Wal78] employed a semantic strategy in the PLANES natural language interface. PLANES performed little syntactic analysis in parsing an utterance, instead relying primarily on a scan of the utterance to identify semantic constituents of the formal query to the database. Once the constituents explicitly present in the user's utterance had been identified, this set of constituents was compared to a set of concept case frames representing reasonably complete queries against the database. If the user's utterance was deemed incomplete due to failure to provide a filler for a necessary constituent, the most recently employed previous filler for that constituent was inserted.

Carbonell [Car83] handled some cases of ellipsis in the XCALIBUR expert system interface using contextual substitution rules similar to those employed by Waltz. These rules used the semantic case frame representation of the last focused user query or command to propose slots that might be filled by subsequent elliptical fragments. The elliptical utterance was then interpreted as this revised instantiation of the case frame representation of the original utterance. For example, consider the following dialogue sequence:

Speaker 1: What is the meeting time of CS360?

Speaker 2: 7:00 P.M. on Monday night.

Speaker 1: The meeting place?

In the interpretation of speaker 1's fragmentary second utterance, Meeting-place replaces Meeting-time as the filler of the project field (the field whose value is being retrieved) in the case frame representation of speaker 1's first utterance, and this results in a case frame representation appropriate to the complete query "What is the meeting place of CS360?" This resembles a syntactic strategy, but Carbonell claimed that a case frame analysis provides a finer-grain substitution method than one that replaces an entire subtree in the parsed representation of a preceding utterance. Consider the following dialogue sequence:

Speaker 1: What is the size of the three largest single port fixed media disks?

Speaker 2: (response appropriate to the system under investigation)

Speaker 1: Disks with two ports?

Carbonell claimed that in the above dialogue Hendrix's syntactic strategy would replace the entire phrase *single port fixed media disks* with *disks with two ports*, whereas in the case frame approach, *two* would replace *one* as the filler of the slot for the number of ports in the case frame representation of speaker 1's first utterance but the fixed media specification would be retained.

Unfortunately, semantic strategies require an extensive case frame representation and are inadequate for handling elliptical fragments that rely on an assumed communication of the underlying task. For example, it is improbable that the case frame for a programming consultant in [EX2] would contain slots for the recommendations of individual faculty.

5.1.3   Plan-Based Strategies

The third potential strategy for interpreting intersentential elliptical fragments utilizes pragmatic knowledge, such as a model of the speaker's task-related plan, beliefs, and expected discourse goals. The power of this approach lies in its reliance on knowledge gleaned from the dialogue, including discourse content and conversational goals, rather than on precise representations of the preceding utterances alone.

Allen [AP80] addressed the problem of understanding sentence fragments occurring at the outset of a dialogue and was the first to relate ellipsis processing to the domain-dependent plan underlying a speaker's utterance. As we saw in chapter 2, Allen viewed the speaker's utterance as part of a plan that the speaker had constructed and was executing to accomplish his overall task-related goals (which, in Allen's domain, were limited to meeting or boarding a train). To interpret an elliptical fragment, Allen's system first constructed a set of representations of possible surface speech acts, constrained by syntactic clues appearing in the fragment. These representations were incompletely specified, usually containing patterns that could be matched with objects and predicates. The task-related goals that the speaker might be pursuing formed a set of expectations. Allen's system attempted to infer the speaker's goal-related plan that included an execution of the transmitted utterance. A part of this inference process involved determining which of the partially constructed plans connecting the expected task-related goals of meeting or boarding a train and the transmitted utterance was reasonable in light of the knowledge and mutual beliefs of the speaker and hearer. The most reasonable inferred plan was selected and analyzed to identify the speaker's obstacles and suggest an appropriate response.

Allen noted that the speaker's fragment must identify the subgoals that the speaker is pursuing but claimed that in very restricted domains, identifying the speaker's overall goal from the utterance was sufficient to identify his current subgoals in terms of the obstacles present in his goal-related plan. For example, the fragment "The train to Windsor?" would suggest two possible surface speech acts: (1) a request that the listener inform the speaker as to whether some proposition involving the train to Windsor is satisfied and (2) a request that the listener inform the speaker about some property involving the train to Windsor. The only two overall goals in Allen's train domain were Meet-train and Board-train. His system would attempt to infer plans connecting each of these goals with each of the possible surface speech acts. The description of the train in the representations of the possible surface speech acts would be incompatible with the Meet-train goal (since the surface speech acts describe a train *to* Windsor), and mutual beliefs about the speaker's knowledge of the domain would eliminate the plan connecting the first possible surface speech act with the Board-train goal. However, the system would find a reasonable plan connecting the second possible surface speech act with the goal of boarding a train and consequently would identify it as the motivation for the speaker's utterance. The system's response would consist of specifying all properties of the Windsor train that appear in the speaker's inferred plan for boarding a train and that the speaker is believed to be unaware of. For isolated sentence fragments occurring in Allen's restricted domain involving train arrivals and departures, his interpretation strategy worked well. To understand elliptical fragments during a dialogue in a more complex domain, it is necessary to identify the particular aspect of the speaker's overall task-related plan addressed by the fragment and to recognize the discourse or communicative goal being pursued.

Litman [Lit86b] also applied her model of plan recognition to understanding intersentential elliptical fragments. To interpret an elliptical fragment, Litman used syntactic clues in the utterance to postulate speech acts (Request or Inform) that the fragment was intended to accomplish. She then attempted to construct an inference path from a postulated speech act to the plan inferred for the speaker. Consider again the following example taken from [FD84] and discussed in chapter 1:

Speaker 1: The Korean jet shot down by the Soviets was a spy plane.

Speaker 2: With 269 people on board?

It appears that Litman's system would handle the elliptical fragment "With 269 people on board?" in much the same way as the complete sentence "Did the Korean jet have 269 people on board?" Thus Litman's strategy would be unable to recognize the surprise and doubt conveyed by the elliptical fragment. In addition, as I mentioned in chapter 2, although Litman's framework for plan inference can model clarification and correction subdialogues, her metaplans (such as Introduce-plan, Continue-plan, and Modify-plan) are more akin to plan-construction metaplans than metaplans representing such communicative goals as expressing surprise or seeking clarification of a question. I contend that recognition of the speaker's discourse or communicative goal must be an integral part of any strategy that fully understands ellipsis.

5.1.4   Other Interpretation Strategies

In addition to syntactic, semantic, and plan-based strategies, a few other heuristics have been devised. Carbonell [Car83] used discourse expectation rules that suggested a set of expected user utterances and that related elliptical fragments to these expected patterns. For example, if the system asked the user whether a particular value should be used as the filler of a slot in a case frame, the system then expected the user's utterance to contain a confirmation or disconfirmation pattern, a different filler for the slot, a comparative pattern such as *too hard*, or a request for other potential fillers or constraints on such fillers. Although these

rules use expectations about how the speaker might respond, they seem
to have little to do with the expected discourse goals of the speaker.
As a result, they are unable to differentiate fragments that merely request information from fragments whose intent is to seek clarification or
express surprise.

Although my intent is not to simulate human processing, consideration of strategies that appear to be employed by humans provides a good
basis for investigating mechanized ellipsis understanding. This is particularly true if accepted rules of communication allow the human speaker
to formulate an utterance under the assumption that his listener will
employ a particular strategy in interpreting it, in which case it is imperative that machines employ that same interpretation strategy. In
the case of processing intersentential elliptical fragments, I believe that
this is exactly what occurs and that expectations about the speaker's
discourse and task-related goals must be a major component of a successful interpretation strategy.

5.2 Requisite Knowledge for Interpreting Ellipsis

According to Grice [Gri57,Gri69], the meaning of an utterance on a
particular occasion is the effect that the speaker intends to produce in
his listener by means of the listener's recognition of that intent. Grice
further notes that the speaker, in making an utterance, must believe
that the listener will be able to deduce these intentions. Therefore, a
speaker can felicitously employ intersentential ellipsis only if he believes
his utterance will be properly understood.

My approach to understanding elliptical fragments is motivated by
the hypothesis that speaker and hearer mutually believe that certain
knowledge has been acquired during the course of the dialogue and that
this factual knowledge, along with other processing knowledge, will be
used to deduce the speaker's intentions. I claim that the requisite factual
knowledge includes the speaker's inferred task-related plan (normally
only a partial plan during the dialogue), the speaker's inferred beliefs,
and the anticipated discourse goals of the speaker; I claim that the
requisite processing knowledge includes plan recognition strategies and
focusing techniques. The next sections discuss these knowledge sources
and their impact on understanding intersentential ellipsis.

5.2.1 The Speaker's Task-Related Plan

In a cooperative information-seeking dialogue the information provider is engaged in helping the information seeker develop a plan for his underlying task. The information seeker is expected to communicate whatever information is necessary for the information provider to fulfill her helping role. However, naturally occurring communication is both imperfect and incomplete. Not only does the information seeker fail to communicate all aspects of his underlying task and partially constructed plan for accomplishing it, but also his utterances are often imperfectly or incompletely formulated. As I argued in chapter 1, the information seeker expects the information provider to facilitate a productive exchange by assimilating the dialogue and using the acquired knowledge about the information seeker's goals and plans to understand his utterances.

According to Grice [Gri57,Gri69], a listener must infer a speaker's intent in making an utterance. Now consider an incomplete utterance. In attempting to deduce the speaker's intent, the listener will be guided by his expectation that the speaker has followed Grice's conversational maxims [Gri75a]. In particular, Grice's maxims of manner and relation suggest that the speaker believes that his utterance is an adequate vehicle for conveying his intentions and is relevant to the current dialogue. Since the listener is assumed to be a cooperative dialogue participant, he will have assimilated the preceding dialogue, inferred much of the underlying task-related plan motivating the speaker's queries, and be focused on that aspect of the task on which the information seeker's attention was centered immediately prior to the new utterance. Given an incomplete utterance, the listener can attempt to deduce the intentions underlying it by reasoning with this acquired knowledge and trying to identify how the utterance relates to the speaker's partially constructed plan.

Dialogues [EX1] and [EX2] illustrated the importance of IS's inferred task-related plan in understanding ellipsis. In [EX1] speaker 1's fragmentary utterance "Small bills only, please." can only be understood in terms of speaker 1's communicated goal of cashing a check and the relevant plans for doing this. Similarly, in [EX2] IS's fragmentary utterance "Tom's recommendation?" can only be understood in terms of IS's communicated goal of hiring programming consultants, the relevant plans for accomplishing that goal, and the subplan (considering and evaluating the applicants) on which IS's attention was currently focused.

This claim that the speaker's underlying task-related plan is an essential component of a strategy for ellipsis interpretation is further supported by research demonstrating the need for considering such plans in understanding other types of utterances. As we saw in chapter 2, Grosz [Gro77a] and Robinson [Rob81] used models of the speaker's task in apprentice-expert dialogues to determine the referents of definite noun phrases and verb phrases, and Perrault and Allen [PA80] used expectations of speaker goals and inferences about their plans for achieving these goals in the interpretation of indirect speech acts. In addition, Allen [AP80] introduced the concept of a plan-based strategy for interpreting fragmentary utterances at the outset of a dialogue in a restricted domain.

5.2.2   Shared Beliefs

Shared beliefs about facts, beliefs that the listener believes speaker and listener mutually hold, are a second component of the factual knowledge required for processing intersentential elliptical fragments. These shared beliefs represent either presumed a priori knowledge of the domain, such as a presumption that dialogue participants in a university domain know that each course has a teacher, or beliefs derived from the dialogue itself. An example of the latter occurs if IP tells IS that CS360 is a four-credit-hour course; IS may not himself believe that CS360 is a four-credit-hour course, but as a result of IP's utterance he does believe that IP believes this.

Understanding and responding to utterances requires that we identify the speaker's discourse goal in making the utterance. Shared beliefs, often called mutual beliefs, form a part of communicated knowledge used to interpret utterances and identify discourse goals in a cooperative dialogue. The following two dialogue sequences illustrate how the listener's beliefs about the speaker's knowledge influence understanding.

IS: When does CS400 meet?

IP: CS400 meets on Monday from 7:00 P.M. until 9:00 P.M.

IS: Who is teaching it?

IP: Dr. Brown.

IS: At night?

Most people would interpret the fragmentary utterance "At night?" as an expression of surprise and a request for corroboration or explanation. Now consider the following dialogue:

IS: Who is teaching CS400?

IP: Dr. Brown is teaching CS400.

IS: At night?

In this case the elliptical fragment "At night?" would be understood as a simple request to know whether CS400 is meeting at night.[2]

The cause of this difference in interpretation is the difference in beliefs about the speaker at the time the elliptical fragment is uttered. In the second case IP believes that it is mutually believed that IS does not know IP's beliefs about the meeting time of CS400. Since IS cannot be surprised about something he doesn't know, a different intention or discourse goal is attributed to him.

As we saw in chapter 2, Allen [PA80] incorporated mutual beliefs into his work on interpreting indirect speech acts. Sidner [Sid83b,Sid85] modeled user beliefs about system capabilities in her work on recognizing speakers' intentions in utterances. Mutual beliefs appear to be a major influence on how human listeners interpret and respond to utterances.

5.2.3   Discourse Expectations

A number of researchers [LF77,SSJ74,MML77] have noted regularities in dialogue and have attempted to capture these regularities in knowledge structures that can be used for comprehending utterances. For example, Mann, Moore, and Levin [MML77] used a knowledge structure called a dialogue game to model goal-related use of language in such joint inter-actions as buying and selling and as learning and teaching. Grosz and Sidner [GS86] and Reichman [Rei78a,Rei84] have investigated discourse structure and have shown that a coherent discourse can be segmented into units that have well-defined relationships to one another.

Reichman further contended that the existing discourse structure established expectations about appropriate next conversational moves. My analysis of naturally occurring dialogue indicates that such expectations about appropriate next steps in a dialogue form a third component of factual knowledge that plays a major role in comprehending elliptical fragments. The dialogue preceding an elliptical utterance may suggest discourse or communicative goals for the speaker, such as seeking clarification of a question, expressing surprise at a question, or answering a question. My transcript analysis leads me to hypothesize that these suggested discourse goals become shared knowledge between speaker and hearer and that as a result the listener is on the lookout for the speaker to pursue these anticipated discourse goals and interprets utterances accordingly.

---

[2]I am considering only typed utterances in terminal-terminal communication and so will ignore considerations such as inflection and intonation.

Consider, for example, the following dialogue:

IS: I want to major in computer science.

IP: Have you taken CS105 or CS180?

IS: At the University of Delaware?

IP: No, anywhere.

IS: Yes, at Penn State.

In this example IP's first question produces a strong anticipation that IS will pursue the discourse goal of providing the requested information. Therefore, subsequent utterances are interpreted with the expectation that IS will eventually address this goal. IS's second utterance is interpreted as pursuing a discourse goal of getting clarification of the question posed by IP. This discourse goal is satisfied by IP's response, and IS's last utterance answers the initial query posed by IP.

However, such discourse expectations do not persist forever with intervening utterances. Consider the following dialogue:

(1) *IP:* Do you want to take CS320?
(2) *IS:* Who is teaching it?
(3) *IP:* Dr. Raff and Dr. Owen.
(4) *IS:* When does Dr. Raff's class meet?
(5) *IP:* At 7:00 P.M. on Wednesday night.
(6) *IS:* Where?
(7) *IP:* At Wilcastle.
(8) *IS:* Does Dr. Owen's class meet on campus?
(9) *IP:* Yes.
(10) *IS:* When?
(11) *IP:* It meets on Tuesday and Thursday at 8:00 A.M.
(12) *IS:* Yes, with Dr. Raff.

IP's initial query produces an expectation that IS will answer the question posed by IP. However, each intervening utterance lessens these expectations to the extent that IS's last utterance is difficult to interpret and therefore should not be used by a cooperative dialogue participant. However, if utterance 12 is substituted for utterance 4 in the above dialogue, the fragment "Yes, with Dr. Raff." is easily understood.

5.2.4   Processing Knowledge

My transcript analysis indicates that plan recognition strategies and focusing techniques are necessary for interpreting intersentential ellipsis. Plan recognition strategies are necessary to infer a model of the information seeker's underlying task-related plan, also an essential component of factual knowledge, and to consider possible expansions of that plan when processing elliptical fragments.

Focusing techniques are necessary to identify that portion of the underlying plan to which a fragmentary utterance refers. Consider again the dialogue in [EX2], repeated below:

Speaker 1: Who are the candidates for programming consultants?

Speaker 2: Mary Smith, Bob Jones, and Ann Doe have applied for the job.

Speaker 1: Tom's recommendation?

The focus of attention in this dialogue is on considering the job applicants and evaluating them. Therefore, speaker 1 is expected to continue with this subtask before considering other aspects of his overall task. As a result, speaker 1's fragmentary utterance "Tom's recommendation?" will be understood as a request for Tom's opinion about the suitability of the job applicants for the job of programming consultant. However, if the focus of attention were instead on determining the number of consultants needed, IS's fragmentary utterance would be understood differently.

As discussed in chapter 2, plan recognition strategies have been used successfully by Allen in the interpretation of indirect speech acts [PA80]. And focusing mechanisms have been used by Grosz in identifying the referents of definite noun phrases [Gro77a], by Robinson in interpreting verb phrases [Rob81], by Sidner in anaphora resolution [Sid81], and by McKeown in natural language generation [McK82,McK83].

5.3 Summary

A robust natural language interface must be able to understand intersentential elliptical fragments. In this chapter I have argued that syntactic and semantic interpretation strategies are limited by their sole reliance on precise representations of preceding utterances and have suggested further investigation of a strategy utilizing the speaker's inferred task-related plan and discourse goals. The power of this approach lies in its reliance on pragmatic information, including discourse content and conversational goals, rather than on precise representations of preceding utterances alone. The next chapter presents such a pragmatic strategy for interpreting intersentential ellipsis.

6 A Pragmatics-Based Approach to Intersentential Ellipsis

Real understanding consists not only of recognizing the propositional content of a particular utterance but also of inferring what the speaker wants to accomplish and the relationship of each utterance to this task. Thus my objective in understanding an intersentential elliptical fragment is to identify the discourse goal that the speaker is believed to be pursuing with the utterance and to determine how the utterance should be interpreted with respect to this discourse goal and the inferred task-related plan motivating the speaker's participation in the dialogue.

My hypothesis is that speaker and hearer mutually believe that certain knowledge has been acquired during the course of the dialogue and that this factual knowledge along with other processing knowledge should be used to deduce the speaker's intentions. These knowledge sources were discussed in the preceding chapter and include the speaker's inferred task-related plan (normally only a partial plan during the dialogue), the speaker's inferred beliefs, the anticipated discourse goals of the speaker, plan recognition strategies, and focusing techniques.

This chapter presents a pragmatics-based approach to understanding intersentential elliptical fragments that occur in information-seeking dialogues. I am assuming that the natural language system plays the role of information provider. I am also assuming that communication is via a typical terminal and have not studied the impact of facial expression and intonation on intended meaning. Since my primary interest in this research is the affect of expectations and inferred knowledge on ellipsis understanding, I have not considered the contribution of clue words to the processing of ellipsis. However, they certainly could be incorporated into my strategy.

In this research I have attempted to ascertain the extent to which pragmatic knowledge can be used to understand ellipsis and the limitations of such an approach. However, I do not maintain that a natural language system should use only pragmatic knowledge; a robust system will need to coordinate syntactic, semantic, and pragmatic techniques to fully understand the wide variety of elliptical utterances used in human communication.

6.1 Overview of the Interpretation Framework

My ellipsis interpretation strategy assumes that the system has assimilated the preceding dialogue and now has access to a context model representing IS's inferred underlying task-related plan, a stack

containing the discourse expectations for IS, and a belief model representing IS's inferred beliefs. These comprise the requisite factual knowledge discussed in the preceding chapter and are part of the overall user
model in the architecture for a robust natural language interface of the
type shown in figure 1.1.

I claim that the dialogue preceding an utterance establishes expectations about discourse goals that IS might pursue and that these expectations should be used to guide interpretation of intersentential elliptical fragments. If IS employs a complete utterance, the utterance
generally gives clues about IS's discourse goal; in this case the discourse
expectations play a secondary role. However, if IS employs an elliptical
fragment, he must intend that the fragment be interpreted according to
these expectations. IS believes that IP expects him to pursue certain
discourse goals and therefore that IP will be anticipating utterances directed toward these goals. If IS does not want his elliptical fragment
interpreted according to these expectations, his utterance must override
them either by not producing an interpretation appropriate to an expected discourse goal or by explicitly suggesting a different discourse
goal (with the use of clue words). Otherwise, IS is assumed to *intend*
that his utterance be interpreted according to IP's expectations.

The following dialogues illustrate this hypothesis:

IP: Do you want to take CS360?

IS: Are you asking me if I want to take it next semester?

IP: Do you want to take CS360?

IS: Will it be offered next semester?

IP: Do you want to take CS360?

IS: Next semester?

In the first dialogue IS's utterance indicates that it is an attempt to
clarify the question posed by IP. In the second dialogue IS's utterance
simply requests information about CS360 in order to formulate an answer to IP's question. However, in the third dialogue IS's utterance is
an elliptical fragment that conceivably could produce several different
interpretations. It might be an attempt to clarify the question posed by
IP, a request for information about when CS360 is offered in order to
formulate an answer to the posed question, or an expression of surprise
that IP would ask such a question (for example, if CS360 is only offered
next semester and IS already has a very full schedule). Such elliptical fragments do not explicitly indicate IS's discourse goal in uttering

the fragment, and thus understanding relies heavily on mutual beliefs, including the discourse goals that IS is expected to pursue.

I thus claim that IS must *intend* his elliptical fragment to be interpreted according to these mutually believed expectations. My ellipsis resolution strategy uses a stack of *discourse expectations* derived from the preceding dialogue to control interpretation of elliptical fragments. Each discourse expectation has an associated *discourse expectation rule* that suggests discourse goals IS might pursue. I view IS's elliptical fragment as highlighting, or bringing to attention, some aspect of his underlying task-related plan. If this aspect of the plan can produce a coherent interpretation appropriate to a discourse goal suggested by the expectation on top of the discourse stack, then the elliptical fragment should be recognized as intending to accomplish this discourse goal, and an appropriate interpretation produced. Otherwise, the discourse stack must be popped, and other less immediate expectations considered.

Figure 6.1 presents an overview of my framework for ellipsis interpretation. The processes in this diagram form one module of the utterance interpreter in figure1.1. Dashed lines represent flow of control, and solid lines represent information flow. Given the semantic representation of an elliptical fragment, the ellipsis processor first invokes the discourse expectation rule associated with the top element of the discourse stack. This rule suggests one or more potential discourse goals that IS might be expected to pursue. Each of the suggested discourse goals has one or more associated *discourse goal rules* that are applied to the fragment in an attempt to produce a coherent interpretation that accomplishes that discourse goal. Discourse goal rules call the *plan analyzer*, which reasons on the context model and a model of IS's beliefs to suggest possible associations of the elliptical fragment with aspects of IS's task-related plan. If multiple associations are suggested, focusing strategies are used to select the association believed to be intended by IS, namely, that most appropriate to the current focus of attention in the dialogue. The conditions tested in a discourse goal rule use the results returned by the plan analyzer, along with other factual and processing knowledge, to determine whether its associated discourse goal should be recognized as the discourse goal being pursued by IS. If these conditions are satisfied, the rule produces an interpretation of the elliptical fragment relevant to the recognized discourse goal. On the other hand, if it is determined that the fragment does not accomplish any of the proposed discourse goals, then the discourse stack is popped, and this interpretation process is repeated using the discourse expectation rule associated with the less immediate expectation now on top of the discourse stack.

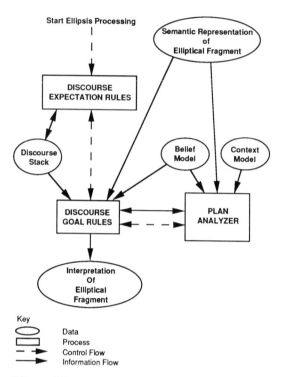

Figure 6.1
Overview of framework for interpreting intersentential ellipsis

This framework is similar to Allen's strategy [AP80] for interpreting elliptical fragments in that it reasons about the user's plan. However, Allen started with potential interpretations of the surface speech act that the speaker's fragment performs and attempted to develop an inference path that connected each potential interpretation with the speaker's possible overall domain goals, where such goals might be to meet or board a train. I am proposing a top-down strategy that uses the information seeker's anticipated discourse goals to guide interpretation of the fragment and that applies focusing rules to determine the aspect of the plan highlighted by it. This model will understand intersentential elliptical utterances by identifying the discourse goal that the information seeker is pursuing and by interpreting the fragment relative to this discourse goal. Discourse expectations will determine the order in which potential discourse goals are considered, and the suggested discourse goals will determine how the aspects of the plan highlighted by the information seeker's utterance are interpreted. Interpretation of elliptical fragments appears to rely heavily on conversational expectations and focus of attention, and this strategy captures such discourse knowledge.

The next sections describe my process model for understanding intersentential ellipsis. Section 6.2 presents the plan analyzer; it is responsible for identifying the aspect of the information seeker's underlying task-related plan highlighted, or brought to attention, by the elliptical fragment. Section 6.3 describes the discourse goals that an information seeker might pursue with an elliptical fragment in a task-oriented dialogue. Section 6.4 presents the discourse component. It discusses the discourse stack, discourse expectation rules, and discourse goal rules, shows how these interact with the plan analyzer to interpret an elliptical fragment, and illustrates my interpretation strategy with a number of examples.

6.2   The Plan Analyzer

As stated earlier, the motivation for my interpretation strategy is the hypothesis that IS and IP share the belief that IP has certain discourse expectations for IS and will be anticipating utterances directed toward discourse goals suggested by these expectations. I view IS's elliptical fragment as highlighting, or bringing to attention, some aspect of his underlying task-related plan. The plan analyzer determines the particular aspect of the plan to which IS's fragment draws attention. If this aspect of the plan can produce a coherent interpretation appropriate to the suggested discourse goal, the elliptical fragment is recognized as intending to accomplish this discourse goal.

I will call the matching of fragments with plan elements *association*. The plan analyzer searches an expansion of the existing task-related plan inferred for IS. It attempts to associate IS's fragment with a term and/or conjunction of propositions in this expanded plan. Focusing heuristics are used to select the most appropriate of several possible associations.

6.2.1   Association of Fragments

I will discuss five classes of elliptical fragments (constants, propositional fragments, variables, terms with attached propositions, and disconnected propositions) and how they are associated with plan elements. The association mechanism should be extendible to other classes of fragmentary utterances.

Constants   A constant fragment can only associate with terms that the system believes IS believes have a semantic type consistent with the semantic type of the constant. Furthermore, each term has a limited set of valid instantiations within the existing plan. A constant associates with a term only if the system's beliefs indicate that IS might believe that the uttered constant is one of the valid instantiations of the term. For example, if a plan contains the proposition Starting-date(AI-CONF, _date:&DATE), the elliptical fragment "February 2?" will associate with the date term in this proposition only if the system believes that IS might believe that the starting date for the AI conference is in February.

Recourse to such a belief model is necessary to allow for yes/no questions to which the answer is no and yet eliminate potential associations that a human listener would recognize as unlikely. If constants are permitted to associate only with terms for which the constant is a valid instantiation in the plan, yes/no questions cannot be handled. Consider, for example, the following dialogue:

IS: What time do the sections of CS440 on Monday meet?

IP: One section of CS440 meets on Monday at 7:00 P.M. and another section meets on Monday at 4:00 P.M.

IS: Dr. Smith? (or With Dr. Smith?)

A portion of IS's expanded underlying task-related plan inferred after the first utterance is shown in figure 6.2. This plan contains the proposition Teaches(_f:&FACULTY, _s:&SECTION). IS's elliptical fragment is a request to know whether the Monday sections of CS440 are taught by Dr. Smith. But if the answer to this question is no, Dr. Smith is not a valid instantiation of the term _f:&FACULTY in this proposition in the expanded plan. If the propositional constraints have little to do with the reasonableness of the interpretation, such constraints must not restrict the association of constants in IS's plan. Thus associations cannot be limited to terms for which the uttered constants are valid instantiations in the expanded plans.

However, if constants are permitted to associate with *any* term with the same semantic type as the constant, associations that a human listener would discard as unreasonable will not be eliminated. Although this discarding of possible associations does not occur often in interpreting elliptical fragments, actual human dialogues indicate that it is a real phenomenon. Consider the following example of an actual dialogue that occurred during April several years ago:

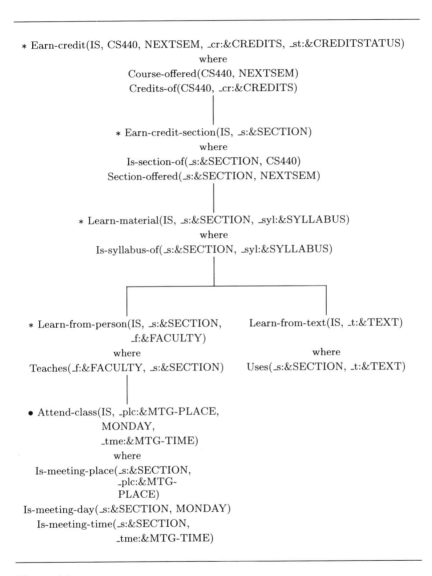

* Earn-credit(IS, CS440, NEXTSEM, _cr:&CREDITS, _st:&CREDITSTATUS)
where
Course-offered(CS440, NEXTSEM)
Credits-of(CS440, _cr:&CREDITS)

* Earn-credit-section(IS, _s:&SECTION)
where
Is-section-of(_s:&SECTION, CS440)
Section-offered(_s:&SECTION, NEXTSEM)

* Learn-material(IS, _s:&SECTION, _syl:&SYLLABUS)
where
Is-syllabus-of(_s:&SECTION, _syl:&SYLLABUS)

* Learn-from-person(IS, _s:&SECTION,
_f:&FACULTY)
where
Teaches(_f:&FACULTY, _s:&SECTION)

Learn-from-text(IS, _t:&TEXT)
where
Uses(_s:&SECTION, _t:&TEXT)

• Attend-class(IS, _plc:&MTG-PLACE,
MONDAY,
_tme:&MTG-TIME)
where
Is-meeting-place(_s:&SECTION,
_plc:&MTG-
PLACE)
Is-meeting-day(_s:&SECTION, MONDAY)
Is-meeting-time(_s:&SECTION,
_tme:&MTG-TIME)

Figure 6.2
A portion of an expanded context model

Speaker 1: Have you received the return receipt for your conference paper?

Speaker 2: Yes, it came yesterday.

Speaker 1: August the _____?

Speaker 2 had submitted a conference paper and had requested a return receipt from the post office upon delivery to the conference committee. Speaker 2 successfully interpreted speaker 1's elliptical fragment as a request for the date that speaker 2 would be attending the conference. However, other terms in speaker 2's overall plan were also of the semantic type DATE and were more relevant to the existing focus of attention. An example of such a term is the date on which the conference paper was delivered to the conference committee. However, speaker 2 believed that it was mutual knowledge that the paper was not delivered in August. Therefore, speaker 2 discarded this term as the aspect of the plan being queried by speaker 1 and selected a term less relevant to the current focus of attention in the dialogue.

Thus constant fragments must associate with plan elements that the system believes that IS might plausibly believe that the uttered constant could instantiate. Therefore, our ellipsis processor uses a simple belief model representing mutual beliefs about the information seeker's beliefs. Included in this belief model are propositions that the information seeker believes are satisfied. These propositions may be fully or partially instantiated; in the latter case they represent the belief that the information seeker believes that the proposition can be satisfied by a constant of the type designated for the argument. So, for example, the system's belief that the information seeker believes that the starting date of the AI conference is in February would be represented in the belief model by the proposition Starting-date(AI-CONF, _date:&FEBRUARY-DATE), where FEBRUARY-DATE is a subclass of DATE. The belief model also contains other beliefs, such as the objects and types that the information seeker knows about and the information seeker's beliefs about the types of constants and about type generalization. My research has not addressed such issues as how beliefs are acquired during a dialogue [KF87] or how they can be efficiently represented and updated in a user model [FD86].

Propositional fragments   A propositional fragment can be of two types. The first is a proposition whose predicate name is the same as the predicate name of a proposition in the plan domain. An example is the proposition Teaches(SMITH, _sect:&SECTION) contained in the semantic representation of the utterance "Taught by Dr. Smith?" The second type is a more general propositional fragment that cannot be associated with a specific plan-based proposition until after the analysis of the relevant propositions appearing in IS's plan. This second type of proposition would be produced by the utterance "With Dr. Smith?" and will be represented as Gen-pred(SMITH), which indicates that the name of the specific plan proposition is as yet unknown, that it is a member of the semantic class Gen-pred, and that one of its parameters must associate with the constant SMITH.

A proposition of the first type *associates* with a proposition of the same name if the parameters of the propositions associate. Propositions can be classified using their predicate names into a generalization hierarchy of such semantic classes as Gen-loc-pred (the class of propositions that specify the location of an entity) and Gen-pred (the top-level semantic class containing all propositions). A proposition of the second type associates with a plan proposition of the same semantic class whose parameters include terms associating with the known parameters of the propositional fragment. Thus the type 2 propositions

Gen-pred(SMITH)
Gen-loc-pred(101-PURNELL)

associate respectively with the plan propositions

Teaches(_f:&FACULTY, _s:&SECTION)
Is-meeting-place(_s:&SECTION, _plc:&MTG-PLACE)

in the plan illustrated in figure 6.2.

Variables The semantic representation of an elliptical fragment consisting of a definite term such as "The meeting time?" contains a variable term _time:&MTG-TIME. Such a term associates with terms of the same semantic type in IS's plan. Note that the system's model of IS's partially constructed plan may contain constant instantiations in place of former variables. A term fragment will still associate with such constant terms.

Terms with attached propositions The semantic representation of an elliptical fragment consisting of a definite noun phrase such as "The meeting place of sections taught by Dr. Smith" contains a term _plc1:&MTG-PLACE with attached propositions:

Is-meeting-place(_ss:&SECTION, _plc1:&MTG-PLACE)
Teaches(SMITH, _ss:&SECTION)

The term and propositions in the semantic representation of such a fragment can associate with individual terms and propositions in IS's plan, with the constraint that a single argument from the semantic representation of the fragment cannot associate with two arguments represented by two different variables in the plan. Thus the propositions

Is-meeting-place(_ss:&SECTION, _plc1:&MTG-PLACE)
Teaches(SMITH, _ss:&SECTION)

in the above example cannot associate respectively with the propositions

Is-meeting-place(_sect1x:&SECTION, _plca:&MTG-PLACE)
Teaches(SMITH, _sect2a:&SECTION),

since then the single argument _ss:&SECTION from the fragment would associate with two different variables from the plan. Without this restriction the term and propositions extracted from IS's plan would not necessarily stand in the same relationship to one another as the terms and propositions in the semantic representation of IS's utterance.

Disconnected propositions   Occasionally the semantic representation of IS's utterance will contain a set of propositions that are not joined to one another by their arguments. An example is the conjunction of the two propositions Gen-pred(SMITH) and Gen-time-pred(MONDAY), which give the semantic representation of the utterance "With Dr. Smith on Monday." Each individual proposition in such a conjunction of propositions will associate with some proposition in IS's underlying task-related plan. The fragment then associates with the conjunction of these individual associations. However, individual associations must occur within the same focus domain. The concept of a focus domain will be presented later in this chapter, but basically this constraint ensures that each proposition has approximately the same relevance to the current focus of attention in the underlying plan. It appears that when speakers employ multiple propositions in an intersentential elliptical utterance, the plan aspects to which the propositions draw attention all reside at the same focus level.

6.2.2   Retaining Established Dialogue Context

Humans seem to retain as much of the established context as possible in interpreting intersentential ellipsis. Carbonell [Car83] demonstrated this phenomenon in an informal poll in which individuals interpreted the fragment in the following dialogue as retaining the *fixed media* specification:

IS: What is the size of the three largest single port fixed media disks?

IP: (response appropriate to the system under discussion)

IS: Disks with two ports?

We have noted the same phenomenon in other domains. Consider the following dialogue:

IS: Is CS440 being taught next semester?

IP: Yes.

IS: Any sections at night?

Humans interpreting the elliptical fragment "Any sections at night?" retain the established context that the course is CS440 during the next semester.

As I described in chapter 3, I represent the system's beliefs about IS's underlying task-related plan in a tree structure called a context model. The set of nodes along the path from the root of the context model to the current focus of attention form a stack of goals and associated plans, the topmost of which is the current focused plan. Each of these goals is part of the plan associated with the goal immediately beneath it in this stack. Along with the most recently considered subgoal in the current focused plan, these nodes will be called *active nodes*. They represent the established global context within which the fragmentary utterance occurs, and the propositions attached to the goals at these nodes (the propositions that restrict the instantiation of arguments in the R-goals) can have the affect of constraining the instantiation of variables in their ancestor nodes in the context model. For example, in figure 6.2 IS's most recently considered subgoal is attending class on Monday; this restricts the sections that he is currently considering taking to those that meet on Monday and thus constrains the possible valid instantiations of the variable _s:&SECTION in the Learn-from-person, Learn-material, and Earn-credit-section subgoals higher up on the active path. These restrictions represent part of the context within which the elliptical fragment occurs and, unless overridden by information in the utterance itself, represent information that may be missing from the sentence fragment but is presumed to be understood by the speaker. Thus if we use the propositions contained in these active nodes, we can retain the restrictions on the variables in ancestor nodes when the focus of attention pops back to them and in this way interpret elliptical fragments within the context established at the time the utterance occurs. In addition, the nodes along the paths from the root of the context model to the nodes at which fragment elements associate with plan elements represent the new context derived from IS's fragmentary utterance.

If the elliptical fragment is a proposition, plan analysis produces a conjunction of propositions that represent the aspect of the plan highlighted by IS's elliptical fragment along with the context within which the fragment should be interpreted. If the elliptical fragment is a constant, variable, or term with attached propositions, plan analysis produces a term associated with the constant or variable term in the fragment as well as a conjunction of propositions. In the remainder of this chapter I will refer to the term and conjunction of propositions identified by the plan analyzer as PLTERM and PLPROPS. PLPROPS consists of all propositions attached to goals along the paths from the root of the context model to the nodes at which an element of the fragment is associated with an element of the plan as well as all propositions attached to goals in the nodes that were active immediately prior to the elliptical fragment. If the substitution of terms from IS's fragment for associated terms in IS's plan is made on PLTERM and PLPROPS, a new term and conjunction of propositions is produced, which I will refer to as STERM and SPROPS respectively. These four elements—PLTERM, PLPROPS, STERM, and SPROPS—are returned by the plan analyzer to the discourse component and will be used in the discourse goal rules.

Example A   Consider the following dialogue:

IS: Is CS440 offered next semester?

IP: Yes.

IS: Do any sections meet on Monday?

IP: Yes, one section of CS440 meets on Monday at 7:00 P.M. and another section meets on Monday at 4:00 P.M.

IS: Taught by Dr. Smith?

Figure 6.2 presents a portion of the expanded plan inferred for IS prior to his elliptical utterance; active nodes are preceded by either an asterisk or a bullet.[1] The semantic representation of the elliptical fragment "Taught by Dr. Smith" is the triple

Teaches(SMITH, _sectx:&SECTION),   Proposition,   ?

---

[1]The active path was defined in chapter 3 as the path from the root of the context model to the current focused goal-plan pair. Note that active nodes extend one node beyond the nodes on the active path and include the most recently considered subgoal in the current focused plan.

which specifies that the fragment is a proposition followed by a question mark. This proposition associates with the proposition Teaches(_f:&FACULTY, _s:&SECTION) at the node for the goal

Learn-from-person(IS, _s:&SECTION, _f:&FACULTY)
where
Teaches(_f:&FACULTY, _s:&SECTION).

The active nodes contain the following propositions restricting the instantiation of arguments in their R-goals:

Course-offered(CS440, NEXTSEM)
Credits-of(CS440, _cr:&CREDITS)
Is-section-of(_s:&SECTION, CS440)
Section-offered(_s:&SECTION, NEXTSEM)
Is-syllabus-of(_s:&SECTION, _syl:&SYLLABUS)
Teaches(_f:&FACULTY, _s:&SECTION)
Is-meeting-place(_s:&SECTION, _plc:&MTG-PLACE)
Is-meeting-day(_s:&SECTION, MONDAY)
Is-meeting-time(_s:&SECTION, _tme:MTG-TIME)

These propositions maintain the established context, namely, that we are talking about the sections of CS440 that meet on Monday during the next semester. The node at which the elliptical fragment associates with a term in the plan is an active node, so the fragmentary utterance does not add any additional propositions to PLPROPS. SPROPS is produced by substituting the terms in IS's fragment for the terms with which they are associated in IS's inferred plan; thus SPROPS contains the following propositions:

Course-offered(CS440, NEXTSEM)
Credits-of(CS440, _cr:CREDITS)
Is-section-of(_sectx:&SECTION, CS440)
Section-offered(_sectx:&SECTION, NEXTSEM)
Is-syllabus-of(_sectx:&SECTION, _syl:&SYLLABUS)
Teaches(SMITH, _sectx:&SECTION)
Is-meeting-place(_sectx:SECTION, _plc:&MTG-PLACE)
Is-meeting-day(_sectx:&SECTION, MONDAY)
Is-meeting-time(_sectx:&SECTION, _tme:&MTG-TIME)

The proposition in SPROPS with which the fragment was associated, Teaches(SMITH, _sectx:&SECTION), gives the individual proposition on which IS's attention is now focused, and the remaining propositions in SPROPS provide the context within which this first proposition should be interpreted. The semantics of the above is that IS is drawing attention to the proposition associated with the fragment such that the conjunction of propositions in SPROPS is satisfied, that is, the proposition Teaches(SMITH, _sectx:&SECTION), where the sections are part of CS440, are offered next semester, and meet on Monday.

Example B Now consider this dialogue:

IS: On what days does CS440 meet next semester?

IP: Two sections meet on Monday and one section meets on Tuesday next semester.

IS: What time do the sections on Monday meet?

IP: One section meets on Monday at 4:00 P.M. and another section meets on Monday at 7:00 P.M.

IS: The texts?

Once again figure 6.2 presents a portion of the expanded plan inferred for IS prior to the elliptical fragment. The semantic representation of the fragment "The texts?" is the triple

_book:&TEXT,   Definite,   ?

which specifies that the fragment is a definite noun phrase followed by a question mark. The term _book:&TEXT from the semantic representation of IS's fragmentary utterance associates with the term _t:&TEXT appearing at the node for the goal

Learn-from-text(IS, _t:&TEXT)
where
Uses(_s:&SECTION, _t:&TEXT)

Thus PLTERM is _t:&TEXT. The propositions restricting the instantiation of arguments in the R-goals at the active nodes are the same as in example A. These propositions maintain the established context, namely, that we are talking about the sections of CS440 that meet on Monday during the next semester. The path from the root of the context model to the node at which the elliptical fragment associates with a term in the plan contains the additional proposition Uses(_s:&SECTION, _t:&TEXT). Thus PLPROPS is the conjunction of this proposition and the nine propositions attached to the goals at the active nodes. STERM and SPROPS are computed by substituting the terms in IS's fragment for the terms with which they were associated in IS's plan. Thus STERM is _book:&TEXT, and SPROPS is the conjunction of the following ten propositions:

Uses(_s:&SECTION, _book:&TEXT)
Course-offered(CS440, NEXTSEM)

Credits-of(CS440, _cr:&CREDITS)
Is-section-of(_s:&SECTION, CS440)
Section-offered(_s:&SECTION, NEXTSEM)
Is-syllabus-of(_s:&SECTION, _syl:&SYLLABUS)
Teaches(_f:&FACULTY, _s:&SECTION)
Is-meeting-place(_s:&SECTION, _plc:&MTG-PLACE)
Is-meeting-day(_s:&SECTION, MONDAY)
Is-meeting-time(_s:&SECTION, _tme:MTG-TIME)

The semantics of this result is that IS is drawing attention to the term _book:&TEXT such that the conjunction of all ten propositions comprising SPROPS is satisfied, namely, textbooks used in sections of CS440 that meet on Monday next semester.

6.2.3   Identifying the Intended Association

Within IS's task-related plan there often are multiple components with which a fragment might associate. Therefore, it is necessary to identify that aspect of the plan that IS intended to draw attention to by using the elliptical fragment. The plan analyzer employs focusing heuristics to select what it believes to be the association intended by IS, that association most relevant to the current focus of attention in the dialogue.

An elliptical fragment by itself often contains very little information, and the fragment is likely to be misunderstood if its relationship to the existing dialogue context is not correctly identified. Although both participants share factual and processing knowledge, discrepancies in such knowledge can exist. For example, their task-related plan structures may not be identical, and thus the depths of a subgoal within the plans may differ. Such minor discrepancies do not seem to be problematic when processing a complete utterance for two reasons:

- Generally sufficient information is conveyed in the utterance to distinguish the subgoal under consideration.

- Even if the relationship between the utterance and the speaker's plan is not precisely identified, a correct interpretation of the utterance itself and a direct response to it is often still possible, although attempts to generate additional helpful information may be unsuccessful.

However, in the case of elliptical fragments, such discrepancies can pose problems. The multitude of possible interpretations and the likelihood of misinterpretation if the relationship between the fragment and the underlying plan is not accurately identified require that speakers using ellipsis not rely on fine-grained plan structures for correct interpretation.

Although a shift in focus occurs every time one moves from a goal to a subgoal in the goal's associated plan, some of these moves may represent relatively small shifts in attention, and others may be quite large. For this reason I employ the notion of focus domains in order to group together goals and plans that appear to be at approximately the same level of focus when a particular plan is the current focused plan. Moving from one goal to another in the same focus domain will be considered a smaller shift in attention than moving from a goal in one focus domain to one in a different focus domain.

In a context model a child node will often be in the same focus domain as its parent. However, if investigating how to achieve a goal represents a significant shift in focus of attention from the plan that contains it, the plan is marked in the plan library to indicate that the goal introduces a new focus domain. This means that in an expanded context model all of the goal's children (representing subgoals in its plan) will be part of a different focus domain than the goal itself. Hence, a move from discussing the goal to considering what one would need to do in order to achieve it represents a large shift in focus of attention. As long as the goal's plan is expanded by substituting plans for just those subgoals that do not introduce another new focus domain, all of the subgoals in the expanded plan will be part of the same focus domain. Since the nodes along the active path in the context model form a stack and focus domains are associated with sequences of goals represented by these nodes, the hierarchy of focus domains along the active path also forms a stack.

The use of focus domains allows the grouping together of those goals that appear to be at approximately the same level of implicit focus when a plan is explicitly focused.[2] For example, figure 6.3 illustrates a context model containing some goals (preceded by an A) in one focus domain and other goals (preceded by a B) in a different focus domain. The subgoals of taking a particular section of a course, learning the material of a course, and learning from a particular teacher reside in the same focus domain within the expanded plan for earning credit in a course, which means that they are in focus to approximately the same degree. The subgoal of being at the cashier's office to pay one's tuition also appears within this expanded plan. However, it is part of a different focus domain introduced by the goal of paying tuition, since it does not come to mind nearly so readily when one thinks about taking a course. The goal Pay-tuition(IS, _cr:&CREDITS) is marked in figure 6.3 as A/B, indicating

---

[2]This is similar to Grosz's focus spaces [Gro77a] and the notion of an object's being in implicit focus.

that it is in focus domain A but that it introduces focus domain B (the goals in its associated plan are in focus domain B).

Focusing heuristics   The focusing heuristics use mutual beliefs about knowledge currently focused on by the dialogue participants and expectations about probable shifts in focus to rank alternative associations of elliptical fragments with elements of IS's underlying task-related plan. These heuristics select that interpretation believed to be intended by IS, that association of fragment and plan components most relevant to the current dialogue context. With the exception of the introduction of focus domains, these focusing heuristics are similar to the focusing heuristics presented in chapter 3.

A *primary focused entity* is an entity that is highlighted by the previous utterance and to which succeeding utterances are very likely to refer. How such primary focused entities are determined is beyond the scope of this book. Other researchers are investigating this problem; my notion of primary focused entities appears to be related to the concept of forward-looking centers, as described in [GJW83]. With respect to my plan structure, it appears that primary focused entities are selected from those entities recently introduced as parameters of subgoals at active nodes in the context model.

Once an entity has been brought into primary focus, we strongly expect IS to continue inquiring about attributes of the entity, even if this necessitates entering a new focus domain in the task-related plan structure. Thus references to attributes of this entity should be preferred interpretations over references to attributes of other entities as long as they are relevant to an expansion of a plan for a goal in the current focus of attention. For example, consider the following dialogue segment:

IS: What text is being used in section 10 of CS440 next semester?

IP: That section is using *Advanced Data Structures* by Lewis.

IS: The cost?

As a result of the first query the current focused plan is

Learn-material(IS, CS440-10-NS, _syl:&SYLLABUS)
where
Is-syllabus-of(CS440-10-NS, _syl:&SYLLABUS)

and the most recently considered subgoal within that plan is

Learn-from-text(IS, _txt:&TEXT)
where
Uses(CS440-10-NS, _txt:TEXT)

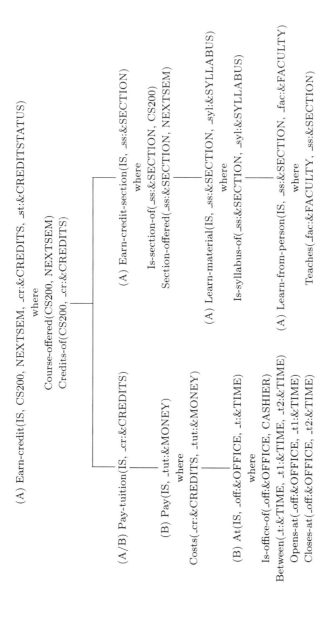

Figure 6.3
Part of a context model illustrating two focus domains

The goal Learn-from-text introduces a new focus domain containing the subgoal Purchase-text(IS, _txt:&TEXT), whose plan in turn contains the subgoal

Pay(IS, _amt:&MONEY)
where
Costs(_txt:&TEXT, _amt:&MONEY).

IP's response causes the textbook *Advanced Data Structures* to become the primary focused entity. The fragment "The cost?" associates with the term _amt:&MONEY in the proposition Costs(_txt:&TEXT, _amt:&MONEY). This interpretation is preferred over other interpretations, such as the costs involved in taking the CS440 course, since the former produces an attribute of the textbook *Advanced Data Structures*, which is the primary focused entity. This reasoning leads to the first focusing heuristic:

> *Association rule 1:* If an association occurs within an expansion of a plan for a goal in the current focus domain and that association represents an attribute of a primary focused entity, select that association.

The current focus domain contains those goals that are most highly focused within IS's underlying task-related plan at the current time, so interpretations relevant to these goals are preferred. For example, consider the following dialogue segment:

IS: Who is teaching CS490?

IP: Dr. Smith.

IS: What textbook is being used?

IP: There is no textbook. However, a set of papers and notes have been assembled into a course manual.

IS: Does the bookstore carry the course manual?

IP: Yes.

IS: Any faculty discounts?

Faculty discounts might be available both on courses taken by faculty and on books purchased at the bookstore. But humans interpret IS's elliptical fragment as asking whether there is a discount for faculty purchases of course manuals at the bookstore. This is explained by noting that the goal of purchasing a text is part of the current focus domain at the time the elliptical fragment is uttered, whereas the goal of paying for the course is not, and interpretations within the current focus domain are preferred over other interpretations in the overall task-related plan.

However, within the current focus domain two preferences exist. The current focused plan is the plan on which IS's attention is currently centered, and he is expected to finish investigating aspects of that plan before considering plans for other goals in his overall task. Therefore, interpretations that address aspects of the current focused plan should be preferred over other interpretations within the focus domain. Furthermore, once IS has introduced consideration of a particular goal, he is most likely to investigate plans for achieving that goal. Therefore, interpretations relevant to the most recently considered subgoal should be preferred over other interpretations in the current focused plan. This reasoning leads to the following focusing heuristic:

> *Association rule 2:* Associations in IS's expanded plan that are in the current focus domain should be preferred. Within the current focus domain, associations in an expansion of the current focused plan should be preferred; within the current focused plan, associations in the expansion of the plan for the most recently considered subgoal should be preferred.

The above two rules account for the large majority of elliptical fragments. This appears to be because such utterances rely on the shared context most strongly focused on by both participants. However, fragments requiring significant focus shift do occur and are generally interpreted correctly by human dialogue participants. Since the current focus domain contains the goals that are most strongly in the focus of attention of the dialogue participants, shifts to focus domains associated with expansions of the plans for these goals should be preferred over shifts to other focus domains. Furthermore, if the most recently considered subgoal introduces a new focus domain, there is a strong expectation that the information seeker will move to consider subgoals in that focus domain. Therefore, movement into a new focus domain introduced by the most recently considered subgoal is the most anticipated of these possible shifts in focus domains.

Consider, for example, the following dialogue:

IS: Who is teaching CS860?

IP: Dr. Herd is teaching CS860.

IS: Which room? (versus Which office? or 450 Purnell?)

Humans interpret the fragment "Which room?" as the room in which CS860 meets, not as the room in which Dr. Herd has his office; thus they remain in the same focus domain. However, the fragment "Which office?" is interpreted as the speaker's wanting to know the location of Dr. Herd's office and thus represents a shift to the new focus domain introduced by the subgoal of discussing CS860 with Dr. Herd before actually taking it. The fragment "450 Purnell?" results in a similar interpretation if speaker and listener mutually believe that IS believes 450 Purnell is a faculty office.

This reasoning leads to the following focusing rule:

> *Association rule 3:* Associations in a focus domain appearing in an expansion of the plan for a goal in the current focus domain should be preferred over other associations that shift to a new focus domain. Among these, if the most recently considered subgoal introduces a new focus domain, associations that appear in an expansion of the plan for that subgoal should be preferred.

The nodes on the active path form a stack of plans to which IS might return once he has completed investigation of the particular subtask on which he is currently focused. Consider, for example, the following dialogue:

IS: Who is teaching CS490?

IP: Dr. Smith.

IS: What textbook is being used?

IP: There is no textbook. However, a set of notes and papers have been assembled into a course manual.

IS: Does the bookstore carry the course manual?

IP: Yes.

IS: Three credits?

The fragment "Three credits?" should be interpreted as asking whether CS490 is a three credit hour course. Purchasing course materials is a subtask in the plan for taking CS490, and interpreting IS's elliptical fragment requires shifting from the focus domain associated with this subtask back to the focus domain associated with taking CS490. This shift is accounted for by the expectation that IS will eventually return to the higher-level plans whose expansion led to the most recently considered goal. Thus elliptical fragments that do not have an interpretation within an expansion of the plan for a subgoal in the current focus domain should be interpreted as reverting back to a previously introduced focus domain. This reasoning leads to the following focusing rule:

> *Association rule 4:* The focus domains of subgoals along the active path form a stack. Among associations that are not in the current focus domain or in an expanded plan for a subgoal in the current focus domain, preference is given to the association that is in the focus domain closest to the top of this stack.

An elliptical fragment whose interpretation requires entering a focus domain that is not strongly suggested by previous utterances must be specific enough to avoid confusion. For example, suppose that IP is a real estate agent and that IS is considering the purchase of a home. Consider the following dialogue:

IS: How large is the lot?

IP: A quarter of an acre.

IS: Who maintains the open areas?

IP: They are county parkland and are maintained by the county crews.

IS: What elementary school do children in this neighborhood attend?

IP: Castle Elementary.

IS: Any nearby Baptist churches?

IS's elliptical fragment will be associated with a term in a new focus domain introduced by a subgoal like Attend-religious-services. This focus domain is not part of the active path in the context model, nor is it a descendant of the most recently considered subgoal of having one's children attend school. However, it is specific enough to avoid ambiguity and can therefore be correctly interpreted as a request to be told whether there are any Baptist churches that the family might attend if they purchase and live in the house under consideration.

In a few instances an elliptical fragment may associate with two alternative elements of IS's underlying task-related plan, with the focusing heuristics rating both equally as the association intended by the speaker. In such a case the utterance will be interpreted as addressing both aspects of the speaker's plan.

6.3   Discourse Goals

Intuitively, a discourse goal is what the speaker is trying to do in making an utterance. The discourse goal itself is content-independent, although its realization in an utterance will involve some term or proposition from the speaker's underlying task-related plan. For example, the discourse goal Express-surprise-obtain-corroboration represents a speaker's attempt to convey to his listener that he is surprised at some proposition and would like a justification of it.

A number of researchers have contended that a coherent discourse consists of segments that are related to one another. The structuring relations have been given many names, including *rhetorical predicates* [Gri75b,McK85b], *coherence relations* [Hob79], *discourse segment purposes* [GS86], and *conversational moves* [Rei84]. My discourse goals are closest to Grosz and Sidner's discourse segment purposes and Reichman's conversational moves. Grosz and Sidner define a discourse segment purpose as the intended role of a discourse segment in achieving an overall discourse purpose. They contend that the discourse segment successfully serves its intended function only if the discourse segment purpose is recognized by the listener. Similarly, I contend that understanding an elliptical fragment requires that the listener identify the discourse goal being pursued by the speaker in uttering the fragment. Reichman differentiated between utterances that continue the current discourse segment and utterances that constitute conversational moves to a segment playing a different role in the overall dialogue. Some of her conversational moves, such as challenging a claim, had the flavor of goals that one might pursue in a dialogue. In a position similar to mine, Reichman contended that conversational moves establish expectations about subsequent conversational moves. However, neither Grosz and Sidner nor Reichman provide the details of a computational mechanism for identifying the role of an utterance in a dialogue. My theory does this for elliptical fragments in an information-seeking dialogue. Given the discourse expectations, it provides a mechanism for understanding an elliptical fragment by recognizing the intentions it communicates.

Understanding the intent behind elliptical fragments requires that the speaker's discourse goals be recognized. Chapter 1 described a set of dialogues that were analyzed as part of this research. From this effort and the consideration of other examples I have identified fifteen discourse goals that occur during information-seeking dialogues and that may be accomplished by means of elliptical fragments. The following is a list of these discourse goals, with definitions and illustrative examples.

- *Provide-for-assimilation:* IS provides information pertinent to constructing his underlying task-related plan.

IS: I want to get a degree. CS major.

In this example IS's second utterance specifies that in formulating a plan for getting a degree, IS wants his major to be computer science.

- *Obtain-information:* IS requests information relevant to constructing his underlying task-related plan or relevant to formulating an answer to a question posed by IP.

IS: Is CS360 being offered this fall?
IP: Yes.
IS: The instructor?

In the above example IS's fragment requests the instructor of CS360 in the fall.

IS: I need to satisfy the Group 4 distribution requirement.

IP: Would you like to take CS105?

IS: The meeting time?

In this example IS's fragment requests the meeting time of CS105 so that he can decide how to answer IP's question.

• *Express-surprise-obtain-corroboration:* IS expresses surprise at some proposition and requests elaboration and justification of it.

IS: When is CS490 being offered?

IP: 9:00 A.M. on Saturday morning.

IS: Who is teaching it?

IP: Dr. Smith.

IS: On Saturday morning?

In this example IS's last utterance expresses his surprise that Dr. Smith is teaching a course on Saturday morning, and in particular, CS490 at 9:00 A.M., and requests corroboration and an explanation of this surprising information.

• *Seek-confirm:* IS echoes some portion of the preceding utterance by IP in order to ascertain if it was transmitted correctly. This discourse goal occurs frequently in verbal dialogues and can occur in teletype dialogues when noisy communication lines exist.

IP: Would you like to take CS360?

IS: CS360? (or CB360?)

In this example IS's fragment may seek to confirm the course specified by IP. In the first sample utterance by IS the course was communicated correctly, but in the second case, erroneous data was transmitted over the communication line.

• *Seek-identify:* IS is unable to satisfactorily identify the referent of an item in IP's utterance and requests help from IP in doing so.

IS: What is Dr. Smith teaching this fall?

IP: CS360.

IS: CS360? (or The course in architecture?)

In this example IS's first fragment may communicate the fact that he has no idea as to what course CS360 is. IS's second fragment asks whether

CS360 is a particular course that IS knows about, the course in architecture. In both cases IS is attempting to identify the object referred to as CS360. I am taking a narrow view of identification in defining this discourse goal. Utterances that are requests for characteristics of an entity will be treated as Obtain-information discourse goals, not as Seek-identify discourse goals. The following is such an example:

IS: Who is teaching CS360?

IP: Dr. Smith.

IS: What other courses has Dr. Smith taught?

• *Seek-clarify-question:* IS requests information relevant to clarifying a question posed by IP.

IP: What course would you like to take?

IS: For credit?

In this example IS inquires whether IP is asking about courses that IS might like to take for credit, as opposed to registering as a listener or merely sitting in on the course.

• *Express-surprise-question:* IS expresses surprise at some aspect of a question posed by IP, either at an inference derived from the question or at the fact that the question was asked at all.

IP: Would you like to take CS360?

IS: With Dr. Smith?

In this example if it is mutual knowledge that Dr. Smith is the only teacher of CS360, IS is communicating his surprise that IP would ask such a question. This indicates that the answer should be obvious: either IS believes that Dr. Smith is known to be such an excellent teacher that no one would pass up such an opportunity or such a poor teacher that he is to be avoided at all costs.

• *Clarify-question:* IS adds additional information in order to extend and clarify a question that he has posed to IP.

IS: What courses can I take next semester to satisfy the CS technical elective requirement? At night.

In this example IS's fragment extends his question by restricting consideration to courses that meet at night.

- *Identify:* IS attempts to identify an entity in his own utterance.

IS: Who is teaching CS360? The course in architecture.

In this example IS's fragment identifies the course CS360, whose teacher is requested.

- *Suggest-answer-own-question:* IS suggests an answer to his own question. IS's intent is to suggest that IP give particular consideration to IS's proposal in formulating an answer to the question.

IS: What course should I take during the winter session? CS370?

In this example IS's fragment indicates that he is considering taking CS370 during the winter session and suggests especial consideration of this course as a possible answer to his question.

- *Answer-question:* IS provides the answer to a question asked by IP.

IP: What course would you like to take?
IS: CS470.

- *Answer-question-with-restrictions:* IS answers a yes/no question, providing restrictions on the relevant underlying task-related plan.

IP: Would you like to take CS440?
IS: With Dr. White. (or Not with Dr. White.)

In this example IS's first response indicates that he wants to take CS440 but that the plan for taking this course should be restricted so that he takes a section taught by Dr. White. IS's second response indicates that he might want to take CS440, but only if the plan for taking the course can be restricted so that he takes a section taught by someone other than Dr. White.

- *Answer-question-suggest-alternative:* IS answers a yes/no question negatively, providing a description of a desirable alternative.

IP: Would you like to take CS360?
IS: No, CS470.

In this example IS answers that he does not want to take the course suggested by IP but would like to take CS470.

• *Answer-question-with-explanation:* IS answers a yes/no question with an explanation of the answer.

IP: Do you want to take CS865?

IS: No, too late at night.

In this example IS's response indicates that he does not want to take CS865 because its meeting time is too late at night.

• *Suggest-answer-to-question:* IS is unsure about how to answer a question posed by IP and therefore suggests a possible answer for further consideration. In such cases IS is indicating that he wants IP's help in deciding whether the suggested answer is a good one.

IP: What course would you like to take to satisfy the science requirement?

IS: Biology 114? (or How about Biology 114?)

In this example IS is unsure whether Biology 114 is a good, or even a possible, way of satisfying the science requirement and is asking IP's considered opinion about the advisability of selecting it.

Although they are not explicitly accomplished by means of elliptical fragments, two other discourse goals play a major role in understanding ellipsis and will be discussed further in the next section.

• *Accept-response:* IP has responded to IS's request for information, and IS explicitly or implicitly accepts this response. Normally dialogue participants implicitly accept responses by failing to pursue discourse goals directed toward obtaining clarification or justification of the response. The following is an example of implicit acceptance:

IS: Who is teaching CS360?

IP: Dr. Smith is teaching CS360.

IS: When does it meet?

In this example IS implicitly communicates his acceptance of IP's response by proceeding on to further queries about the task-related plan being constructed. This acceptance can also be conveyed explicitly (perhaps with a complete sentence, although this rarely occurs). The following is an example of explicit acceptance:

IS: What course should I take to satisfy the CS technical electives?

IP: Statistics 370 would be a good course, since you do not have any statistics background and it is a prerequisite for CS421.

IS: I understand what you are saying. Does Statistics 370 have any prerequisites?

• *Accept-question:* IP has posed a question to IS, and IS explicitly or implicitly accepts the question. Normally dialogue participants implicitly accept such questions by failing to pursue discourse goals whose purpose is to get a question clarified or justified so that it can be understood and accepted. The following example illustrates implicit acceptance of a question posed by IP:

IP: Would you like to take CS360 next semester?

IS: Yes, but I would like to take it during the day if possible.

IS can explicitly accept the question, as illustrated in the following dialogue, but this rarely occurs.

IP: Would you like to take CS360 next semester?

IS: I understand what you are asking. But before I answer, can you tell me what other CS courses are being offered?

6.4   The Discourse Component

6.4.1   Discourse Expectations and the Discourse Stack

When IS makes an utterance, he is attempting to accomplish a discourse goal; this discourse goal may in turn establish expectations about what IS will do next. For example, if IS asks a question, one anticipates that IS may want to expand on his question by further identifying an entity or by clarifying the question. Similarly, utterances made by IP also establish expectations for IS. Chapter 5 discussed the importance of these expectations on the interpretation of elliptical fragments.

The discourse stack contains expectations about IS's discourse behavior along with the semantic representation of the utterance that prompted the expectation. I contend that ellipsis understanding is heavily dependent on discourse expectations that are pushed onto or popped from the stack as a result of utterances made by IS and IP. Precisely how this is accomplished in all cases is an issue that requires further study. My intent in this section is to show the motivation for the contents of the discourse stack by giving a set of stack processing rules that hold for simple utterances. However, in the current implementation the system does not actually construct the discourse stack from the dialogue preceding the elliptical fragment; this requires further research into recognizing discourse goals from complete utterances and must take into account indirect speech acts.

My stack-processing rules capture expectations about subsequent discourse behavior. Consider what happens when IP poses a question to IS.[3] In a cooperative dialogue we expect IS to answer the question. But before that can occur, IS must understand the question and accept it as relevant and valid. Normally dialogue participants implicitly accept such questions by answering the question or by proceeding to seek information relevant to formulating an answer; that is, the question is implicitly accepted by failing to communicate that it is not yet accepted. However, IS may be unable to accept the question posed by IP because he does not understand it (perhaps some of the terms were not clearly transmitted, or he is unable to identify some of the entities mentioned in the question, or the question seems ambiguous) or because he is surprised by it. This leads IS to pursue such discourse goals as seeking confirmation, seeking the identity of an entity, seeking clarification of the posed question, or expressing surprise at the question. The following is an example of such a dialogue:

IP: Would you like to take CS360 with Dr. Smith?

IS: Since when is Dr. Smith teaching CS360? I thought Dr. Brown always taught it.

Thus when IP poses a question to IS, our discourse expectations are that IS will first accept the question (or if that is not yet possible, he will work toward accepting it) and then answer it. Thus these two expectations must be pushed onto the discourse stack and should serve to guide our understanding of elliptical fragments. This reasoning leads to the following stack processing rule:

> *Rule SP1:* When IP asks a question of IS with the discourse goal of seeking information, Answer-question and Accept-question are pushed onto the discourse stack.

Similarly, when IP answers a question posed by IS, IS is expected to accept the response either explicitly or implicitly and then pursue other discourse goals. But before IS can accept the response, he must understand it and believe that it is relevant and valid. Once again, dialogue participants normally implicitly accept such responses by proceeding to formulate other queries pertinent to constructing their underlying task-related plan. However, IS may be unable to accept IP's response because he does not understand it (perhaps some of the terms in the response were not clearly transmitted or he is unable to identify some of the entities mentioned in the response) or because he is surprised by it. This

---

[3]IP may ask IS a question to decide what information IS needs.

leads IS to pursue such discourse goals as seeking confirmation, seeking the identify of an entity, or expressing surprise at some aspect of the response. The following is an example of such a dialogue:

IS: Who is teaching CS360?

IP: Dr. Smith is teaching CS360.

IS: Dr. Smith? (or Who in the world is Dr. Smith? Don't you mean Dr. Smythe?)

Thus when IP answers a question, our discourse expectations are that IS will first accept the response (or if that is not yet possible, work toward accepting it). This reasoning leads to the following stack-processing rule:

> *Rule SP2:* When IP answers a question posed by IS, Accept-response is pushed onto the discourse stack.

When IS pursues a discourse goal, such as seeking information or clarification, one's expectation is that IS will continue pursuing this discourse goal with subsequent utterances. For example, once IS has begun seeking information to formulate a task-related plan, one expects him to continue executing this discourse goal unless a subsequent utterance suggests otherwise. This leads to the next stack-processing rule

> *Rule SP3:* When IS actively pursues a discourse goal, the discourse goal is pushed onto the discourse stack.

If IS poses a question felicitously, he wants an answer to the question. So he is expected either to wait for an answer or to expand on the question with subsequent utterances. Similarly, when IS makes a statement or answers a question, we expect IS to believe that the statement or answer adequately conveys his intentions or else to expand on it until he is satisfied with it. This reasoning leads to the following stack-processing rules:

> *Rule SP4:* When IS poses a question to IP, Expand-question is pushed onto the discourse stack.

> *Rule SP5:* When IS answers a question posed by IP, Expand-answer is pushed onto the discourse stack.

> *Rule SP6:* When IS makes a statement, Expand-statement is pushed onto the discourse stack.

> *Rule SP7:* Once IP begins responding to IS, the discourse stack is popped up to and including the Expand expectations associated with IS's question, answer, or statement.

Although the strongest expectations are that IS will pursue a goal suggested by the top element of the discourse stack, this expectation can be passed over, at which point it no longer suggests expectations for utterances. This produces the following stack-processing rule:

> *Rule SP8:* When IS's utterance does not pursue a goal suggested by the top entry on the discourse stack, this entry is popped from the stack.

When IP begins responding to an utterance by IS, rule SP7 is applied followed by rule SP1 or SP2, according to whether IP is asking or answering a question. When IS makes an utterance, rule SP8 is applied until it fails, at which point rule SP3 is applied, followed by one of rules SP4, SP5, and SP6.

The following example illustrates operations on the discourse stack:

IS: Who is teaching CS440?

IP: Dr. Jones and Dr. White.

IS: I'd like to take CS440.

IP: Do you want to take CS440 on Monday night?

IS: Are you asking me if I want to take CS440 on Monday night next semester?

IP: Yes.

IS: Monday night will be fine.

Initially, the discourse stack is empty. IS's first query causes the entries Obtain-information and Expand-question to be pushed onto the stack (stack processing rules SP3 and SP4); after IP's first response, stack processing rules SP7 and SP2 cause the discourse stack to appear as follows. (The top of the stack here is the top of the list.)

Accept-response
Obtain-information

IS's next utterance pursues a Provide-for-assimilation discourse goal. Since the utterance conveys no difficulty with IP's preceding response, that response is implicitly accepted, and the top element of the discourse stack is popped (rule SP8). The utterance is not a request for further information, as is suggested by the expectation Obtain-information that is now on top of the discourse stack, so the stack is again popped (rule SP8). The new discourse goal Provide-for-assimilation is pushed onto the stack (rule SP3), followed by Expand-statement (rule SP6). IP then poses a question for IS, which pops Expand-statement from the discourse stack and pushes Answer-question and Accept-question onto the stack (rules SP7 and SP1), with the result that the discourse stack is now the following:

Accept-question
Answer-question
Provide-for-assimilation

IS's third utterance is an attempt to obtain clarification of the question, which indicates that IS cannot yet accept it. The following discourse stack results (rules SP3 and SP4):

Expand-question
Seek-clarify-question
Accept-question
Answer-question
Provide-for-assimilation

Once IP begins responding with the requested clarification, Expand-question is popped from the discourse stack and Accept-response is pushed onto the stack (rules SP7 and SP2). IS's last utterance does not convey difficulty with IP's response, nor does it attempt further clarification of IP's earlier question, so Accept-response and Seek-clarify-question are popped from the discourse stack. The utterance does not pursue a discourse goal suggested by Accept-question, as described in the next section, so the existing question is implicitly accepted. It does provide an answer to the question posed by IP and thereby addresses the expectation represented by what is now the top entry of the discourse stack, Answer-question.

I contend that listeners develop (from the dialogue) expectations about discourse goals that the speaker is likely to pursue. However, further research is needed to determine precisely how utterances affect these expectations. For example, I showed in the preceding chapter that expectations do not persist forever with intervening utterances. Thus some mechanism must exist to drop entries from the bottom of the stack after lengthy exchanges. In addition, further study is needed to ascertain exactly how utterances by IP affect the stack. For example, a response by IP that does more than IS requested appears to insert entries onto the stack as if IP's response had been requested by IS. The following dialogue illustrates this:

IP: Would you like to take CS470 from Dr. Smith?

IS: Is this Dr. Mary Smith?

IP: No, Dr. Joe Smith is teaching CS470. He is a new professor who will also be teaching a seminar in operating systems.

In this example IP's last response does more than merely identify Dr. Smith; the introduction of additional information appears to affect the discourse stack in a manner similar to an actual request for this knowledge. Our rules do not presently account for such complex interactions.

6.4.2 Suggested Discourse Goals

I have argued that an ongoing dialogue establishes discourse expectations for IS and have represented these expectations as a discourse stack. I have further claimed that elliptical fragments do not explicitly indicate the discourse goal being pursued, and so IS must *intend* that elliptical fragments be interpreted according to mutually believed expectations.

My analysis of naturally occurring dialogue has led to the formulation of discourse expectation rules that specify the affect of discourse expectations on the identification of IS's discourse goal. Each discourse expectation has an associated discourse expectation rule that suggests a set of one or more discourse goals that IS might pursue and the order in which they should be considered.

Suppose that IP poses a question to IS. The strongest discourse expectation is that IS will understand and accept the posed question or work toward understanding and accepting it. To understand a question, the question must have been satisfactorily transmitted. If not, IS will attempt to confirm the components that he believes may have been miscommunicated. Thus the first suggested discourse goal for IS under this discourse expectation is Seek-confirm. Once IS believes that the question has been properly transmitted, he must be able to satisfactorily identify the referents of the entities mentioned in the question. If he cannot do so, he may attempt to obtain further identification of an entity. Thus the second suggested discourse goal for IS under this discourse expectation is Seek-identify. Once the components of the question are understood, IS must believe that he fully comprehends what is being asked. If he does not, he must obtain clarification of the question before he can answer it. Thus the third suggested discourse goal for IS under the discourse expectation of accepting the question is Seek-clarify-question. Once the question is understood, IS may refuse to accept it by expressing surprise at an inference drawn from the question or at the fact that the question was asked at all. Thus the fourth suggested discourse goal under the discourse expectation of accepting the question is Express-surprise-question. If the elliptical fragment does not accomplish any of these discourse goals, IS has implicitly accepted the question and discourse stack rule SP8 pops the top element of the discourse stack. This reasoning leads to the following discourse expectation rule:

> *Rule DE1:* The discourse expectation Accept-question suggests the following ordered set of discourse goals for IS:
> 1. Seek-confirm
> 2. Seek-identify
> 3. Seek-clarify-question
> 4. Express-surprise-question

In a cooperative dialogue, once IS has understood and accepted a question, IP expects him to answer it and so is on the lookout for an answer. Therefore, preference should be given to interpretations that accomplish this goal. Thus the first discourse goals suggested for IS in this situation are those that directly or indirectly answer the question. If IS is unsure of the best answer to the question, he may suggest one or more possible answers and request IP's help in evaluating them. Thus the second suggested discourse goal for IS is Suggest-answer-to-question. In a cooperative dialogue we expect IS to answer questions posed to him. If he does not, he must not have sufficient knowledge to formulate a good answer. In this case we expect IS to work toward being able to answer the question by gathering whatever extra information he needs. Thus the third discourse goal suggested for IS under the discourse expectation of answering the question is Obtain-information. This analysis leads to the following discourse expectation rule:

> *Rule DE2:* The discourse expectation Answer-question suggests the following partially ordered set of discourse goals:
> 1. Answer-question, Answer-question-with-restrictions, Answer-question-suggest-alternative, or Answer-question-with-explanation
> 2. Suggest-answer-to-question
> 3. Obtain-information

Suppose that IP has responded to IS's request for information. Then the strongest expectation is that IS will understand and accept the response or work toward understanding and accepting it. To understand a response, the response must have been satisfactorily transmitted, and IS must be able to identify the referents of the entities mentioned in the response. Otherwise, IS may attempt to confirm any components that he believes may have been miscommunicated and identify any components whose extension he cannot recognize. Thus the first two suggested discourse goals for IS under the discourse expectation of accepting the response are Seek-confirm and Seek-identify. Once IS understands the response, he may still refuse to accept it by expressing his surprise at the response and indicating a desire for elaboration and corroboration.

Thus the third suggested discourse goal under this discourse expectation is Express-surprise-obtain-corroboration. If the elliptical fragment does not accomplish any of these suggested discourse goals, IS has implicitly accepted the response, and discourse stack rule SP8 pops the top element of the discourse stack. This reasoning leads to the following discourse expectation rule:

> *Rule DE3:* The discourse expectation Accept-response suggests the following ordered set of discourse goals for IS:
> 1. Seek-confirm
> 2. Seek-identify
> 3. Express-surprise-obtain-corroboration

The next three discourse expectation rules concern how IS might expand on a preceding utterance. If IS felicitously poses a question, he is expected either to wait for IP's response or to expand on the question in order to help IP understand the question and construct a useful reply. I claimed that when asked a question, a respondent can seek confirmation of a component, seek identification of a component, seek clarification of the question, express surprise at the question, answer the question, suggest an answer to the question, or obtain information relevant to answering the question. Similarly, having posed a question, a questioner can anticipate his respondent's needs and attempt to help his respondent understand and answer the question by himself pursuing the goals of identifying a component, clarifying the question, or suggesting an answer to which he thinks the respondent should give especial consideration. However, he will not confirm a component, since he has no reason to suspect it was miscommunicated, and he will not express surprise at the question or answer it if it was felicitously posed. Thus elliptical fragments uttered by IS immediately after a question posed by IS should be interpreted as directed toward helping the other dialogue participant answer the question. Similarly, if IS makes a statement or answers a question, he may decide to further identify one of the components of his utterance, and in the case of an answer to a question, he may elaborate on his answer by providing constraints on the task-related plan that he is trying to construct. This reasoning leads to the following discourse expectation rules:

> *Rule DE4:* The discourse expectation Expand-question suggests the following ordered set of discourse goals for IS:
> 1. Identify
> 2. Clarify-question
> 3. Suggest-answer-own-question

Rule DE5: The discourse expectation Expand-statement suggests the
following discourse goal for IS:
1. Identify

Rule DE6: The discourse expectation Expand-answer suggests the following ordered set of discourse goals for IS:
1. Identify
2. Provide-for-assimilation

If IS has been informing IP about certain aspects of his underlying
task-related plan, we expect him to elaborate on the plan by providing
further detail. However, in an information-seeking dialogue we anticipate that IS is providing this knowledge as background information to
help IP formulate cooperative responses to subsequent questions. Thus
we expect that IS will eventually request information about the domain
to achieve his objective of constructing a plan for his underlying task.
This leads to the following discourse expectation rule:

Rule DE7: The discourse expectation Provide-for-assimilation suggests
the following ordered set of discourse goals for IS:
1. Provide-for-assimilation
2. Obtain-information

Once IS begins actively pursuing a discourse goal, we expect that
subsequent utterances will repeat that discourse goal. Thus we have the
following discourse expectation rule:

Rule DE8: Discourse expectations other than Accept-question, Accept-
response, Answer-question, Provide-for-assimilation, and the three Expand expectations suggest that IS will pursue the discourse goal named
by the discourse expectation.

As described earlier, discourse expectations are represented in the discourse stack and are used to suggest anticipated behavior for IS. When IS
utters an elliptical fragment, these discourse expectations are analyzed
in turn until a coherent interpretation is identified. The top element
of the discourse stack represents the most immediate discourse expectation at the current point in the dialogue and the rule associated with it
is used to suggest discourse goals that IS might pursue. If it is determined that IS is not pursuing any of the discourse goals suggested by the
discourse expectation on top of the stack, the stack is popped and the
process is repeated. Thus, for example, when IP asks IS a question, the
discourse expectations Answer-question and Accept-question are pushed
in turn onto the discourse stack. If IS then uses an elliptical fragment,
the discourse expectation Accept-question will first be used to suggest
discourse goals that IS might be pursuing. However, if an interpretation

of the fragment accomplishing one of these suggested discourse goals cannot be constructed, this discourse expectation will be popped from the discourse stack; this indicates that IS has understood and implicitly accepted the question asked by IP. The top element of the stack will then be Answer-question, and it will be used to suggest discourse goals that IS might be pursuing by means of the fragment. (Note that although discourse expectations can be popped from the discourse stack, a cooperative dialogue participant can never pass over the discourse goal of answering a question.)

6.4.3   Discourse Goal Rules

I have claimed that the processing of elliptical fragments should be controlled by the discourse expectations in effect at the time the fragment is uttered. Discourse expectations suggest discourse goals that IS might be expected to pursue. If an elliptical fragment can be interpreted as pursuing a suggested discourse goal, this interpretation should be recognized as the one intended by IS; otherwise IS would have overridden these expectations, since he is aware that they will be used in understanding his utterances.

For each discourse goal I have formulated a set of discourse goal rules that are invoked when the discourse goal is suggested by the current discourse expectations. Each rule applies factual and processing knowledge to analyze a fragment and determine whether it could be understood as pursuing the discourse goal with which the rule is associated. My model views fragments as highlighting terms and/or propositions in the underlying task-related plan. The conditions tested in a discourse goal rule determine whether IP believes that it is mutually believed that the discourse goal might be pursued by IS in the current situation and whether the highlighted aspect of the plan as identified by the plan analyzer provides sufficient information for recognizing the discourse goal. If the conditions in a rule associated with a suggested discourse goal are satisfied, the discourse goal is recognized and the rule produces a related interpretation of the elliptical fragment.

To demonstrate how discourse goal rules facilitate recognition of the discourse goal that IS is pursuing, let us examine how IS might seek identification of an entity appearing in IP's utterance. Below are two plans, Seek-identify-1 and Seek-identify-2.

Seek-identify-1(IS, _entity1)
Applicability conditions:
  ¬Know(IS, referent(_entity1))
  Want(IS, Know(IS, referent(_entity1)))
Plan body:
  Request(IS, IP, Informref(IP, IS, referent(_entity1)))
Primary effects:
  Seek-identify(IS, _entity1)

Seek-identify-2(IS, _entity1, _entity2)
Applicability conditions:
  ¬Know(IS, referent(_entity1))
  Want(IS, Know(IS, referent(_entity1)))
  Know(IS, referent(_entity2))
  ¬Believe(IS, ¬Same-referents(_entity1, _entity2))
Plan body:
  Request(IS, IP, Informif(IP, IS, Same-referents(_entity1, _entity2)))
Primary effects:
  Seek-identify(IS, _entity1)

Although their primary effect is the same, namely to seek identification
of an entity, the two plans differ in that in the body of the first plan IS
directly requests further identification of the entity in question, whereas
in the second plan IS attempts to determine the referent by asking if it
is the same as an entity with which he is familiar. Now let us consider
how an elliptical fragment might be recognized as pursuing one of these
plans. Suppose we have the following dialogue:

IS: What CS courses are being offered during the summer?

IP: CS105 and CS461.

IS: CS461?

Suppose further that Seek-identify has been suggested as a discourse
goal for IS. If IS intends IP to recognize Seek-identify-1 as the discourse
plan that he is pursuing, he must indicate _entity1, the entity whose
identification he is requesting. The elliptical fragment "CS461?" may
be viewed as doing this. The applicability conditions for Seek-identify-1
specify constraints that must be satisfied if it is a reasonable plan for
IS to pursue. Only if IP believes that it is mutually believed that these
constraints are satisfied can IP infer that IS intends him to recognize
that he is pursuing the discourse goal that is the effect of the plan.
In the above dialogue IP believes that it is mutually believed that IS
wants to know the referent of CS461, since CS461 was mentioned in IP's
previous response. It is also reasonable for IP to believe that IS may not
know the referent of CS461.

Let us examine this latter belief in greater detail. Why didn't IP provide an extended description of CS461 in her previous response if she believes that IS cannot satisfactorily identify the course from its department and number? Though this is not an issue with which this chapter is concerned, I will suggest one possibility. In constructing a description, IP uses knowledge about the listener to produce a concise reference that she believes will be acceptable [App85,Goo86b]. Sometimes she will be quite certain that the listener will be able to identify the referent of her description; for example, perhaps the same description has been used successfully before. At other times IP will be uncertain whether the description is sufficiently detailed. If she goes to the extreme and includes every detail at her disposal, she risks confusing the listener and hampering identification [Goo86b]. Therefore, if IP is uncertain whether her description will be adequate, she must wait for IS's response to the description to determine its success. In the case of the above dialogue IS does not explicitly or implicitly accept the description (which he would do if he passed over the discourse goal of Seek-identify), and IP is left with the belief that her description was unsatisfactory.

In contrast, consider the following variation of the above dialogue:

IS: What courses is Dr. Jones teaching next fall?

IP: CS440 and CS461.

IS: What days is CS461 offered?

IP: Monday evenings.

IS: What courses are being offered during the summer?

IP: CS105 and CS461.

IS: CS461?

Since IS implicitly accepted IP's first response, implying that he understood the description *CS461*, and subsequently used it himself, IP is led to believe that IS can satisfactorily identify the referent of the term *CS461*. Consequently, IP is unlikely to interpret IS's last utterance as seeking identification of it. If IS really wants to pursue this discourse goal, he must override IP's beliefs with an utterance such as "I haven't heard of CS461. What course is it?" This leads to the following discourse goal rule:

> *DG rule Seek-identify-1:* Check whether the following conditions are satisfied:
>
> • IS's elliptical fragment terminates in a question mark.
>
> • The fragment highlights a component of IS's underlying task-related plan and matches a description used in the utterance by IP that is closest to the top of the discourse stack.

- It is mutually believed that IS might not know the referent of this description.

    If these conditions are satisfied, interpret the fragment as seeking further identification of the highlighted plan component.

There are many ways for IP to identify an entity for IS. For example, a faculty member can be identified by specifying any unique characteristic, such as the faculty member's full name, office location, or special research area. IP should choose identifying characteristics useful to IS, and here recourse can be made to IS's underlying task-related plan. This plan and the focus of attention in it suggest characteristics that might be useful to IS. For example, if IS is interested in taking a course, helpful identifying characteristics of the instructor might include his full name, position, departmental affiliation, research area, and status (full-time, part-time, visiting, extension faculty member). On the other hand, if IS is seeking advisement, helpful identifying characteristics of a faculty advisor include his full name and office address. Thus if IP believes that IS is unfamiliar with Dr. Smith, IS's elliptical fragment in each of the following dialogues will be interpreted as seeking identification of Dr. Smith, but IP's response providing the identification will differ.

IS: Who is teaching CS360?

IP: Dr. Smith is teaching CS360.

IS: Dr. Smith?

IS: Who is the advisor for CS freshmen?

IP: Dr. Smith is the CS freshman advisor.

IS: Dr. Smith?

It should be noted that IP could also provide identification by noting unusual characteristics of the entity, such as a faculty member's unique appearance or some reason he has recently been in the news. Such features exceed the scope of this work.

Now let us consider how an elliptical fragment might be recognized as seeking identification of an entity by pursuing the plan Seek-identify-2. If IS intends IP to recognize Seek-identify-2 as the discourse plan that he is pursuing, its applicability conditions must be satisfied, and IS must indicate both _entity1 (the entity whose identification he is requesting) and _entity2 (the entity with which he is familiar). _entity2 must be explicitly provided by the elliptical fragment, since it is new information not currently focused on in the dialogue, and _entity1 can be implicitly provided by the plan element with which the fragment is associated. For example, consider the following dialogue segment:

IS: What upper-level computer science courses are being offered during the summer?

IP: Dr. Smith will be teaching CS461 at 9:00 A.M.

IS: The course in simulation of discrete systems?

IS's elliptical fragment associates with the entity CS461 in IS's under-lying task-related plan. If IP believes that the applicability conditions for Seek-identify-2 are not violated, IS's fragment can be interpreted as attempting to accomplish the discourse goal of seeking identification of CS461 by ascertaining whether it is the course in simulation of discrete systems. Once again, since IP believes that it is mutually believed that she will use discourse expectations to guide interpretation of elliptical fragments, she is justified in believing that IS intended the fragment to be interpreted in this manner. This reasoning leads to the following discourse goal rule:

> *DG rule Seek-identify-2:* Check whether the following conditions are satisfied:
>
> • IS's elliptical fragment terminates in a question mark.
>
> • The fragment highlights a component of IS's underlying task-related plan, and this component is referred to with a description D in the utterance by IP that is closest to the top of the discourse stack.
>
> • It is mutually believed that IS might not know the referent of the description D.
>
> • It is mutually believed that IS does not believe that the fragment and the description D refer to different entities.[4]
>
> If these conditions are satisfied, interpret the fragment as seeking fur-ther identification of the highlighted plan component. In particular, IS's fragment describes an entity with which he is familiar and asks whether this entity and the highlighted plan component are the same.

Thus my framework for understanding intersentential elliptical frag-ments is a top-down procedure, with expectations about appropriate discourse goals guiding the interpretation process. The ellipsis proces-sor employs discourse expectation rules and discourse goal rules. The discourse expectation rules use the discourse stack to suggest possible discourse goals for IS, and then the system activates the associated dis-course goal rules. The discourse goal rules use the plan analyzer to help determine the best interpretation of the fragmentary utterance rel-evant to the suggested discourse goal. If a discourse goal rule succeeds

---

[4]Note that ¬Believe(IS, ¬P) does not imply Believe(IS, P).

in producing an interpretation, the ellipsis processor identifies that discourse goal and its associated interpretation as its understanding of the utterance.

The idea of using a general plan recognition strategy to recognize discourse goals as well as domain goals is appealing. However, such a strategy has not been adequately worked out even for complete utterances, although Litman's process model that handles clarification and correction subdialogues [LA87] is a step in this direction. Furthermore, as I argued in chapter 5, elliptical fragments require special treatment. My discourse goal rules are compilations of the kind of reasoning that must be done on discourse plans to ascertain if an elliptical fragment is intended to be recognized as pursuing a suggested discourse goal. They test the applicability conditions associated with a plan for a suggested discourse goal and determine whether the elliptical fragment can be interpreted with respect to the suggested discourse goal. The next sections present additional discourse goal rules along with the motivation for each.

Other discourse goals suggested by Accept expectations   Once IP has posed or answered a question, the question or response must be accepted by IS. This suggests the discourse goals of seeking confirmation, seeking identification of an entity in the utterance, seeking clarification if the utterance is a question, and expressing surprise at the question or response.

If IS cannot accept a question or response because he is unsure that it has been transmitted correctly, he may seek confirmation of the utterance. If IS's fragment is similar to, but not an identical match with, a component of IP's utterance, we strongly suspect that the fragment was improperly transmitted. In terminal-terminal dialogues, several interpretations exist for a fragment that is identical to a component of IP's preceding utterance. Interpreting such a fragment as an echo is highly dependent on whether we believe that IS believes that the communication line is noisy. Consider, for example, the following dialogue segment:

IP: Dr. Smith is teaching CS360.

IS: CB360? (or CS360?)

Since the fragmentary utterance "CB360?" typographically closely resembles the constant *CS360*, which should have been transmitted to IS, there is a suspicion that *CS360* was incorrectly transmitted. Thus IP is led to believe that IS could not recognize the transmitted component and that IS believes that the communication line is noisy. As a result, IS's fragment produces a mutual belief that the communication line is noisy and that IS is seeking confirmation of this constant. On the other hand, the fragmentary utterance "CS360?" will be interpreted as seeking confirmation of the transmitted component only if IP believes that it is mutually believed that the probability of noise on the line is high; otherwise a different discourse goal will be attributed to IS. This reasoning leads to the following discourse goal rule associated with the discourse goal Seek-confirm:

> *DG rule Seek-confirm:* Check whether the following conditions are satisfied:
>
> • IS's elliptical fragment terminates in a question mark.
>
> • The fragment appears to be a miscommunication of a component of the utterance by IP that is closest to the top of the discourse stack, or the fragment matches a component of the utterance by IP that is closest to the top of the discourse stack and IP believes that it is mutually believed that the probability of noise is high.
>
> If these conditions are satisfied, interpret the fragment as seeking confirmation that the component was correctly transmitted to IS.

Once IS believes that a posed question has been properly transmitted and that he can identify the entities mentioned in it, IS may still be unable to accept it because it is ambiguous or he is surprised by it. If IS's fragment highlights a term or proposition in his underlying task-related plan and IS already knows IP's beliefs regarding the possible values of the term or the truth of the proposition, IS has no need for this information again. At this juncture two possibilities exist:

• IS is referring to a term with multiple valid instantiations and is asking IP to clarify whether the question is intended to include a specific instantiation for the term.

• IS is expressing surprise about some inference drawn from the question or that the question was even asked.

If IS is seeking clarification of the question posed by IP, IS must believe that several possible alternatives exist. IS can request that IP specify the intended alternative, if any, or IS can ask if a specific alternative was implicitly intended by IP. On the other hand, if IS is expressing surprise at the posed question or an inference drawn from it, IS must believe that the aspect of the plan to which IS's elliptical fragment draws attention is entailed by the posed question and its associated plan.

Similarly, once IS believes that a response has been properly transmitted and that he can identify the entities mentioned in it, he may still
be unable to accept it because he is surprised by some aspect of the
response. In such cases his elliptical fragment may call attention to a
term or proposition whose value it is mutually believed that IS knows
(or at least that IS knows IP's beliefs about) and that, along with the
new information communicated in IP's response, is the source of IS's
surprise.

This reasoning leads to the following discourse goal rules:[5]

DG rule Seek-clarify-question: Check whether the following conditions
are satisfied:

• IS's elliptical fragment terminates with a question mark.

• The fragment highlights a term and/or one or more propositions *P*
in the context of a conjunction of propositions SPROPS (which include
P) in IS's underlying task-related plan.

• It is mutually believed either that (a) the fragment results in SPROPS
containing a term whose valid instantiations are restricted to what IS
believes is a proper subset of its multiple valid instantiations in PL-
PROPS, or (b) that the fragment is a singular reference to a term that
IS believes has multiple possible valid instantiations in his plan.

If these conditions are satisfied, interpret the fragment as seeking clarification of IP's question. In particular, in case (a) IS wants to know if
IP intended the proposition SPROPS to be understood as part of the
question, and in case (b) IS wants to know the value IP intended for
the specified term in the posed question.

DG rule Express-surprise-question: Check whether the following conditions are satisfied:

• IS's elliptical fragment terminates with a question mark.

• The fragment highlights a term STERM and/or one or more propositions *P* in the context of a conjunction of propositions SPROPS (which
include *P*) in IS's underlying task-related plan.

• It is mutually believed that IS already knows IP's beliefs about the
value of the term STERM and the truth of SPROPS.

• IS's fragment does not reduce the possible instantiations of the term
STERM or the conjunctive proposition SPROPS from what IS believes
are the valid instantiations possible in PLTERM or PLPROPS before
IS's fragment.

---

[5]Recall from section 6.2.2 that PLTERM and PLPROPS are the term and conjunction of propositions in IS's expanded plan that are highlighted by IS's elliptical
fragment, and STERM and SPROPS are produced by substituting into PLTERM
and PLPROPS the terms in IS's fragment for the corresponding terms in IS's plan.

> If these conditions are satisfied, interpret the fragment as expressing surprise at the question posed by IP.

This expression of surprise may be divided into three categories:

- If the truth of the conjunctive proposition SPROPS was known prior to the posed question, IS may be expressing surprise that the question was asked, since IS believes that mutual knowledge of the truth of SPROPS should make the answer to the question obvious.

- If the truth of the proposition SPROPS was just communicated in the posed question and it is mutually believed that IS did not know that SPROPS was satisfied, IS may be expressing surprise at the truth of SPROPS.

- If the fragment is a reference to a newly specified instantiation of a term in IS's task-related plan and IP believes that it is mutually believed that this term could have other values, IS may be expressing surprise at IP's selection of this particular instantiation.

> *DG rule Express-surprise-obtain-corroboration:* Check whether the following conditions are satisfied:
>
> - IS's elliptical fragment terminates in a question mark.
>
> - The fragment highlights a term STERM and/or one or more propositions P in the context of a conjunction of propositions SPROPS (which include P) in IS's underlying task-related plan.
>
> - It is mutually believed that IP already knows IS's beliefs about the value of the term STERM and the truth of SPROPS.
>
> If these conditions are satisfied, interpret the fragment as expressing surprise at IP's response and seeking corroboration of it. In particular, IS is surprised at the known value of STERM or the known truth value of SPROPS in light of the new information provided by IP's response and the term or proposition P highlighted by IS's fragment.

The following examples illustrate these discourse goal rules.

Example 1: Seeking clarification   Consider the following dialogue:

IS: I need to satisfy the Group 4 distribution requirement.

IP: Do you want to take CS105?

IS: During the next semester? (or The semester?)

If it is mutually believed that IS believes CS105 is offered every semester, this example illustrates an elliptical fragment that seeks clarification of the question posed by IP.

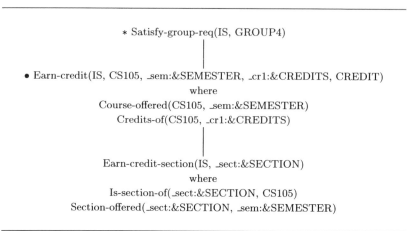

* Satisfy-group-req(IS, GROUP4)

|

• Earn-credit(IS, CS105, _sem:&SEMESTER, _cr1:&CREDITS, CREDIT)
where
Course-offered(CS105, _sem:&SEMESTER)
Credits-of(CS105, _cr1:&CREDITS)

|

Earn-credit-section(IS, _sect:&SECTION)
where
Is-section-of(_sect:&SECTION, CS105)
Section-offered(_sect:&SECTION, _sem:&SEMESTER)

Figure 6.4
A portion of an expanded context model for example 1

The semantic representation of the elliptical fragment "During the next semester?" is the triple

Gen-time-pred(NEXTSEM),   Proposition,   ?

which indicates that the fragment is followed by a question mark and is a general propositional fragment that must associate with a plan proposition that predicates a time relationship and has an argument associating with NEXTSEM.

Similarly, the semantic representation of the fragment "The semester?" is the triple

_sm1:&SEMESTER,   Definite,   ?

which specifies that the fragment is a definite noun phrase whose head noun is of type SEMESTER followed by a question mark.

A portion of an expansion of the task-related plan inferred for IS is shown in figure 6.4.

The belief model indicates that IS believes that CS105 is offered every semester. The top two entries of the discourse stack are Accept-question and Answer-question, which indicates that IS is first expected to accept IP's question and then answer it. The discourse expectation rule associated with Accept-question, rule DE1, first suggests the discourse goals of Seek-confirm and Seek-identify. The discourse goal rules associated with these discourse goals fail to produce an interpretation, since the fragment does not associate with a term in IS's plan that was a component of IP's question.

Rule DE1 next suggests the discourse goal Seek-clarify-question. DG rule Seek-clarify-question checks whether the fragment ends with a question mark and invokes a plan analysis on the context model shown in figure 6.4. The plan analyzer finds that IS's first elliptical fragment associates with the proposition Course-offered(CS105, _sem:&SEMESTER), and IS's second elliptical fragment with the term _sem:&SEMESTER in this proposition.

In both cases PLPROPS is the conjunction of the propositions Course-offered(CS105, _sem:&SEMESTER) and Credits-of(CS105, _cr1:&CREDITS). IS's first fragment results in SPROPS containing the propositions Course-offered(CS105, NEXTSEM) and Credits-of(CS105, _cr1:&CREDITS). Thus the first fragment instantiates a term with what the belief model indicates that IS believes is a valid instantiation. In addition, the belief model indicates that IS believes that this term has multiple valid instantiations in the inferred plan. Therefore, IS's elliptical fragment is interpreted as seeking clarification of IP's question by inquiring whether IP intended this instantiation to be assumed as part of the question, namely, as seeking clarification as to whether IP was asking if IS wanted to take CS105 during the next semester. IS's second elliptical fragment "The semester?" is a singular reference to the term _sem:&SEMESTER and is interpreted as seeking to clarify IP's question by requesting the particular semester intended by IP in the posed question.

Example 2: Expressing surprise at a question Consider next this dialogue:

IS: I need to satisfy the Group 4 distribution requirement.

IP: Do you want to take CS105 during summer session?

IS: Summer session?

This example illustrates an elliptical fragment that conveys IS's surprise at some aspect of IP's question. The semantic representation of the elliptical fragment is the triple

SUMMER-SEMESTER,   Constant,   ?

which indicates that the fragment is a constant followed by a question mark. The expanded context model is similar to the one shown in

figure 6.4 except that the term _sem:&SEMESTER is instantiated with
the constant SUMMER-SEMESTER.

Let us assume that the belief model indicates that IS believes that
CS105 is taught regularly during the fall and spring semesters, that IS
knows what the summer session is, and that IS does not believe that
the communication line is noisy. As a result of the utterances preceding
the elliptical fragment, the top two entries of the discourse stack are
Accept-question and Answer-question, which indicates that IS is first
expected to accept IP's question and then to answer it.

The discourse expectation rule associated with Accept-question, rule
DE1, first suggests the discourse goals Seek-confirm, Seek-identify, and
Seek-clarify-question. The conditions in the discourse goal rules associated with Seek-confirm and Seek-identify are not satisfied, since the
belief model indicates that IS does not believe that the communication
line is noisy and that IS knows the referent of the term *summer session*.
The conditions in the discourse goal rule associated with Seek-clarify-
question are not satisfied, since the fragment associates with a term
that has only one possible value (because it is a constant in the context
model) and the conjunction of propositions SPROPS computed during
plan analysis does not further restrict any of the terms in IS's plan.

Rule DE1 next suggests the discourse goal Express-surprise-question.
Its associated rule, DG rule Express-surprise-question, checks that the
fragment terminates with a question mark, and then begins testing the
other conditions that must be satisfied for its discourse goal to be recognized. The plan analyzer determines that the fragment associates with
the term SUMMER-SEMESTER in IS's task-related plan. The fragment
must be interpreted within the context of the propositions attached to
goals in the active nodes and along the path to the node at which the
fragment associates with a plan element. These propositions (which
comprise both PLPROPS and SPROPS, since IS's fragment is identical
to the plan element with which it associates) are Course-offered(CS105,
SUMMER-SEMESTER) and Credits-of(CS105, _cr1:&CREDITS).

As a result of IP's question the belief model indicates that IS knows
that IP believes that SPROPS is satisfiable, or that CS105 is offered
during the summer session for some amount of credits. Since STERM is
identical to PLTERM (both are the constant SUMMER-SEMESTER)
and SPROPS is identical to PLPROPS, IS's fragment does not place
additional restrictions on terms in IS's task-related plan. Thus IS is
bringing to attention some facet of the underlying task-related plan that
it is mutually believed must be satisfied no matter how the plan is further
instantiated.

Since the conditions in DG rule Express-surprise-question are satisfied, IS's elliptical fragment is interpreted as expressing surprise at the question posed by IP. Two possibilities exist. Since the posed question conveys the truth of SPROPS, IS may be expressing surprise at the information that CS105 is taught during summer session. Second, since the fragment "Summer session?" associates with a term newly instantiated with a constant in IS's task-related plan and it is mutually believed that IS believes that this term could have been instantiated differently, IS may be expressing surprise at IP's selection of this particular constant.

Example 3: Expressing surprise at a response   Now consider the following dialogue:

IS: I want to take CS310 next semester. Who is teaching it?

IP: Dr. Smith is teaching CS310 next semester.

IS: What time does it meet?

IP: It meets at 8:00 A.M.

IS: With Dr. Smith?

This example illustrates an elliptical fragment that conveys IS's surprise at IP's response and seeks elaboration and corroboration of it. The semantic representation of the elliptical fragment is the triple

Gen-pred(SMITH),   Proposition,   ?

which specifies that the fragment is followed by a question mark and is a general propositional fragment that must associate with a plan proposition that has Smith as an argument. The context model immediately prior to the elliptical fragment is shown in figure 6.5, with active nodes preceded by an asterisk or a bullet.

The belief model indicates that IS knows that Dr. Smith is teaching a section of CS310 next semester, since this was communicated and accepted prior to the fragment. The top two entries of the discourse stack are Accept-response and Obtain-information, which indicates that IS is first expected to accept IP's response to his previous question and then to proceed to seek other information that he needs to construct his underlying task-related plan.

The discourse expectation rule associated with Accept-response, rule DE3, suggests the discourse goals Seek-confirm, Seek-identify, and Express-surprise-obtain-corroboration. The discourse goal rules associated with the first two of these discourse goals fail to produce an interpretation, since the fragment does not associate with a term in IS's

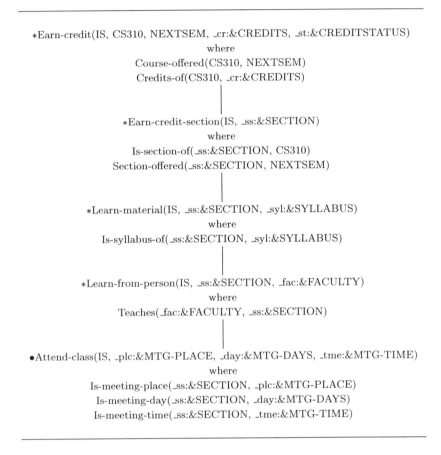

*Earn-credit(IS, CS310, NEXTSEM, _cr:&CREDITS, _st:&CREDITSTATUS)
where
Course-offered(CS310, NEXTSEM)
Credits-of(CS310, _cr:&CREDITS)

*Earn-credit-section(IS, _ss:&SECTION)
where
Is-section-of(_ss:&SECTION, CS310)
Section-offered(_ss:&SECTION, NEXTSEM)

*Learn-material(IS, _ss:&SECTION, _syl:&SYLLABUS)
where
Is-syllabus-of(_ss:&SECTION, _syl:&SYLLABUS)

*Learn-from-person(IS, _ss:&SECTION, _fac:&FACULTY)
where
Teaches(_fac:&FACULTY, _ss:&SECTION)

•Attend-class(IS, _plc:&MTG-PLACE, _day:&MTG-DAYS, _tme:&MTG-TIME)
where
Is-meeting-place(_ss:&SECTION, _plc:&MTG-PLACE)
Is-meeting-day(_ss:&SECTION, _day:&MTG-DAYS)
Is-meeting-time(_ss:&SECTION, _tme:&MTG-TIME)

Figure 6.5
A portion of an expanded context model for example 3

plan that was a component of IP's previous utterance. DG rule Express-surprise-obtain-corroboration checks that the fragment ends with a question mark and invokes plan analysis on the context model shown in figure 6.5. The plan analyzer finds that IS's elliptical fragment associates with the proposition Teaches(_fac:&FACULTY, _ss:&SECTION).

In order to retain the existing dialogue context, this proposition must be interpreted within the context of the propositions attached to goals in the active nodes in figure 6.5. SPROPS is computed by substituting

SMITH for _fac:&FACULTY in these propositions. Thus SPROPS is the conjunction of the following propositions:

Teaches(SMITH, _ss:&SECTION)
Course-offered(CS310, NEXTSEM)
Credits-of(CS310, _cr:&CREDITS)
Is-section-of(_ss:&SECTION, CS310)
Section-offered(_ss:&SECTION, NEXTSEM)
Is-syllabus-of(_ss:&SECTION, _syl:&SYLLABUS)
Is-meeting-place(_ss:&SECTION, _plc:&MTG-PLACE)
Is-meeting-day(_ss:&SECTION, _day:&MTG-DAYS)
Is-meeting-time(_ss:&SECTION, _tme:&MTG-TIME)

Since the belief model indicates that IS already knows the truth value of SPROPS, that is, he already knows that Dr. Smith is teaching a section of CS310 next semester, DG rule Express-surprise-obtain-corroboration identifies the elliptical fragment as expressing surprise at, and requesting corroboration of, IP's response. In particular, the system believes this surprise is a result of the new information presented in IP's response, namely that 8:00 A.M. is the value of the term _tme:&MTG-TIME in the SPROPS proposition Is-meeting-time(_ss:&SECTION, _tme:&MTG-TIME), and the aspect of the plan highlighted by IS's elliptical fragment, namely the proposition Teaches(SMITH, _ss:&SECTION). Precisely the reason why this data surprises IS would require an additional inference mechanism. Perhaps Dr. Smith is known to be a notoriously late riser in the morning, or perhaps Dr. Smith holds a full-time job elsewhere and only teaches occasional evening courses at the university.

Questions and Statements   The discourse goals of obtaining information and providing information for assimilation are commonly encountered in information-seeking dialogues. Fragments terminating in a question mark may highlight a term or proposition whose value IS needs either to construct his task-related plan or to answer a question posed by IP and that IS wants IP to provide. On the other hand, fragments terminating in a period may provide the value of a term or proposition in IS's intended plan. These situations are captured in the following two discourse goal rules.

> *DG rule Obtain-information:* Check whether the following conditions are satisfied:
>
> • IS's elliptical fragment terminates with a question mark.
>
> • The fragment highlights a term *T* and/or proposition *P* in the context of a conjunction of propositions SPROPS (which include *P*) in IS's underlying task-related plan.

• It is mutually believed that IS does not know the value of the highlighted term or proposition.

If these conditions are satisfied, interpret the fragment as requesting information about the value of the highlighted term T or proposition P within the context of the propositions in SPROPS.

DG rule Provide-for-assimilation: Check whether the following conditions are satisfied:

• IS's elliptical fragment terminates with a period.

• The fragment highlights a term T and/or proposition P in the context of a conjunction of propositions SPROPS (which include P) in IS's underlying task-related plan.

If these conditions are satisfied, interpret the fragment as specifying that the user-specified term replace the term with which it is associated in the plan or that the proposition be satisfied as part of the plan being constructed.

Example 4: Obtaining information   Consider the following dialogue:

IS: I want to register for a course for next semester. But I missed pre-registration. The cost?

In this example the first two utterances establish a plan context of taking a course, with attention directed to the subtask of registering late for it. The elliptical fragment should be interpreted as the cost of registering late. (Note that IS's first utterance in this dialogue segment is pragmatically ill-formed, since students register for sections of courses, not courses.)

An expansion of the context model immediately prior to the elliptical fragment is shown in figure 6.6. In the belief model the only proposition about costs asserts that IS believes that the cost of any item is of type MONEY, so the system assumes that IS does not know the specific cost of individual items. The semantic representation of the elliptical fragment is the triple

_cost1:&MONEY,   Definite,   ?

which specifies that the fragment is a definite noun phrase whose head noun is of type MONEY, followed by a question mark. As a result of the dialogue preceding the elliptical fragment, the top two entries of the discourse stack are Expand-statement and Provide-for-assimilation.

Rule DE5, the discourse expectation rule associated with the expectation Expand-statement, suggests the discourse goal Identify. Its discourse goal rule, presented later in this section, fails to produce an interpretation, since the fragment does not terminate with a period. The discourse stack is popped, and rule DE7, the discourse expectation rule associated with Provide-for-assimilation, suggests that the strongest expectation is for IS to continue providing information to the system and that the next strongest expectation is for IS to seek the information that he needs for constructing his task-related plan. The conditions in the discourse goal rule associated with Provide-for-assimilation, DG rule Provide-for-assimilation, are not satisfied, since the elliptical fragment does not terminate with a period. Next DG rule Obtain-information is invoked. It checks that the fragment terminates with a question mark and calls the plan analyzer to associate the fragment with an aspect of IS's inferred underlying task-related plan.

In the context model shown in figure 6.6, the parenthesized letters preceding goals indicate the focus domain of each goal, and active nodes are preceded by an asterisk or a bullet. Immediately prior to IS's elliptical fragment the current focused plan is the plan associated with the goal of registering late, and the most recently considered aspect of this plan is missing preregistration. The goal of registering introduces a new focus domain of goals preceded by (B) in figure 6.6. IS's fragment associates with the term _lreg:&MONEY in IS's inferred plan, as well as with terms elsewhere in parts of the expanded plan not shown in figure 6.6. However, none of the other terms appear in the current focus domain (goals preceded by (B) in figure 6.6), and so the association of the fragment with _lreg:&MONEY is selected as most relevant to the current dialogue context. The fragment must be interpreted within the context of the propositions attached to goals in the active nodes and along the path from the root of the context model to the node at which the fragment associates with a plan element. Thus SPROPS, which represents this context, is the conjunction of the following propositions:

Course-offered(_crse:&COURSE, NEXTSEM)
Credits-of(_crse:&COURSE, _cr:&CREDITS)
Is-section-of(_ss:&SECTION, _crse:&COURSE)
Section-offered(_ss:&SECTION, NEXTSEM)
Costs(LATE-REG, NEXTSEM, _cost1:&MONEY)

Since the belief model does not contain a proposition indicating that IS knows the value of the term _cost1:&MONEY, DG rule Obtain-information interprets the fragment as seeking information about the

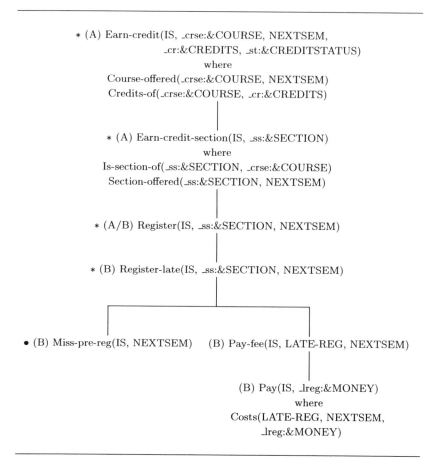

Figure 6.6
A portion of the expanded context model for example 4

charge for late registration in order to formulate the task-related plan; in particular, IS is requesting the value of the term _cost1:&MONEY such that the conjunction of the following propositions is satisfied:

Course-offered(_crse:&COURSE, NEXTSEM)
Credits-of(_crse:&COURSE, _cr:&CREDITS)
Is-section-of(_ss:&SECTION, _crse:&COURSE)
Section-offered(_ss:&SECTION, NEXTSEM)
Costs(LATE-REG, NEXTSEM, _cost1:&MONEY)

Example 5: Obtaining information   Consider the following dialogue:

IS: I need to take one more CS course.

IP: Do you want to take CS310 with Dr. Smith next semester?

IS: The meeting time?

This example illustrates an elliptical fragment that requests information to construct an answer to IP's question. The semantic representation of the elliptical fragment is the triple

_time:&MTG-TIME,   Definite,   ?

which specifies that the fragment is a definite noun phrase whose head noun is of type MTG-TIME, followed by a question mark. Suppose that the belief model indicates that IS knows that there is only one section of CS310 taught by Dr. Smith next semester and that sections have only one meeting time, but it gives no reason to believe that IS knows when that section meets.

As a result of stack processing rule SP1 and IP's question, the top two entries of the discourse stack immediately prior to IS's elliptical fragment are Accept-question and Answer-question. IS must understand and accept IP's posed question before answering it; discourse goals suggested by this expectation are seeking confirmation, seeking identification of an entity in the question, seeking clarification of the question, and expressing surprise at the question (rule DE1). The discourse goal rule associated with seeking confirmation fails to produce an interpretation, since the fragment does not match, or appear to be a miscommunication of, a component of IP's question. Similarly, the discourse goal rules associated with seeking identification fail to produce an interpretation, since the fragment does not associate with a term in IS's plan that was a component of IP's previous utterance.

Next the discourse goal rules associated with seeking clarification of the question and expressing surprise at the question are tried. The context model immediately prior to the elliptical fragment is similar to the one shown in figure 6.5, except that the node preceded by a bullet (Attend-class) is not active and the term _fac:&FACULTY is instantiated with the constant SMITH. Plan analysis associates the elliptical fragment with the term _tme:&MTG-TIME in this context model. The propositions attached to goals in the active nodes and along the path to the node at which the fragment associates with a term in the context model are collected to form PLPROPS. STERM and SPROPS are computed from PLTERM and PLPROPS by substituting the term from IS's fragment for the term with which it is associated in IS's plan. Thus STERM is _time:&MTG-TIME and SPROPS is the conjunction of the following nine propositions:

Course-offered(CS310, NEXTSEM)
Credits-of(CS310, _cr:&CREDITS)
Is-section-of(_ss:&SECTION, CS310)
Section-offered(_ss:&SECTION, NEXTSEM)
Is-syllabus-of(_ss:&SECTION, _syl:&SYLLABUS)
Teaches(SMITH, _ss:&SECTION)
Is-meeting-place(_ss:&SECTION, _plc:&MTG-PLACE)
Is-meeting-day(_ss:&SECTION, _day:&MTG-DAYS)
Is-meeting-time(_ss:&SECTION, _time:&MTG-TIME)

One seeks clarification of a question when one tries to ascertain additional information that one believes the questioner might have intended to communicate either explicitly or implicitly. If the fragment in the above dialogue were an attempt to seek clarification, it would represent a request that IP clarify which section she is asking IS about (by giving its meeting time). The discourse goal rule associated with seeking clarification fails to produce an interpretation, since the fragment associates with a term that the belief model indicates IS believes has only one instantiation in the inferred plan.

The belief model does not indicate that IS knows the value of the term STERM within the context of SPROPS; that is, IS is not believed to know the meeting time of the section of CS310 taught by Dr. Smith. The discourse goal associated with expressing surprise at the question fails to produce an interpretation, since one cannot be surprised about something one does not know.

Thus the question is implicitly accepted, since the fragment is not interpreted as pursuing one of the discourse goals suggested by the Accept-question discourse expectation, and Accept-question is popped from the discourse stack. Rule DE2, the discourse expectation rule associated with the new top element of the discourse stack, suggests the discourse goals of answering the question and suggesting an answer to the question. The rules associated with these discourse goals, discussed later in this section, similarly fail to produce an interpretation. The last discourse goal suggested by rule DE2 is obtaining information to answer the posed question. DG rule Obtain-information checks that the fragment terminates in a question mark, and plan analysis associates the fragment with _tme:&MTG-TIME in IS's underlying task-related plan. PLTERM, PLPROPS, STERM, and SPROPS are the same as before. Since it is mutually believed that IS does not know the value of the term _time:&MTG-TIME (the STERM) such that SPROPS is satisfied, DG rule Obtain-information interprets the fragment as seeking information about the meeting time of the section of CS310 taught by Dr. Smith next semester.

Answering a question   The next several discourse goal rules deal with elliptical fragments that answer a question posed by IP or suggest an answer to a question. If the question is a request for the value of a term in the underlying task-related plan, we expect IS to provide the desired value. So we anticipate elliptical fragments that provide that instantiation.

Traditional approaches have viewed the set of appropriate responses to yes/no questions as consisting of "Yes," "No," and "Unknown." However, several researchers have shown that speakers often respond indirectly to yes/no questions. Hirschberg [Hir84] investigated a type of conversational implicature and proposed representing yes/no questions as scalar queries, which would enable inferences to be drawn from indirect responses. For example, knowledge about the order of actions in a task allows one to draw the inference that the bookcase is as yet unfinished from the response in the following dialogue:

Speaker 1: Have you finished building the bookcase?

Speaker 2: I've sanded the shelves.

Indirect responses can address an aspect of the task-related plan associated with the question, and such responses often take the form of elliptical fragments. If IP poses a yes/no question and IS wants to answer the question affirmatively, IS may want to place some restrictions on that answer. Thus we anticipate elliptical fragments that restrict the underlying task-related plan associated with the question. On the other hand, if IS wants to answer a yes/no question negatively, we anticipate that he may provide some alternative or an explanation of his answer. Thus we anticipate elliptical fragments that provide an alternative value for a term or proposition in the underlying task-related plan under consideration or that explain why the suggested plan is unacceptable.[6] The following discourse goal rules cover these cases.

DG rule Answer-question: Check whether the following conditions are satisfied:

• IS's elliptical fragment terminates with a period.

• The elliptical fragment highlights a term and/or one or more propositions in the context of a conjunction of propositions SPROPS in IS's underlying task-related plan.

• The highlighted term and propositions provide an instantiation of the term whose value was requested in the question posed by IP at the top of the discourse stack, and this question has not yet been answered.

If these conditions are satisfied, interpret the fragment as answering the question by providing the value of the requested term along with any restrictions represented by the highlighted propositions.

DG rule Answer-question-with-restrictions: Check whether the following conditions are satisfied:

• IS's elliptical fragment terminates with a period.

• The question posed by IP at the top of the discourse stack is a yes/no question, and this question has not yet been answered.

• The elliptical fragment highlights a term and/or one or more propositions in the context of a conjunction of propositions SPROPS in IS's underlying task-related plan.

• The highlighted term and propositions do not provide an alternative instantiation of a term in the proposition queried by IP.

If these conditions are satisfied, interpret the fragment as answering yes, with the restriction that the instantiated terms and highlighted propositions be part of the plan.

DG rule Answer-question-suggest-alternative: Check whether the following conditions are satisfied:

• IS's elliptical fragment terminates with a period.

• The question posed by IP at the top of the discourse stack is a yes/no question, and this question has not yet been answered.

• The elliptical fragment highlights a term and/or one or more propositions in the context of a conjunction of propositions SPROPS in IS's underlying task-related plan.

---

[6]For completeness I have included providing an explanation of the answer as one way of answering a question with an elliptical fragment. However, the kinds of elliptical fragments that we are currently considering cannot be used to do this.

- The highlighted term and propositions provide an alternative instantiation of a term in the proposition queried by IP.

If these conditions are satisfied, interpret the fragment as answering no and providing an alternative instantiation of the proposition queried by IP, along with possibly additional restrictions given by the highlighted propositions, under which the answer is yes.

DG rule Suggest-answer-to-question: Check whether the following conditions are satisfied:

- IS's elliptical fragment terminates with a questions mark.

- The question posed by IP at the top of the discourse stack is not a yes/no question, and this question has not yet been answered.

- The elliptical fragment highlights a term and/or one or more propositions in the context of a conjunction of propositions SPROPS in IS's underlying task-related plan.

- The highlighted term and propositions provide an instantiation of the term whose value was requested by the question.

If these conditions are satisfied, interpret the fragment as suggesting an answer to the question by providing a possible value for the requested term along with any restrictions represented by the highlighted propositions.

DG rule Suggest-answer-own-question is the same as DG rule Suggest-answer-to-question except that the unanswered question closest to the top of the discourse stack was asked by IS.

Example 6: Answering a question and popping the discourse stack   Consider the following discourse:

IP: Do you want to take CS105 next semester?

IS: Who is teaching it?

IP: Dr. Brown and Dr. Ames.

IS: On Monday, Wednesday, Friday with Dr. Ames.

This example illustrates a situation in which multiple expectations must be popped from the discourse stack in processing a fragment that answers a question posed earlier in the dialogue. IP's first utterance establishes an expectation that IS will accept and answer the question asked by IP. So stack processing rule SP1 pushes Answer-question and Accept-question onto the discourse stack. IS's first utterance does not convey any difficulty with IP's question, which indicates that the question has been implicitly accepted. So stack processing rule SP8 pops Accept-question from the discourse stack. IS's first utterance is a request for information in order to formulate an answer to IP's posed question,

which results in the expectation that IS will continue gathering such information. Thus stack processing rules SP3 and SP4 respectively push
Obtain-information and Expand-question onto the discourse stack. Once
IP responds, stack processing rule SP7 pops Expand-question from the
discourse stack, and rule SP2 pushes Accept-response onto the stack.
Thus the discourse stack passed to the ellipsis processor contains the
following three entries:

Accept-response
Obtain-information
Answer-question

The context model at this point in the dialogue is shown in figure 6.7,
with active nodes preceded by an asterisk or a bullet. The semantic
representation of IS's elliptical fragment is the triple

[Gen-time-pred(MON-WED-FRI), Gen-pred(AMES)],   Proposition,

which specifies that the fragment is a conjunction of two propositions,
followed by a period.

   The discourse expectation rule associated with the top element of the
discourse stack, rule DE3, suggests the discourse goals Seek-confirm,
Seek-identify, and Express-surprise-obtain-corroboration. The conditions in the discourse goal rules associated with these discourse goals
are not satisfied, since the fragment does not end with a question mark.
Therefore, stack processing rule SP8 pops Accept-response from the discourse stack. The discourse expectation rule associated with the new top
element of the discourse stack, rule DE8, suggests the discourse goal of
obtaining further information. Once again, the conditions in the associated discourse goal rule, DG rule Obtain-information, are not satisfied,
since the fragment does not terminate in a question mark, and stack
processing rule SP8 pops the discourse stack.

   The discourse expectation rule associated with the expectation Answer-
question, rule DE2, suggests, among others, the discourse goal of answering the question by providing restrictions on the underlying task-related
plan. DG rule Answer-question-with-restrictions invokes plan analysis
on the context model produced from the preceding dialogue and finds
that the propositions comprising the fragment associate with the plan
propositions

Is-meeting-day(_ss:&SECTION, _day:&MTG-DAYS)
Teaches(_fac:&FACULTY, _ss:&SECTION),

to result in the instantiated propositions

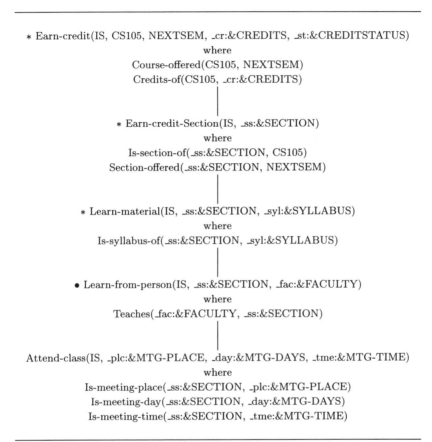

Figure 6.7
A portion of an expanded context model for example 6

Is-meeting-day(_ss:&SECTION, MON-WED-FRI)
Teaches(AMES, _ss:&SECTION).

The active nodes immediately prior to the elliptical fragment indicate that the fragment should be interpreted within the context established by the following additional propositions:

Course-offered(CS105, NEXTSEM)
Credits-of(CS105, _cr:&CREDITS)
Is-section-of(_ss:&SECTION, CS105)
Section-offered(_ss:&SECTION, NEXTSEM)
Is-syllabus-of(_ss:&SECTION, _syl:&SYLLABUS)

Since the utterance that prompted the top element of the discourse stack is IP's unanswered question "Do you want to take CS105 next semester?" and since IS's fragment terminates with a period and associates with plan propositions without providing an alternative to the instantiated terms, such as *CS105*, in the proposition queried by IP, DG rule Answer-question-with-restrictions interprets the question as answering IP's question affirmatively with the restriction that the conjunction of the SPROPS propositions

Course-offered(CS105, NEXTSEM)
Credits-of(CS105, _cr:&CREDITS)
Is-section-of(_ss:&SECTION, CS105)
Section-offered(_ss:&SECTION, NEXTSEM)
Is-syllabus-of(_ss:&SECTION, _syl:&SYLLABUS)
Teaches(AMES, _ss:&SECTION)
Is-meeting-day(_ss:&SECTION, MON-WED-FRI)

be satisfied in IS's task-related plan, that is, that the section of CS105 he enrolls in be taught by Dr. Ames and meet on Monday, Wednesday, and Friday next semester.

Example 7: Answering a question by suggesting an alternative
To briefly illustrate another use of an elliptical fragment to answer a question, consider the following dialogue:

IS: I need to satisfy the Group 4 distribution requirement.

IP: Would you like to take CS105?

IS: CS106 at Wilcastle.

IS's first utterance establishes the goal of satisfying the Group 4 distribution requirements. This can be accomplished by earning credit in the appropriate number of Group 4 courses. Therefore, an expansion of IS's underlying task-related plan will contain the subgoal

Earn-Credit(IS, _crse:&GROUP4-COURSE, NEXTSEM,
            _cred:&CREDITS, CREDIT)

IP's question instantiates the term _crse:&GROUP4-COURSE with the constant CS105. However, IS's fragment provides an alternative instantiation of this term, namely CS106 (a similar course that uses Fortran instead of Pascal), along with an additional proposition that plan analysis will associate with the plan proposition specifying the meeting place of the section taken. The fragment will be interpreted as answering IP's question no but providing an alternative instantiation that, along with IS's added restrictions, will result in a yes answer. Thus IS is saying that he does not want to take CS105 but is interested in taking CS106 at the Wilcastle Center.

Identifying and clarifying In a cooperative dialogue IS wants IP to be able to understand the intended meaning of his utterance. Therefore, if IS follows one utterance with another that is an elliptical fragment terminating in a period, IS might be trying to further identify a component of his preceding utterance or, if the previous utterance was a question, to clarify it. The next two discourse goal rules handle these situations:

> *DG rule Identify:* Check whether the following conditions are satisfied:
>
> • IS's elliptical fragment is a constant or definite term with attached propositions followed by a period.
>
> • The fragment highlights a term in IS's task-related plan that is referred to by a description D in the utterance by IS that is at the top of the discourse stack.
>
> If these conditions are satisfied, interpret the fragment as further identifying the entity referred to by the description D.
>
> *DG rule Clarify-question:* Check whether the following conditions are satisfied:
>
> • IS's elliptical fragment terminates with a period.
>
> • The fragment highlights a term and/or one or more propositions in the context of a conjunction of propositions SPROPS in IS's underlying task-related plan.
>
> If these conditions are satisfied, interpret the fragment as clarifying the question to include the highlighted term and propositions.

6.5   Implementation

I have implemented a prototype system demonstrating this pragmatics-based framework for processing intersentential ellipsis in a university domain. My implementation handles ten of the discourse goals discussed in this chapter and, with the exception of Answer-question-with-explanation, could be extended to handle the others. The system is presented with a semantic representation of an elliptical fragment, a context model representing the system's beliefs about the information seeker's underlying task-related plan, a belief model representing the system's beliefs about the information seeker's beliefs, and a discourse stack containing discourse expectations. The semantic representation of the fragment gives the structure of the fragment as discussed in section 6.2.1 and its terminating punctuation. The context model is inferred and constructed from the preceding dialogue using the incremental plan recognition algorithm implemented in the TRACK system and described in chapter 3. The belief model is very primitive and is only intended to facilitate illustration of the ellipsis processor. The examples in the preceding section illustrate how elliptical fragments are processed by this system.

6.6   Extensions and Future Work

The main limitation of this pragmatics-based framework appears to be in handling such intersentential elliptical utterances as the following:

IS: Who is the teacher of CS200?

IP: Dr. Herd is the teacher of CS200.

IS: CS263?

Obviously IS's elliptical fragment requests the teacher of CS263. My model cannot currently handle such fragments. This limitation is caused by the mechanisms for retaining dialogue context; they assume that IS constructs a plan for a task in a depth-first fashion and completes his investigation of a plan for taking CS200 before moving on to investigate a plan for taking CS263. Since the *teacher* of CS200 has nothing to do with the plan for taking CS263, the mechanisms for retaining dialogue context will fail to identify the teacher of CS263 as the information requested by IS.

One might argue that the elliptical fragment in the above dialogue relies heavily on the syntactic representation of the preceding utterance and thus that a syntactic strategy is required for interpretation. This may be true. However, dialogues such as the above really investigate task-related plans in a kind of breadth-first fashion. For example, in the above dialogue IS is first analyzing the teachers of each course under consideration and will then move on to consider other aspects of the courses. It appears that my plan-based framework could be extended to handle many such dialogues by reasoning about IS's plan-construction strategy [Ram89b], as discussed in chapter 2.

Litman [LA87] uses metaplans in her formalism and is able to handle the fragment in the above dialogue. However, she views IS as changing the plan from consideration of CS200 to CS263, not as possibly considering several plans simultaneously. As a result her system cannot handle such fragments as IS's last utterance in the following dialogue:

IS: Who is teaching CS105?

IP: Dr. Brown and Dr. Ames are teaching sections of CS105.

IS: Who is teaching CS106?

IP: Dr. Derr is teaching CS106.

IS: The meeting time of Dr. Brown's section?

Successfully handling such fragments appears to require that we consider several potential plans in parallel, and we are now considering mechanisms for doing so.

6.7   Conclusions

This chapter has presented a pragmatics-based framework for understanding intersentential ellipsis occurring during an information-seeking dialogue in a task domain. Understanding the intent behind elliptical fragments requires that the speaker's discourse goal be recognized. My ellipsis interpretation strategy is a top-down procedure that utilizes expectations gleaned from the preceding dialogue to suggest discourse goals that the speaker might be expected to pursue. If the aspect of the speaker's plan highlighted by his elliptical fragment can produce a coherent interpretation relevant to a suggested discourse goal, the fragment is recognized as intending to accomplish that discourse goal and the appropriate interpretation is produced.

My ellipsis resolution strategy uses many pragmatic knowledge sources, including the information seeker's inferred task-related plan, his inferred beliefs, his anticipated discourse goals, and focusing strategies. I do not contend, however, that a natural language system should use only pragmatic knowledge; a robust system will need to coordinate syntactic, semantic, and pragmatic techniques to fully understand the wide variety of elliptical utterances employed in human communication.

7 Plan Inference: The Next Generation

In the preceding chapters I have described what some have characterized as first-generation plan-inference systems. Chapter 2 discussed the
roots of plan recognition work and described several major research efforts. Chapter 3 presented the details of one such system, TRACK, and
chapters 4, 5, and 6 presented strategies for reasoning on the system's
model of the information seeker's plan to handle two classes of problematic utterances: pragmatically ill-formed queries and intersentential
elliptical fragments.

Pollack [Pol87b] was the first to characterize the assumptions underlying the correct functioning of first-generation systems and to analyze how
these assumptions limit the system's ability to infer plans from naturally
occurring dialogue. Other limiting assumptions were subsequently noted
in my research [Car86,Car90]. This chapter discusses these assumptions
and the need for more robust plan inference systems. It describes a substantially different approach to plan recognition developed by Martha
Pollack [Pol86a], an approach that appears to form the basis for a second generation of plan inference systems. It then discusses other recent
and ongoing research that addresses issues not handled by Pollack's system. Thus this chapter both presents second-generation plan inference
research and indicates directions for future work.

7.1 Limitations of First-Generation Systems

7.1.1 Limiting Assumptions

The examples of plan inference in the preceding chapters all had several
common features: the information seeker was pursuing a valid plan that
was part of the system's knowledge base, no default inferences were necessary, and the system never erred in incrementally building its model of
the information-seeker's plan from the dialogue. This was not accidental. First-generation models of plan inference make several assumptions
that render them capable of handling only dialogues of this kind. Below
are listed five restrictive assumptions underlying first-generation plan
inference systems.

> System's domain knowledge
> 1. Explicit representation of all necessary knowledge about
>   domain goals and plans for achieving them
> 2. No incorrect or outdated domain knowledge

User's domain knowledge

3. No incorrect knowledge about domain plans

System's beliefs

4. No incorrect beliefs about the user's goals and plans for achieving them

5. Attribute to the user all of the goals and plans that the user intended to be recognized

The first three concern the system's and user's knowledge and were identified by Pollack [Pol87b]. The last two concern the system's beliefs about the user's goals and plans. In addition, these assumptions imply four assumptions about the behavior of the user and the system:

User

6. Constructs only valid plans

7. Asks only questions appropriate to a correct means of achieving his goal

8. Makes only precise utterances

System

9. Always makes the right choice among possible inferences

The first assumption is a variation of the closed world assumption often used in question-answering systems. Reiter [Rei78b] differentiated between *open world* and *closed world* reasoning. In an open world a proposition or its negation is true only if it can be proved true; otherwise the truth value of the proposition is unknown. In a closed world a proposition is assumed false if it cannot be proved true. In query evaluation a system that maintains the *closed world assumption* presumes that all answers to the query can be inferred from its knowledge base. For example, a student advisement system might know that Dr. Smith and Dr. Jones teach CS105. A query such as "Who teaches CS105?" will cause the system to retrieve Dr. Smith and Dr. Jones from its knowledge base. Since nothing in the system's knowledge indicates whether Dr. Brown teaches CS105, a system that uses closed world reasoning will assume that Dr. Brown does not teach CS105 since it cannot prove that he does. One of the main advantages of maintaining the closed world assumption is that only positive facts need be explicitly represented in the system's knowledge base in order to answer queries correctly. On the other hand, the closed world assumption means that the system's world knowledge cannot be incomplete in some areas [Rei85]. First-generation plan inference systems maintain a stronger version of the closed world assumption, namely, that the system's knowledge base contains an explicit representation of all domain-related goals and possible plans for accomplishing them that might be needed to recognize what the user is trying to do (1) [Pol87b]. They also presume that the system's knowledge is perfect in the sense that it is always accurate and up-to-date (2) (the *correct knowledge assumption* [Pol87b]).

In addition, first-generation systems assume that although the user's knowledge about goals and plans may be incomplete, it is not erroneous (3). This limits how extensive the system's knowledge base must be. Since the user's knowledge is assumed to be correct, the partial plan that a user has in mind will always be valid (6) (the *valid plan assumption* [Pol87b]), although not necessarily fully expanded and instantiated. An implication of this is what Pollack has termed the *appropriate query assumption* [Pol87b], the assumption that the user's queries will always be appropriate to a correct means of achieving his goal (7). In a university setting, for example, the appropriate query assumption means that a student pursuing a Bachelor of Science degree would always know enough about the domain not to ask about how to satisfy a nonexistent foreign language requirement. Consequently, the system's knowledge base need not contain any information about invalid or buggy plans (incorrect ways of pursuing a goal), since it is assumed that the user will never have such a plan in mind. This feature of first-generation systems, that only valid plans are included in the system's knowledge base, has been called the *principle of parsimony* [Pol87b].

First-generation plan inference systems also assume that immediately preceding each new utterance, the system's beliefs about the user's goals and plans for achieving them are accurate (4). This assumption is valid only if the system's data (the user's utterances) are precise and not misleading (8) and the system's inference mechanisms never err in processing the data (9). I will call these the *precise data assumption* and the *infallible-inference-mechanism assumption*. In addition, first-generation systems assume that the system has successfully inferred all of the goals and plans that the user intended it to recognize (5), since the system must make inferences on this acquired knowledge to understand and assimilate the user's subsequent utterances.

Now let us examine how realistic these assumptions are and determine what a system will need to do if any unrealistic assumptions are removed. Pollack [Pol87b] argues convincingly that assumptions 1 and 3 in the list above are too strong and discusses the results of removing each of the three assumptions on the system's and user's domain knowledge along with the first two assumptions about the user's

behavior. The correctness of the user's domain knowledge is probably
the least tenable assumption. Users interact with an information system precisely because they do not know enough about the domain to
construct their task-related plans on their own. Therefore, it is unreasonable to expect that they will always have accurate beliefs about how
to achieve their goals and as a result will always ask the right questions. But once this assumption is removed, the assumptions about the
system's knowledge become a problem. If we assume that the system's
knowledge base explicitly contains a representation of all the plans a user
might have in mind, we cannot adhere to the principle of parsimony but
must instead provide the system with a library of buggy plans. However, as Pollack argues, although the system designer can include typical
erroneous plans, he cannot possibly anticipate all the misconceptions a
user might have. Thus the first assumption—that all necessary domain
knowledge, including knowledge about user domain plans, is explicitly
represented in the system's knowledge base—must at least be weakened
to the extent that the system's knowledge base is assumed to explicitly
contain only all the valid plans that the user might pursue. This means
that the system will need the ability to reason with its knowledge of
correct plans to recognize invalid plans when they occur.

Next let us consider the assumption that the system's knowledge of
valid plans is correct and complete. System designers are not omniscient.
Thus it is quite reasonable to expect that a user might devise a novel and
workable plan that has not been included in the system's knowledge base.
Furthermore, in a rapidly changing world, knowledgeable users may have
more accurate information about some aspects of the domain than the
system does. Therefore, it appears necessary to remove the first and
second assumptions on the system's domain knowledge. Consequently,
a plan inference system that handles naturally occurring dialogue must
be able to recognize user plans that are not explicitly represented in the
system's plan library and reason about their validity [Pol87b].

The assumptions concerning the system's beliefs are also untenable.
Errors can enter the system's beliefs about the user's plans and goals
if the precise data assumption and the infallible-inference-mechanism
assumption are not maintained, that is, if we do not assume that the
data (the user's utterances) and the system's inference mechanisms are
perfect. Inaccurate and inappropriate queries are examples of imperfect
data that can produce errors in the system's beliefs about the user. For
example, a user of a student advisement system might say that he is a
junior when in fact he is a few credits short of junior standing, thereby
leading the system to mistakenly infer that he is eligible for certain

programs or awards that he does not qualify for. Unfortunately, even cooperative users are often imprecise, especially when they do not realize that minor perturbations in the data can be significant. In addition, if we drop the appropriate query assumption, the user may ask an irrelevant question that seems perfectly reasonable to the system, thereby leading the system to develop incorrect beliefs about the user's objectives. Consider, for example, a student advisement system. If only BA degrees have a foreign language requirement, the query "What courses must I take to satisfy the foreign language requirement in French?" may lead the system to infer that the user is pursuing a Bachelor of Arts degree. If only BS degrees require a senior project, a subsequent query such as "How many credits of senior project are required?" is problematic. Either the second query is inappropriate to the user's goal of obtaining a Bachelor of Arts degree, or the system's context model does not accurately reflect what the user wants to do. Note that in both cases the user has a misconception, but in the latter case the misconception went undetected and was allowed to introduce errors into the system's context model.

The assumption that the system has infallible inference mechanisms is also unrealistic. Even in the simplest of cases the system must decide how individual utterances relate to one another. Since speakers sometimes shift their focus of attention without accurately conveying this to their listeners, the system's decisions are imperfect.

Grosz [Gro81] claimed that miscommunication can occur if both dialogue participants are not focused on the same subset of knowledge. Joshi [Jos82] contended that successful communication requires that the mutual beliefs of the dialogue participants be consistent. Extending this to inferred plans, I claim that a successful cooperative dialogue requires that the system's beliefs about the user's plan be consistent with what the user is actually considering doing. But clearly it is unrealistic to expect that the system's model will always be correct in view of the different knowledge bases of the two participants and the imperfections of communication via dialogue. So once we drop the assumption that the system's beliefs about the user's plan are always correct, the system must be able to detect inconsistencies between its inferred model and the user's actual plan and repair its model whenever possible.

The second assumption concerning the system's beliefs, that they attribute to the user all of the plans and goals that the user intended be recognized, is certainly unreasonable if the system's inference mechanisms are imperfect. Furthermore, analysis of naturally occurring dialogues suggests that information seekers often intend for and expect an information provider to use default reasoning in inferring and evaluating their plans and goals, and current models of plan inference lack this ability.

Plan inference in dialogue is a difficult task. If the system's knowledge about goals and plans is correct, sufficient for the domain, and explicitly represented, the user holds no misconceptions about domain plans, the data (the user's utterances) are accurate and not misleading, the system does not need to make any default inferences, and the system never makes erroneous inferences in processing the data, then a first-generation system will be able to infer a plan for the user, and there will be no discrepancies between this inferred plan and the actual plan under construction by the user. These limiting assumptions simplify the plan recognition problem and have allowed basic principles and strategies to be identified. However, these assumptions are clearly unrealistic and must be removed in the next generation of plan inference systems.

7.1.2   Cooperative Behavior

Examples of naturally occurring dialogues illustrate the kind of behavior that a robust natural language system must exhibit. Consider the following example taken from [Pol87b].

IS: I want to talk to Kathy. Do you know the phone number at the hospital?

IP: She's already been discharged. Her home number is 555-1238.

In this example IS wants to talk to Kathy and, since he believes Kathy is at the hospital, requests the phone number there. Since Kathy has been discharged, IS has an invalid plan for accomplishing his goal. IP's response indicates that she has not only recognized this invalid plan but has also reasoned about how the plan is wrong and generated a helpful response [Pol87b]. An intelligent, cooperative information system must exhibit similar behavior.

The following is a second example of a dialogue that cannot be handled by first-generation systems:

(1) *IS:* I wish I could transfer files between the Vax and my PC.

(2) *IP:* Kermit lets you do that.

(3) *IS:* How do I get Kermit?

(4) *IP:* The computing center will give you a copy if you bring them a floppy disk.

(5) *IS:* How late is the university bookstore open?

Upon completion of utterance (4) IP will most likely believe that IS wants to get a copy of the Kermit file transfer program in order to transfer files between the Vax and his PC. Suppose that IS knows that the university bookstore sells floppy disks, whereas IP does not know how to obtain floppy disks on campus. Then from IP's limited knowledge, IS's next query (5) will not appear to address an aspect of what she believes IS is trying to do. Despite IP's limited knowledge, she should be able to reason about what IS's plan might be. IP's response should include a direct answer to IS's posited question. But this alone is insufficient. If IP limits herself to a direct answer, IS may infer that IP has related IS's current utterance to what she believes IS is trying to do and that IP's knowledge supports this plan, that is, that IP also believes that IS can purchase a floppy disk at the bookstore. Joshi's revised maxim of quality [Jos82] asserts that IP's response must block false inferences. In addition, as a helpful participant, IP should include whatever evidence she has for or against IS's proposed plan. An appropriate response would be "The university bookstore is open until 4:30 P.M. But I don't know whether it sells floppy disks. However, it does sell many other items of an educational nature besides books, so it is perhaps a good place to try." Thus a cooperative natural language system must be able to recognize and reason about *novel plans*, plans that are not part of the system's domain knowledge.

The dialogue below illustrates a case in which default inferencing accounts for the information provider's response and results in the information provider having to revise her beliefs. This dialogue was transcribed from a radio talk show on investments. At that time individual retirement accounts (IRAs) were available as tax-sheltered investments in the United States as long as a person had earned income and was not covered by a company-sponsored pension program.

(1) *IS:* I'm a retired government employee but I'm still working. I'd like to start out an IRA for myself and my wife—she doesn't work.

(2) *IP:* Did you work outside of the government last year?

(3) *IS:* Yes I did.

(4) *IP:* There's no reason why you shouldn't have an IRA for last year.

(5) *IS:* I thought they just started this year.

(6) *IP:* Oh no. IRA's were available as long as you are not a participant in an existing pension.

(7) *IS:* Well, I do work for a company that has a pension.

(8) *IP:* Ahh. Then you're not eligible for '81.

IP's response in utterance (4) can be explained by postulating the following default reasoning:

> Since IS is retired but still working, he has earned income. Since he is working outside the government after retirement, he is *probably* working in a part-time or temporary position that is *probably* not covered by a company-sponsored pension program. Therefore, he is probably eligible for an IRA for 1981.[1]

In utterance (5) IS expresses surprise at IP's response, cuing the possibility that the beliefs on which IP's response was based are wrong. IP's beliefs as a result of the default inferences are a probable source of disparity. In utterance (6) IP identifies one of the beliefs added to her model of IS (that IRA's are available to IS for 1981) and attempts to justify it (with the participant's not being part of a company-sponsored pension program). IS's next utterance informs IP that the assumption that led IP to infer that IS is eligible for a 1981 IRA is incorrect. IP then notifies IS that she recognizes the error and that her beliefs about IS have been corrected. Analysis of naturally occurring dialogues such as this suggest that a cooperative natural language system should use default inference rules to expand the context model and provide a more detailed and tractable arena in which to understand and respond to subsequent utterances. But then the system must be able to repair its context model when errors are detected in it.

The preceding examples illustrate the kind of behavior that humans expect of cooperative information providers. If natural language systems are to attain their full capability as intelligent assistants in human problem solving and decision making, they must be able to interact as effectively with humans as humans interact with one another. This means that more sophisticated strategies must be developed for reasoning about the user's plans and goals and the system's own beliefs about them. The next sections describe research on richer and more robust models of plan inference that overcome some of the limitations of first-generation systems.

---

[1] At the time of this dialogue, rules on IRA's were different from those in subsequent years.

7.2   A Second-Generation Model of Plan Inference

7.2.1   A New Approach

The rules of plan inference operate on beliefs about relationships among goals, actions, effects, and plans. First-generation systems are unclear about exactly where these beliefs come from [Pol87b]. Intuitively, they should be the system's beliefs about the user's beliefs, since it is the user's plan that is being inferred and it is the system that is doing the inferring [Pol87b]. By assuming that both system and user have correct knowledge about domain goals and plans, first-generation systems were able to use the system's knowledge of domain plans as a model of the user's knowledge. Of course, since the user's knowledge was necessarily incomplete (or else he wouldn't be interacting with the system), there had to be gaps in the user's knowledge that weren't present in the system's knowledge, but first-generation systems ignored this.

If a plan inference system does not make the limiting assumptions of the preceding section, it must be able to represent and reason about the beliefs motivating a user query. One way of doing this is to construct a model of the user's knowledge so that it is available for the plan inference rules to operate on. Kass [KF87] developed heuristics for hypothesizing user knowledge on the basis of the user's statements and queries about the domain. For example, if a user states that he has successfully performed an action, it is reasonable to believe that he knows the preconditions of the action. Although such a model will provide insight into many aspects of the user's knowledge, this approach will be inadequate, since it is extremely unlikely that at the time of a user query the model will already represent all of the user's domain knowledge relevant to that query. The only other possibility is for the system to reason about what beliefs the user might plausibly have on the basis of the user's query, the system's existing beliefs about the user's beliefs and intentions, and the system's own domain knowledge.

This was the approach taken by Pollack [Pol86a,Pol86b]. Since the dialogues she was considering were brief, usually consisting of only a stated goal and a subsequent query followed by the information provider's response, she assumed that the system's existing beliefs about the user's beliefs and intentions consisted of the goal that the user wanted to achieve. The problem then was to infer the user's goal-related plan that motivated the observed query. Instead of having the plan inference rules merely chain on the system's knowledge of goals, actions, and plans, Pollack's model required that the system explicitly ascribe beliefs and intentions to the user and permitted a plan to be inferred and attributed to the user when the user was missing beliefs about some conditions essential to the plan's success. Of course, the system might ascribe its own beliefs about goals and plans to the user, in which case a valid plan *might* be inferred (though not necessarily). However, the system could also ascribe to the user variations of its own beliefs, in which case the resulting inferred plan might be deemed ill-formed by the system.

The major contribution of Pollack's work was a model of plan inference based on explicit reasoning about plausible user beliefs. Although the model makes several simplifying assumptions, it sets the stage for a second generation of plan inference systems that are far more robust and able to handle a wider range of dialogue. The next sections describe Pollack's model.

7.2.2   Plans as Mental Models

Pollack equated having a plan for a goal with having a set of beliefs and intentions about how one is going to achieve the goal. She adopted Goldman's view of plans [Gol70], in which actions are related to one another by either *generation* or *enablement*. An action A_i is said to *generate* an action A_k if performing A_i counts as an instance of doing A_k. A_i is said to *enable* A_k if performing A_i establishes some conditions that must hold for A_k to be generated by an action A_j. For example, under the appropriate circumstances one can express approval by clapping one's hands—the latter action generates the former. On the other hand, purchasing a ticket only enables one to attend a concert.

Pollack dealt only with plans whose constituent actions formed a sequence related by generation. She called these *simple plans*. In addition, as mentioned earlier, she assumed that the recognizing agent already knew the planning agent's goal, the last action in the sequence, and could identify the first action in the sequence from the planning agent's query. A planning agent (PA) was said to have a simple plan (SP) containing the sequence of actions $A_1, A_2, \ldots, A_n$ if the following conditions were satisfied:

1. PA believes that each of the actions A_i is executable.

2. PA believes that each action in the sequence generates its successor (except A_n, which has no successor).

3. PA intends to perform each action in the sequence and intends to do so *by* performing its predecessor in the sequence (except A_1,

which has no predecessor and whose explicit execution will start the generation process).

Inferring an agent's plan consisted not only of ascribing to the agent an intended action sequence $A_1, A_2, \ldots, A_n$ and the belief that each action would successfully fulfill its intended role in the plan but also of being able to justify or explain the basis for this recognition. Pollack captured this notion by saying that the recognizing agent had to believe not only (1) through (3) above but also the following:

4. For each action A_i, PA believes that there is a set of conditions C_i (perhaps null) under which A_i generates its successor A_{i+1}.

5. For each action A_i, PA believes that all of the conditions in the set C_i will be satisfied at the time A_i is executed.

Let a plan segment be a subsequence of the actions contained in a simple plan. The recognizing agent's hypothesizing a plan segment for the planning agent means that the recognizing agent holds a set of beliefs about an action sequence $A_i, A_{i+1}, \ldots, A_j$ such that the recognizing agent believes that (1) through (5) are satisfied. Condition (4) was the crux of Pollack's model of plan inference. If the recognizing agent can identify a particular set of conditions C that suggests either that the planning agent might believe that an action A_{new} generates A_i under conditions C or that the planning agent might believe that A_j generates an action A_{new} under conditions C, the recognizing agent's hypothesis about the planning agent's plan segment can be expanded to include A_{new}, which means that the recognizing agent now holds the belief that the extended action sequence, either $A_{\text{new}}, A_i, A_{i+1}, \ldots, A_j$ or $A_i, A_{i+1}, \ldots, A_j, A_{\text{new}}$, satisfies conditions (1) through (5). Pollack referred to this collection of beliefs about the planning agent's beliefs and intentions regarding the action sequence as an *explanatory plan*; I will say that the beliefs of the recognizing agent (RA) explain and plausibly attribute to the planning agent (PA) the hypothesized plan segment (figure 7.1).

7.2.3   Attributing Belief

The question that must be addressed is how the recognizing agent arrives at a set of beliefs that she attributes to the planning agent. The recognizing agent may know some of the planning agent's beliefs, either from prior knowledge about the planning agent or by inferring them from the preceding dialogue [KF87]. If these beliefs are not sufficient to

1. RA believes that PA believes that each of the actions A_i is executable.

2. RA believes that PA believes that each action in the sequence generates its successor (except A_n, which has no successor).

3. RA believes that PA intends to perform each action in the sequence and intends to do so *by* performing its predecessor in the sequence (except A_1, which has no predecessor and whose explicit execution will start the generation process).

4. RA believes that for each action A_i, PA believes that there is a set of conditions C_i (perhaps null) under which A_i generates its successor A_{i+1}.

5. RA believes that for each action A_i, PA believes that all of the conditions in the set C_i will be satisfied at the time A_i is executed.

Figure 7.1
Attributing a plan segment $A_1, A_2, \ldots, A_n$ to a planning agent

explain the planning agent's utterance, the recognizing agent must reason on her own beliefs about the domain and her knowledge about the planning agent to hypothesize plausible beliefs that the planning agent might hold. To some extent this is a circular process. Only *plausible* beliefs should be hypothesized in relating the planning agent's utterance to his desired goal, but beliefs that succeed in explaining his utterance will automatically seem more plausible.

Pollack's plan inference rules captured some of the ways in which the recognizing agent might construct a set of beliefs that she attributes to the planning agent. In the simplest case, since the recognizing agent has certain beliefs about the world, it is reasonable for her to believe in the absence of contradictory evidence that the planning agent holds the same beliefs. This leads to Pollack's first plan inference rule:

> If RA's beliefs explain and plausibly attribute to PA a hypothesized plan segment $A_i, A_{i+1}, \ldots, A_j$, RA believes that action A_j generates action A_{new} under conditions C, and RA has no reason to doubt that PA believes that action A_j generates A_{new} under conditions C, then RA can infer the necessary beliefs (conditions (1) through (5) in figure 7.1) to explain and plausibly attribute to PA the extended plan segment $A_i, A_{i+1}, \ldots, A_j, A_{new}$.

Since the planning agent is not an expert in the domain, it is reasonable for the recognizing agent to hypothesize that the planning agent might not know all of the conditions that must hold for one action to generate another. Therefore, the recognizing agent might attribute to the planning agent the belief that two actions are related by generation under conditions C^*, where C^* is deficient. This reasoning leads to Pollack's second plan inference rule:

> If RA's beliefs explain and plausibly attribute to PA a hypothesized plan segment $A_i, A_{i+1}, \ldots, A_j$, RA believes that action A_j generates A_{new} under conditions C, C^* is a proper subset of C, and RA has no reason to doubt that PA believes that action A_j generates A_{new} under conditions C^*, then RA can infer the necessary beliefs (conditions (1) through (5) in figure 7.1) to explain and plausibly attribute to PA the extended plan segment $A_i, A_{i+1}, \ldots, A_j, A_{\text{new}}$.

Similar plan inference rules capture the same kind of reasoning to allow A_{new} to be appended to the front of the plan segment.

Given a goal action A_n and a queried action A_1, Pollack's system constructed two plan segments consisting of the single actions A_1 and A_n and then repeatedly applied the plan inference rules to infer plausible extended plan segments. Pairs of extended plan segments in which the first segment began with the action A_1 and the second terminated with A_n can be viewed as similar to the partial plans inferred from alternatives and expectations in Allen's system [AP80] described in chapter 2. Inferencing terminated and the status of a partial plan was upgraded from plausible to recognized when the two extended plan segments merged to form a single sequence of actions related by generation.

Pollack's model of plan inference is a substantially different approach that overcomes some significant limitations of first-generation systems. Yet much work remains before it can be successfully applied to a wide range of dialogues. First, Pollack's plan inference rules do not fully capture the reasoning that might lead the recognizing agent to attribute beliefs to the planning agent. For example, Pollack postulated an additional plan inference rule that permitted the recognizing agent to infer an extended plan segment by hypothesizing that the planning agent had confused an action with a similar action. However, she provided no mechanism for suggesting the similar action or the source of the confusion. This is not an easy problem. Second, as mentioned earlier, she limits herself to consideration of plans whose constituent actions are related by generation. But in most dialogues, actions in the user's underlying plan are related in ways other than just generation, and plan inference will be considerably more complex. In addition, reasoning about inappropriate plans will necessitate considering not only plans that omit essential conditions but also ones that incorporate unnecessary constraints and actions. Nonetheless, Pollack's concept of reasoning on the recognizing agent's beliefs to identify a set of beliefs and intentions that can be ascribed to the planning agent and that will serve to explain the actions contained in the agent's plan was a major change from previous models of plan inference. This approach enables recognition of invalid as well as valid plans and, as will be shown in the next section, provides the basis for generating the kind of cooperative responses found in naturally occurring dialogue.

Recently Pollack's model of plan recognition and belief ascription has been cast as defeasible reasoning and the process represented using a formal argumentation system developed by Konolige [KP89]. A formal argument is a triple consisting of a set of premises, an inference rule, and a conclusion. Extended arguments for a proposition consist of a formal argument whose conclusion is the proposition, along with extended arguments for all premises that are not initial facts of the world. In this paradigm extended arguments are developed as support for various propositions but an argument for one proposition can be defeated by other arguments that support conflicting conclusions. For example, if the planning agent intends to perform an action A_i and he believes that A_i will cause a proposition P to be satisfied, one formal argument ascribes to the planning agent the intention of performing A_i to achieve P. In addition if P is satisfied, a second formal argument ascribes to the planning agent belief in P. One of the defeat rules states that arguments of the first type defeat arguments of the second type since agents don't perform purposeless actions. Another defeat rule states that an initial world fact defeats any argument whose conclusion it conflicts with. Thus many lines of inference and associated ascriptions of belief and intention are possible but some are preferred over others. Although this model of plan recognition is in its early stages, it offers an elegant formalism for choosing among competing inferences.

7.2.4 Analyzing the Inferred Plan

Once the planning agent's plan has been inferred, it must be analyzed and evaluated to generate an appropriate response. If the plan is deemed correct and executable, a cooperative respondent will provide the information that she believes that the information seeker (planning agent) intended her to provide. In addition, as in Allen's generation of helpful responses [AP80] and in Joshi, Webber, and Weischedel's and van Beek and Cohen's research on identifying the appropriate content of expert responses [JWW84,vBC86,vB87], the respondent may include additional information that removes obstacles hampering execution of the plan or suggests better ways of achieving the information seeker's overall goal.

Several researchers have addressed the problem of correcting misconceptions that result in an invalid plan. Allen's system, for example, does not expressly eliminate partial plans that are not executable but rather weights them less favorably than executable ones. If the inferred plan is not executable, a cooperative respondent might identify obstacles to the success of the plan. In this case the plan must be altered, since the obstacles cannot be removed, whereas in the former case of a correct executable plan, the obstacles might be additional knowledge that the information provider can provide (such as the departure gate of the train when only the departure time was requested). Although Quilici [QDF88,Qui89] has studied different kinds of misconceptions that a planning agent might have and appropriate responses for removing these misconceptions, he has not investigated how the invalid plan was identified. Only Pollack has related inference and evaluation of unexecutable and ill-formed plans to the generation of appropriate responses.

Pollack identified several ways in which a plan might be invalid and suggested response strategies appropriate to each. Although the user may have constructed a plan whose actions are correctly related to one another by generation, it might happen that one of the conditions necessary for an action in the plan to generate its successor action will not hold at the time the plan is executed. A cooperative response should inform the user of this obstacle to the success of the plan. In this situation the system will have inferred the user's plan by ascribing to him the system's own presumably correct beliefs about the conditions under which actions generate one another, but the system and user differ in their beliefs about whether the conditions are met. A dialogue that illustrates this kind of misconception is "I want to get a soda. May I borrow 75 cents for the machine downstairs?" If the agent's queried action is identified as Transfer-money-to-soda-machine, the goal action of obtaining a soda will be generated if the machine is working and contains sodas. The system could infer this plan by ascribing these beliefs to the planning agent, in which case it could understand how his query relates to his stated goal. However, if the soda machine is empty, then even though the agent's plan is a generally correct way of getting a soda, it will not work in this instance. An appropriate response might be "I'd be happy to lend you 75 cents, but unfortunately the machine downstairs is empty. You might try the one over in Purnell Hall."

On the other hand, the user's plan may be ill-formed because the actions comprising the plan are not really related by generation. A cooperative response should correct the user's misconceptions about the conditions under which actions will generate one another. This situation occurs when the system has had to ascribe to the user beliefs that differ from its own presumably correct beliefs about the relationships between actions. For example, suppose that a university requires that a writing course be taken during a student's junior or senior year, and that a first-semester sophomore says "I want to satisfy the writing requirement. What are the prerequisites for E410, technical writing?" Although the student may have satisfied the prerequisites for E410, he cannot yet take it to fulfill the writing requirement, since he is only a sophomore. To understand how the action identified by the student's query (taking E410) relates to his stated goal (satisfying the university writing requirement), the system must ascribe to him the belief that taking E410 automatically satisfies the writing requirement. In this case the student's plan is ill-formed because of his misconception about the conditions that must be satisfied for the queried action to generate the goal action. An appropriate response might be "The only prerequisite for E410 is E110, which you've taken. However, taking E410 right now won't satisfy the university writing requirement, since the latter can be done only after you've earned at least 60 credits."

Thus Pollack's system was able to recognize and reason about invalid as well as valid plans. Previous research had not specifically addressed the problem of recognizing invalid plans, and in any case, the systems could not recognize a plan that was ill-formed because the recognizing agent held incorrect beliefs about how actions fit together. The main contributions of Pollack's work were the realization that the recognizing agent must explicitly ascribe beliefs and intentions to the planning agent in deducing his plan and the formalization of a model of plan inference that worked within this paradigm.

7.3   Other Research on More Robust Models

7.3.1   Generalized and Default Inferences

Suppose you observe a student carrying a drop/add form. Although you do not know whether he intends to drop a course, add a course, or change his status in a course (perhaps from credit to listener), you would be justified in believing that he intends to change his registration in some way and in predicting that he will go to the records office in the near future to turn in his completed form. Current models of plan inference are either unable to make such inferences or their control strategies make it very difficult. In my TRACK system, upward expansion of the context model is terminated once a choice among mutually exclusive inferences has to be made; Sidner [Sid85] employed a similar heuristic. Allen [AP80] used a branching heuristic that reduced the rating of the alternative inferred plans, since the speaker could not intend the hearer to know which inference to choose.

Kautz [KA86] proposed a model of plan recognition intended to make generalized inferences from a set of observations and thereby to capture more of the knowledge that humans typically acquire from their observations. His model made two strong assumptions: that the plan library was complete and that the number of higher-level actions containing any specific subaction could not grow so as to make reasoning about all possibilities computationally intractable. Kautz's plan library contained actions related by specialization and decomposition. *Specialization* was similar to Goldman's and Pollack's generation; *decomposition* had the traditional meaning of an action broken down into a set of simpler subactions. Figure 7.2 illustrates such a hierarchy of actions. Specialization is represented by solid lines, and decomposition by dashed lines. Since the plan library is asserted to be complete, the only more specific ways of performing Purchase-item are Purchase-in-store and Purchase-by-mail. Similarly, the only higher-level actions that a subaction can be part of are those actions whose successive decompositions contain it.

Using the action hierarchy and the notion of completeness, Kautz demonstrated how a system can recognize general aspects of an overall plan from specific observations. For example, if an agent were observed signing a form in a store, by reasoning up the action hierarchy in figure 7.2, the system could infer that the agent was either making a layaway purchase or a credit card purchase, was therefore making a store purchase, was therefore purchasing an item, and was therefore performing the top-level action of making use of a new item. From this and knowledge about the decomposition of a Make-use-of-new-item action, the system could predict that the agent would utilize the item either by letting a friend use it or by using it himself.

Kautz recognized that terminating plan inference at choice points prevents the identification of many useful generalizations that should be made from observations. However, it is not computationally tractable to continue working up the action hierarchy when each action can

254

Chapter 7

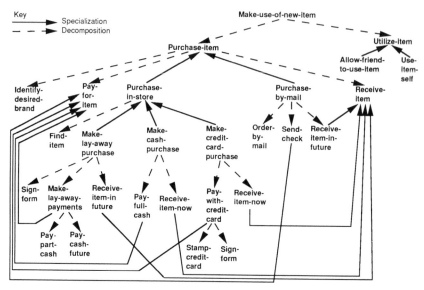

Figure 7.2
An action hierarchy

potentially be part of several higher-level actions. In the absence of evidence to the contrary, some choices are generally favored over others. For example, if one observes an agent signing a form at a store counter, one is likely to temporarily assume that he is making a credit card purchase until presented with conflicting evidence (such as a violation of the expectation that he will receive the purchased item immediately). From such default inferences one can continue inferencing upward in the action hierarchy to identify relevant generalizations. One focus of my current research is the development of a model of plan recognition that permits default inferences [Car90].

7.3.2 Handling Disparate Models

Earlier in this chapter I argued that it is unrealistic to assume that the system's beliefs about the user's plans are always correct. For example, errors may enter the system's context model if the user's statements are inaccurate or misleading or if the system's inference mechanisms, such as focusing heuristics or default rules, are fallible. Thus the system must be able to detect inconsistencies between its inferred model and the user's actual plan and repair its model whenever possible.

As described in chapter 2, Schmidt, Sridharan, and Goodson [SSG78] proposed a hypothesize-and-revise paradigm for inferring a user's goal by observing his noncommunicative actions. They formulated a set of revision critics for altering a plan upon observing actions that conflict with expectations, but they failed to provide a principled mechanism for selecting the appropriate revision. Furthermore, their revision critics were primarily concerned with revising plans affected by unforeseen subsequent events rather than with revisions necessitated by an incorrect hypothesis on the part of the observer. Although the model of plan recognition for an office environment formulated by Carver, Lesser, and McCue [CLM84] attempted to repair the inferred plan when actions inconsistent with it were observed, it did not reason about where the plan might be wrong but merely backtracked to select another interpretation.

My concern here is with modeling the user's plan when his planning is correct but for some reason the system's model fails to reflect that plan. Rarely will an information seeker be aware that the system has constructed an incorrect model of what he wants to accomplish, and even less often will he know exactly where the model is wrong. Instead, the information seeker may express surprise with the system's response or in some way convey that his needs are not being satisfied. The system must then determine the cause of this dissatisfaction.

My own research indicates that detecting and recovering from disparate plan structures requires a four phase approach:

1. Detecting clues to possible disparity between the system's context model and the user's actual goals and plans for accomplishing them

2. Reasoning on the system's context model and the system's domain knowledge to hypothesize the source of these disparities

3. Negotiating with the user to isolate the errors. The negotiation phase should be guided by the system's hypothesis about the source of errors in the context model.

4. Appropriately repairing the context model as indicated by the negotiation dialogue

This approach is motivated by the way humans appear to respond in similar situations, as determined through an analysis of dialogue transcripts. Therefore, a natural language system that pursues this strategy will be viewed as acting naturally by human users. The next sections briefly discuss each of these phases.

Detection   As was claimed earlier, since the system is presumed to be
a cooperative dialogue participant, it must be on the lookout for plan
disparity. I have identified four sources of clues to the existence of such
disparity:

- The discourse goals of IS, such as expressing surprise or confusion

- Conflicts between inferences drawn from IS's current utterance and
  the existing context model

- The relevance of IS's current utterance to the context model

- Abrupt shifts in focus of attention in the context model

IS may express surprise or confusion about the system's response and
thereby cue the possibility of plan disparity. For example, in the IRA
dialogue presented on page 243, plan disparity is suggested when IS in
utterance (5) expresses confusion at IP's previous response by postulating a contradiction to it. Although no one as yet has a general account of
how utterances should be recognized as expressing confusion, my work
on understanding intersentential elliptical fragments in chapter 6 is a
step toward such a theory. In addition, IS's query may contradict or
appear irrelevant to what the system believes is IS's overall task, which
would lead the system to suspect that its context model may not reflect
IS's plan. Or IS's query may require so sharp an unsignaled shift in
focus as to suggest possible problems in the system's model of what IS
wants to accomplish; the strongest expectations are for speakers to address aspects of the task closely related to the current focus of attention
[Sid81,McK85b,Car87a].

Hypothesis Formation   I believe that the knowledge acquired from
the dialogue and how it was used to construct the context model are
important factors in hypothesizing the cause of disparity between the
system's context model and the actual plan under construction by the
information seeker. To do the kind of inferencing exhibited in dialogue
transcripts and provide the most helpful responses, natural language
systems must employ such various techniques for understanding and
relating utterances as focusing heuristics and default rules. Confidence
in individual components of the resultant context model appears to be
important in hypothesizing errors. I believe that the system's context
model should be enriched so that its representation of the plan inferred
for the user differentiates among its components according to the support
that the system accords each component as a correct and intended part

of that plan. The system can then reason on this enriched context model to hypothesize the most likely sources of suspected disparities.

For example, if the system believes that the information seeker intends the system to recognize from his utterance that G is a component of his plan, the system can confidently add G to its context model and have the greatest faith that it really is a component of IS's plan. Therefore, such components are unlikely sources of disparity between the system's context model and IS's plan.

Components that the system adds to the context model because of the system's domain knowledge should be less strongly believed. This distinction resembles intended recognition versus keyhole recognition [CPA81]. My analysis of naturally occurring dialogue suggests that keyhole recognition is often critical to expanding beliefs about what the information seeker is trying to do and how it should be done. For example, if CS180 is an introductory course restricted to majors in computer science and electrical engineering, the system might infer from the utterance "Can you tell me what time CS180 meets?" not only that the user wants to know the meeting time for CS180 but also that the user is pursuing a major in computer science or electrical engineering. The user may intend the system to recognize the first goal, but it is questionable whether the user actually *intends* the system to recognize that the user is pursuing a major in computer science or electrical engineering. This latter inference is based on the system's beliefs about who can take CS180, knowledge that the user may not have. Therefore, since the user may not have intended to communicate these model components, they are more likely sources of error than components that the user intended the system to recognize.

The particular rules used to add a component to the context model should affect the system's faith in that component as part of the information seeker's overall plan. Analysis of naturally occurring dialogues suggest that natural language systems should use such mechanisms as default inference rules and focusing heuristics to expand the context model and provide a more detailed and tractable arena in which to understand and respond to subsequent utterances. However, since these rules select from among multiple possibilities, they add components that are likely sources of suspected errors.

Response Generation and Model Repair Webber [Web86] distinguishes between answers and responses. She defines an *answer* as the production of the information or the execution of the action requested by the speaker. She defines a *response* as "the respondent's complete

informative and performative reaction to the question which can include
... additional information provided or actions performed that are salient
to this substitute for an answer." ([Web86] page 366) Our analysis of
naturally occurring dialogue indicates that humans respond, rather than
answer, once disparate models are detected. This third phase often entails additional actions, including a negotiation dialogue to ascertain the
cause of the discrepancy and to enable the models to be *squared away*
[Jos82] so that they are once again in alignment. Otherwise, the participants might lack confidence that they understand the other's utterances
or that their own responses are being understood. In the ensuing negotiation dialogue each participant may attempt to identify errors by making
relevant assertions, asking questions, or justifying suspect portions of his
own model.

The IRA example illustrates a negotiation dialogue. In utterance (6)
IP identifies a suspect component of her context model (that IRA's are
available to IS for 1981) and justifies it. IS's next utterance informs IP
that the assumption that led IP to infer that IS was eligible for an IRA
is incorrect. IP then notifies IS that IP recognizes the error and that
her beliefs have been repaired. The information-seeking dialogue then
resumes.

Once the cause of model disparity is identified, the system must adjust
its context model as determined through the negotiation dialogue. The
system may communicate to IS the changes that are being made so that
IS can assure himself that the models now agree.

I believe that if a plan recognition system builds such an enriched
context model, uses it to hypothesize the source of suspected errors in
the model, and attempts to negotiate with the user to isolate and repair
its model, the system will be able to handle a much larger set of dialogues
than can current models of plan inference and will be likely to produce
responses resembling those found in transcripts of naturally occurring
information-seeking dialogues.

7.4 Other Models of Plan Recognition

Chapter 2 discussed the importance of plan recognition in story understanding. Goldman and Charniak [GC88] are investigating the problem
of choosing from among multiple explanations for a character's actions
in a story. They are developing an overall probabilistic approach to plan
recognition that uses a multiple-context, truth-maintenance system and
associates probabilities with each of the potential contexts. Only the

contexts with the highest probabilities are investigated, which thus limits the search for an explanation.

Goodman and Litman [GL88,GL89] have been working on a model of plan recognition that they term *constructive*. Instead of trying to fit a user's utterances into the system's knowledge of plans and goals as encoded in a plan library, their model reasons about how the actions fit together in a purposeful manner. Although their intent is eventually to extend their model to plan recognition in dialogue, the current focus of their work is on recognizing user plans in a computer-aided design system. In such a domain, users are generally constructing novel designs and so it is unreasonable to expect that expanding plans from the system's plan library will produce the user's intended plan. Thus their paradigm of constructive plan recognition is intended to facilitate the recognition and acquisition of novel user plans. Goodman [Goo86a] is also investigating using relaxation to identify an initial user plan from ambiguous utterances.

7.5 Summary

Both planning and plan recognition are mental phenomena and produce cognitive structures. The first generation of research in plan recognition made several simplifying assumptions whose effect was to assume that the planning agent's knowledge was similar to that of the recognizing agent and that the recognizing agent could infallibly identify from the dialogue the plan under construction by the planning agent. Although these assumptions are often violated in naturally occurring dialogue, they served to simplify the problem so that fundamental principles and strategies could be identified and tested.

More recent research, beginning with the work of Pollack, has begun to view plans and models of plans as mental phenomena. Since plan inference requires that the recognizing agent deduce the plan that the planning agent has in mind, the recognizing agent must explicitly reason about plausible beliefs of the planning agent that might have influenced the planning process. Similarly, since the recognizing agent cannot be certain that she has correctly deduced the planning agent's plan, she must be on the lookout for clues to discrepancies between her inferred plan and the actual plan under construction by the planning agent, be capable of reasoning about potential discrepancies, and be able to negotiate with the planning agent to repair her model. Although much progress has been made on plan recognition in dialogue, much work remains before cooperative, intelligent systems will be a reality.

8 Summary and Conclusions

This book has investigated models of plan recognition, with emphasis on my own research into computational strategies for assimilating an ongoing dialogue and using the acquired knowledge to facilitate robust understanding. This chapter summarizes the results of the preceding chapters and briefly explores other language problems, besides understanding pragmatically ill-formed input and intersentential elliptical fragments, that have been addressed by reasoning on a model of the user's plan. The chapter then concludes by highlighting several important areas of current and future work.

8.1 Modeling the User's Plans and Goals

The primary themes of this book have been that a model of the underlying plans and goals motivating an information seeker's utterances must be incrementally inferred from an ongoing dialogue and that reasoning on such a model must play a major role in an intelligent, cooperative, and robust natural language system. I believe that if computer systems are to attain their full capability as cooperative, helpful assistants in problem solving and decision making, they must be able to communicate as effectively with humans as humans communicate with one another. Studies by Schmidt, Sridharan, and Goodson [SSG78] and by Cohen, Allen, and Perrault [CPA81] provide compelling evidence that humans perform plan recognition and that they often expect other agents to recognize and respond to their unstated plans and goals. Therefore, it appears that a natural language system must be able to model its user's plans and goals and reason with this acquired knowledge if it is to exhibit the kind of behavior observed in cooperative, naturally occurring dialogues.

Plan recognition research has built on work in other areas, most notably planning, philosophy of language and meaning, and focusing. We have seen how the representations and basic inference mechanisms used in models of plan recognition are based on those developed for robot planning and problem solving. Many philosophers have been interested in communication, and their work has had a major impact on strategies for identifying the intended meaning of an utterance. In fact, Allen's seminal work on intended plan recognition [PA80] produced a computational strategy that captured

- Austin's view of language [Aus62] by treating utterances as actions and modeling them with operators in a planning system,

- Grice's theory of meaning [Gri57,Gri69] by equating understanding with recognition of speaker intent,

- Searle's view of language as rule-governed behavior [Sea70] by using syntactic analysis of an utterance to identify the communicated surface speech act and by capturing Searle's conditions on speech acts either in the system's representation of speech act operators or as conditions satisfied during the planning process,

- Searle's view that the illocutionary force of an indirect speech act can be identified by inferencing on shared knowledge [Sea75].

Although Allen's system for plan inference modeled the process of recognizing an agent's plan from an agent's utterance and differentiated between keyhole and intended recognition, it was limited by its inability to handle dialogue. To incrementally construct a model of a speaker's task-related plan from multiple utterances, plan recognition systems must identify the intended relationship of a new utterance to the established dialogue context. To develop such process models, researchers drew on earlier work on focusing that addressed such problems as resolving referents and generating text. Building on the hypothesis that speaker and hearer must maintain the same focus of attention in the dialogue in order to avoid miscommunication [Gro81], researchers developed focusing heuristics that ordered expectations about shifts in a speaker's focus of attention within the plan structure. These focusing heuristics were used to identify the relationship of a new utterance to the partial plan inferred from the preceding dialogue and to expand the system's model of the user's plan to account for the goal associated with the new utterance (chapter 3).

In addition to his domain goals, a planning agent involved in an information-seeking dialogue has two other kinds of goals: plan-construction or problem-solving goals that he is pursuing to further instantiate and construct his task-related plan and discourse or communicative goals such as answering a question or seeking clarification. Wilensky [Wil78,Wil80,Wil81] argued that a plan inference system must reason not only about how actions achieve domain goals but also about how an agent's selection and ordering of actions is influenced by such planning goals as minimizing the expenditure of resources. This requires recognizing the agent's plan for constructing his domain plan. Wilensky contended that if knowledge about the planning process is expressed declaratively, the same mechanism used to infer domain plans can be used to recognize the metaplans motivating actions taken to achieve planning goals. Litman [LA87] extended this concept of reasoning about higher-order goals to speech acts and communication. She developed an elegant model of plan recognition that differentiated between a domain plan and an agent's currently executing plan for constructing it and that captured the possible relationships between utterances and plans. As a result, her model was able to handle clarification and correction sub-dialogues. Ramshaw [Ram89a,Ram89b] extended Litman's work and developed a rich model of the plan construction process.

Unfortunately, current models of plan inference make a number of re-strictive assumptions that limit their ability to handle naturally occur-ring dialogue. Pollack [Pol87b] was the first to characterize some of these assumptions, and other limiting assumptions were subsequently identi-fied in my research [Car86,Car90]. These include the assumption that the user is pursuing a valid plan that the system knows about [Pol87b] and the assumption that the system never errs in incrementally build-ing its model of the user's plan from the dialogue [Car86,Car88,Car89a]. These assumptions simplified the plan recognition problem and allowed basic principles and strategies to be identified. However, they are clearly unrealistic and must be removed.

The first step in this direction was taken by Pollack [Pol86b]. She developed a substantially different approach to plan recognition, an ap-proach that appears to form the basis for a second generation of plan inference systems. Pollack was concerned with removing the appropriate query assumption, the assumption that although the user's knowledge may be incomplete, it is not erroneous, and that the user thus will not ask a question that is inappropriate to achieving his overall goal. Pollack developed a richer model of plans as mental phenomena and identified how a system might use its own beliefs to reason about user beliefs. Her process model of plan inference explicitly ascribed plausible beliefs and intentions to the user and permitted a plan to be inferred and attributed to the user when the user was missing beliefs about some conditions es-sential to the plan's success.

Recent and ongoing research on plan inference has been addressing other issues. Kautz [KA86] proposed a model of plan recognition in-tended to make generalized inferences from a set of observations and thereby to capture more of the knowledge that humans typically acquire from their observations. Goldman and Charniak [GC88] have been de-veloping a probabilistic approach to plan recognition that controls search and limits consideration of low probability contexts. Goodman and Lit-man [GL88] have been addressing the problem of recognizing novel user plans in the context of a computer-aided design system. My own research has been concerned with default inferences in plan recognition [Car90] and with handling suspected disparity between the system's model of the user's plan and the actual plan under construction by the user [Car86].

8.2   Intelligent Person-Machine Interfaces

In the preceding chapters we have seen examples of computational strategies that reason about the user's plans and goals in order to understand several kinds of utterances that have been problematic for natural language systems. Allen's seminal work in plan recognition produced a technique for identifying the illocutionary force of an utterance and therefore a mechanism for recognizing the intended meaning of indirect speech acts (chapter 2). In chapter 6 we saw how a model of the user's domain goals, plans, and anticipated discourse goals contributes to proper understanding of intersentential elliptical fragments.

When an utterance is ill-formed, the context in which the utterance occurs has a major impact on the listener's repair of the utterance and her recognition of the speaker's intended meaning. Chapter 4 presented a strategy for handling one class of ill-formed utterances that violate the structural properties of the listener's world model. This strategy involved reasoning on a model of the user's underlying task-related plan and focus of attention to suggest variants of the ill-formed utterance that might represent his intended meaning. But clearly a model of the existing dialogue context in terms of the user's plans and goals should be useful in dealing with other kinds of ill-formedness as well.

Ramshaw [Ram89b] investigated how pragmatic knowledge extracted from the dialogue can be used to repair alias errors, or errors that evaded the layers of constraints that were intended to catch them. He concentrated mostly on misspellings that produced a valid but unintended word and therefore were not detected by lexical constraints.[1]

Unfortunately, when such errors occur, it is difficult even to identify the erroneous word, since substitutions for each of several words can often result in legal sentences. To use a naval domain example from [Ram89b], single-word substitutions in the ill-formed utterance "Where is the case in Iceland?" can produce several valid sentences,

---

[1] Granger [Gra77,Gra83] studied the use of pragmatic knowledge in identifying the meaning of unknown words. However, since he was concerned with understanding naval ship-to-shore messages and not user utterances in information-seeking dialogues, a model of a particular user's domain goals and problem-solving strategy was not needed.

including "What is the case in Iceland?" and "Where is the base in Iceland?"

Ramshaw's strategy had two aspects: analyzing the ill-formed query to identify any constraints imposed by syntax and semantics on potential word substitutions and using pragmatic knowledge provided by the existing dialogue context to suggest and rank possible corrections. Ramshaw proposed that each word in the ill-formed utterance be "wildcarded" and treated as a slot that could be filled with a word satisfying the syntactic and semantic constraints imposed by the other words in the sentence. He argued for parsing the sentence multiple times, with the ith word wildcarded during the ith parse, and for the use of a unification parser that would collect the constraints imposed on the wildcarded word in generating a valid parse and partial interpretation. His experiments suggested that only a limited number of valid parses result from wildcarding, and therefore that relatively few partial semantic interpretations are produced for consideration. Once generated, the set of partial interpretations containing constraints on wildcarded slots were related to expectations about follow-on queries suggested by the preceding dialogue. This was done by expanding a metaplan model of the user's domain and problem-solving goals and using the heuristics described in section 2.7.3 to rate matches of partial interpretations with query metaplans, with the matched metaplans suggesting fillers for the wildcarded word. Thus Ramshaw's research not only produced a rich model of problem-solving behavior; it also showed how reasoning on a model of an agent's plans and goals could be used to suggest relevant interpretations of unparsable utterances.

Besides being useful in identifying the intended meaning of a user's utterance, reasoning on a model of the user's plans and goals also contributes to generating cooperative, helpful responses. Allen [AP80] was the first to provide a computational strategy that accounted for extra helpful information included in a response. Using bidirectional inferencing from an agent's observed utterance and from his expected goals, Allen's interpretation strategy inferred an agent's top-level goal and partially developed plan and identified the intended meaning of the utterance. However, Allen noted that a respondent might include extra information not requested by the agent. He characterized this behavior as cooperative and explained it as the respondent's recognition of obstacles in the agent's plan and his attempt to help the agent overcome them. Thus, for example, in Allen's train domain a request for the departure gate of a train might result in a response that provided not only the departure gate but also the departure time, since not knowing the

departure time appeared to be an obstacle to the information seeker's
inferred goal of boarding the train. This notion of cooperative behavior was further developed in [JWW84] and [vBC86,vB87], in which appropriate responses were explored for situations in which the user's
plan would fail to achieve his goal or was not the most effective
means for achieving it. In addition, as described in chapter 7, Pollack [Pol86a,Pol86b] and Quilici [QDF88,Qui89] both studied appropriate responses for removing a planning agent's misconceptions, although
Pollack was more concerned with recognizing the user's invalid plan than
with actually generating a response.

Even when the user's partially developed plan appears to be correct
and efficient, reasoning on a model of the user's plans and goals can
lead to more helpful responses. McKeown [MWM85] developed a strategy that generated answers and associated explanations tailored to the
user's perspective on the domain and reasons for asking the question.
The knowledge base was partitioned into overlapping hierarchies of information, each associated with a particular perspective. To explain an
answer to a question, the system accessed the information in the perspective indexed by the user's overall goal and used this information
to generate an explanation appropriate to the user's needs. Thus the
same question asked by two users motivated by different overall domain
goals might result in the same answer but with very different explanations for the answer. Cohen and Jones [CJ89a,CJ89b] also investigated
user-oriented responses and developed a strategy that took into account
both a user's background knowledge and his domain goals to effectively
answer questions in an expert system for educational diagnosis.

Sarner [SC88] extended this notion of responses tailored to the user's
plans and goals by proposing a strategy for generating definitions most
helpful to the user. The strategy relied on a dynamically inferred model
of the user's domain knowledge, task-related plans and goals, and recep-
tivity to different kinds of information. It constructed a definition by
weighting both the strategic predicates that might comprise a definition
and the propositions that might be used to fill them. These weights
could be used to rank what might be included in a response based on
anticipated usefulness to the user, and rules could then be used to produce an utterance that incorporated the most important information
while adhering to common rhetorical practices. This strategy reflected
the hypothesis that beliefs about the appropriate content of a definition
should guide the selection of a rhetorical strategy instead of the choice
of a rhetorical strategy determining content.

Thus we see that plan recognition plays an important role both in robust natural language understanding and in generating appropriate responses.

8.3   Future Directions

Although the past decade has produced a great deal of interest in plan recognition research, much work remains in developing computational strategies capable of handling naturally occurring dialogue and in integrating them into an intelligent, robust system. I believe that one of the most important directions for plan inference research is to follow Pollack's lead and develop a model of plan recognition that relaxes the assumptions made by previous systems and produces a richer model of the user's plans and goals. Such a system must be able to make default and generalized inferences about what the user is trying to do and be able to recognize and reason about novel user plans. In addition, since communication is imperfect and the system's reasoning processes are fallible, the system must be able to detect possible disparities between its inferred model and the actual plan under construction by the user and to negotiate with the user to repair these discrepancies.

Further research is needed on computational strategies for reasoning on a model of the user's plans and goals in order to understand user utterances and generate effective responses. Along this line, research is needed on how individual reasoning strategies should interact with one another and be integrated into an overall natural language system. In addition, many other problems need to be addressed, such as coordinating plan recognition with other aspects of user modeling and recognizing hidden plans in adversarial interactions. Plan recognition in dialogue offers a rich and potentially fruitful source of research topics.

Bibliography

[AFFH86]   Jerome Azarewicz, Glenn Fala, Ralph Fink, and Christof Heithecker.
            Plan recognition for airborne tactical decision making. In *Proceedings
            of the Fifth National Conference on Artificial Intelligence*, pages 805–
            811, Philadelphia, 1986.

[AFH89]   Jerome Azarewicz, Glenn Fala, and Christof Heithecker. Template-
            based multi-agent plan recognition for tactical situation assessment. In
            *Proceedings of the Fifth IEEE Conference on Artificial Intelligence Ap-
            plications*, Miami, 1989.

[All79]   James F. Allen. A plan-based approach to speech act recognition. Ph.D.
            thesis, University of Toronto, 1979.

[AP80]   James F. Allen and C. Raymond Perrault. Analyzing intention in ut-
            terances. *Artificial Intelligence* 15:143–178, 1980.

[App82]   D. Appelt. Planning natural language referring expressions. In *Pro-
            ceedings of the Twentieth Annual Meeting of the Association for Com-
            putational Linguistics*, pages 108–112, Toronto, 1982.

[App85]   Douglas E. Appelt. *Planning English Sentences*. Cambridge University
            Press, Cambridge, England, 1985.

[Aus62]   J. L. Austin. *How to Do Things with Words*. Harvard University Press,
            Cambridge, Massachusetts, 1962.

[BN78]   Bertram Bruce and Denis Newman. Interacting plans. *Cognitive Sci-
            ence* 2:195–233, 1978.

[Bru86]   Bertram Bruce. Generation as a social action. In Barbara Grosz, Karen
            Sparck Jones, and Bonnie Lynn Webber, editors, *Readings in Natural
            Language Processing*, pages 419–422, Morgan Kaufmann, Los Altos,
            California, 1986.

[Car83]   Jaime G. Carbonell. Discourse pragmatics and ellipsis resolution in
            task-oriented natural language interfaces. In *Proceedings of the Twenty-
            First Annual Meeting of the Association for Computational Linguistics*,
            pages 164–168, Boston, 1983.

[Car86]   Sandra Carberry. User models: The problem of disparity. In *Pro-
            ceedings of the Eleventh International Conference on Computational
            Linguistics*, pages 29–34, Bonn, 1986.

[Car87a]   Sandra Carberry. Pragmatic modeling: Toward a robust natural lan-
            guage interface. *Computational Intelligence* 3:117–136, 1987.

[Car87b]   Sandra Carberry. Using inferred knowledge to understand pragmati-
            cally ill-formed queries. In Ronan Reilly, editor, *Communication Fail-
            ure in Dialogue*, pages 187–200, North-Holland, Amsterdam, 1987.

[Car88] Sandra Carberry. Modeling the user's plans and goals. *Computational Linguistics* 14(3):23–37, 1988.

[Car89a] Sandra Carberry. Plan recognition and its use in understanding dialogue. In Alfred Kobsa and Wolfgang Wahlster, editors, *User Models in Dialog Systems*, pages 133–162, Springer Verlag, Berlin, 1989.

[Car89b] Sandra Carberry. A pragmatics-based approach to ellipsis resolution. *Computational Linguistics* 15(2):75–96, 1989.

[Car90] Sandra Carberry. Incorporating default inferences into plan recognition. In *Proceedings of the Eighth National Conference on Artificial Intelligence*, AAAI, Boston, 1990.

[Cha78] C. L. Chang. Finding missing joins for incomplete queries in relational databases. Technical report RJ2145, IBM Research Laboratory, San Jose, California, 1978.

[Che76] P. P. Chen. The entity-relationship model—Towards a unified view of data. *ACM Transactions on Database Systems* 1(1):9–36, 1976.

[Chi88a] David N. Chin. Exploiting user expertise in answer expression. In *Proceedings of the Seventh National Conference on Artificial Intelligence*, pages 756–760, Saint Paul, 1988.

[Chi88b] David N. Chin. Knome: Modeling what the user knows in UC. In Alfred Kobsa and Wolfgang Wahlster, editors, *User Models in Dialog Systems*, pages 74–107, Springer Verlag, Berlin, 1988.

[CJ89a] Robin Cohen and Marlene Jones. Incorporating user models into expert systems for educational diagnosis. In Alfred Kobsa and Wolfgang Wahlster, editors, *User Models in Dialogue Systems*, pages 313–333, Springer Verlag, Berlin, 1989.

[CJ89b] Robin Cohen and Marlene Jones. Providing responses specific to a user's goals and background. *International Journal of Expert Systems*, 1989.

[CLM84] Norman F. Carver, Victor R. Lesser, and Daniel L. McCue. Focusing in plan recognition. In *Proceedings of the Fourth National Conference on Artificial Intelligence*, pages 42–48, Austin, 1984.

[Coh84] Robin Cohen. A computational theory of the function of clue words in argument understanding. In *Proceedings of the Tenth International Conference on Computational Linguistics*, pages 251–258, Stanford, 1984.

[Coh87] Robin Cohen. Analyzing the structure of argumentative discourse. *Computational Linguistics* 13(1–2):11–24, 1987.

[CP79] Philip R. Cohen and C. Raymond Perrault. Elements of a plan-based theory of speech acts. *Cognitive Science* 3:177–212, 1979.

[CPA81]   Philip R. Cohen, C. Raymond Perrault, and James F. Allen. Beyond
            question answering. In W. Lehnert and M. Ringle, editors, *Strategies
            for Natural Language Processing*, pages 245–274, Lawrence Erlbaum
            Associates, Hillsdale, New Jersey, 1981.

[Dav80]   Randall Davis. Meta-rules: Reasoning about control. *Artificial Intelli-
            gence* 15:179–221, 1980.

[EN69]   G. Ernst and Allen Newell. *GPS: A Case Study in Generality and
            Problem Solving.* Academic Press, New York, 1969.

[FD84]   M. Flowers and M. E. Dyer. Really arguing with your computer. In
            Proceedings of the National Computer Conference, pages 653–659, 1984.

[FD86]   Tim Finin and David Drager. GUMS: A general user modeling sys-
            tem. In *Proceedings of the Sixth Canadian Conference on Artificial
            Intelligence*, pages 24–30, Montreal, 1986.

[Fin83]   Timothy Finin. Providing help and advice in task oriented systems. In
            *Proceedings of the International Joint Conference on Artificial Intelli-
            gence*, pages 176–178, Karlsruhe, West Germany, 1983.

[FN71]   R. E. Fikes and N. J. Nilsson. STRIPS: A new approach to the ap-
            plication of theorem proving to problem solving. *Artificial Intelligence*
            2:189–208, 1971.

[GC88]   Robert Goldman and Eugene Charniak. A probabilistic ATMS for plan
            recognition. In *Proceedings of the AAAI Workshop on Plan Recogni-
            tion*, Saint Paul, 1988.

[Gen79]   M. R. Genesereth. The role of plans in automated consultation. In
            *Proceedings of the 1979 International Joint Conference on Artificial
            Intelligence*, pages 311–319, Tokyo, 1979.

[Gen82]   M. R. Genesereth. The role of plans in intelligent teaching systems.
            In D. Sleeman and H. S. Brown, editors, *Intelligent Tutoring Systems*,
            pages 137–155, Academic Press, New York, 1982.

[GJW83]   B. Grosz, A. K. Joshi, and S. Weinstein. Providing a unified account
            of definite noun phrases in discourse. In *Proceedings of the Twenty-
            First Annual Meeting of the Association for Computational Linguistics*,
            pages 44–50, Cambridge, Massachusetts, 1983.

[GL88]   Bradley Goodman and Diane Litman. Aiding design with constructive
            plan recognition. In *Proceedings of AAAI Workshop on Plan Recogni-
            tion*, Saint Paul, 1988.

[GL89]   Bradley Goodman and Diane Litman. Design interfaces and plan recog-
            nition. Technical report 7103, BBN Systems and Technologies Corp.,
            Cambridge, Massachusetts, 1989.

[Gol70]   Alvin Goldman. *A Theory of Human Action.* Prentice-Hall, Englewood
            Cliffs, New Jersey, 1970.

[Goo86a]   Bradley A. Goodman. Miscommunication and plan recognition. Paper
            presented at International Workshop on User Modeling, Maria Laach,
            West Germany, 1986.

[Goo86b]   Bradley A. Goodman. Reference identification and reference identifica-
            tion failures. *Computational Linguistics* 12(4):273–305, 1986.

[Gra77]   R. H. Granger. FOUL-UP: A program that figures out meanings of
            words from context. In *Proceedings of the Fifth International Joint
            Conference on Artificial Intelligence*, pages 172–178, Cambridge, Mas-
            sachusetts, 1977.

[Gra83]   R. H. Granger. The NOMAD system: Expectation-based detection and
            correction of errors during understanding of syntactically and semanti-
            cally ill-formed text. *American Journal of Computational Linguistics*
            9(3–4):188–196, 1983.

[Gre69]   Cordell Green. Theorem-proving by resolution as a basis for question-
            answering systems. In B. Meltzer and D. Michie, editors, *Machine
            Intelligence*, pages 183–205, American Elsevier, New York, 1969.

[Gri57]   H. Paul Grice. Meaning. *Philosophical Review* 56:377–388, 1957.

[Gri69]   H. Paul Grice. Utterer's meaning and intentions. *Philosophical Review*
            68:147–177, 1969.

[Gri75a]   H. Paul Grice. Logic and conversation. In P. Cole and J. L. Mor-
            gan, editors, *Syntax and Semantics*, vol. 3, *Speech Acts*, pages 41–58,
            Academic Press, New York, 1975.

[Gri75b]   J. E. Grimes. *The Thread of Discourse.* Mouton, the Hague, 1975.

[Gro77a]   B. Grosz. The representation and use of focus in dialogue understand-
            ing. Technical report 151, SRI International, Menlo Park, California,
            1977.

[Gro77b]   Barbara J. Grosz. The representation and use of focus in a system
            for understanding dialogs. In *Proceedings of the International Joint
            Conference on Artificial Intelligence*, pages 67–76, Cambridge, Mas-
            sachusetts, 1977.

[Gro79]   Barbara J. Grosz. Utterance and objective: Issues in natural language
            processing. In *Proceedings of the International Joint Conference on
            Artificial Intelligence*, pages 1067–1076, Tokyo, 1979.

[Gro81]   Barbara J. Grosz. Focusing and description in natural language di-
            alogues. In B. Webber, A. Joshi, and I. Sag, editors, *Elements of
            Discourse Understanding*, pages 85–105, Cambridge University Press,
            Cambridge, England, 1981.

[GS86]   Barbara Grosz and Candace Sidner. Attention, intention, and the struc-
            ture of discourse. *Computational Linguistics* 12(3):175–204, 1986.

[HE80]   Jerry R. Hobbs and David A. Evans. Conversation as planned behavior.
            Cognitive Science 4:349–377, 1980.

[Hir84]   Julia Hirschberg. Toward a redefinition of yes/no questions. In *Pro-
            ceedings of the International Conference on Computational Linguistics*,
            pages 48–51, Stanford, 1984.

[Hob79]   Jerry R. Hobbs. Coherence and coreference. *Cognitive Science* 3:67–90,
            1979.

[HSSS78]   Gary G. Hendrix, Earl D. Scerdoti, Daniel Sagalowicz, and Jonathan
            Slocum. Developing a natural language interface to complex data. *ACM
            Transactions on Database Systems* 3(2):105–147, 1978.

[Jos82]   Aravind K. Joshi. Mutual beliefs in question-answer systems. In N.
            Smith, editor, *Mutual Beliefs*, pages 181–197, Academic Press, New
            York, 1982.

[JWW84]   Aravind Joshi, Bonnie Webber, and Ralph Weischedel. Living up to ex-
            pectations: Computing expert responses. In *Proceedings of the Fourth
            National Conference on Artificial Intelligence*, pages 169–175, Austin,
            1984.

[KA86]   Henry Kautz and James Allen. Generalized plan recognition. In *Pro-
            ceedings of the Fifth National Conference on Artificial Intelligence*,
            pages 32–37, Philadelphia, 1986.

[Kap79]   S. J. Kaplan. Cooperative responses from a portable natural language
            database query system. Ph.D. thesis, University of Pennsylvania, 1979.

[Kap82]   S. J. Kaplan. Cooperative responses from a portable natural language
            query system. *Artificial Intelligence* 19(2):165–187, 1982.

[KF87]   Robert Kass and Tim Finin. Rules for the implicit acquisition of knowl-
            edge about the user. In *Proceedings of the Sixth National Conference
            on Artificial Intelligence*, pages 295–300, Seattle, 1987.

[KP89]   Kurt Konolige and Martha Pollack. Ascribing plans to agents: Pre-
            liminary report. *Proceedings of the International Joint Conference on
            Artificial Intelligence*, 924–930, Seattle, 1989.

[LA84]   Diane Litman and James Allen. A plan recognition model for clarifica-
            tion subdialogues. In *Proceedings of the Tenth International Conference
            on Computational Linguistics*, pages 302–311, Stanford, 1984.

[LA87]   Diane Litman and James Allen. A plan recognition model for subdia-
            logues in conversation. *Cognitive Science* 11:163–200, 1987.

[LF77]   W. Labov and D. Fanshel. *Therapeutic Discourse: Psychotherapy as Conversation.* Academic Press, New York, 1977.

[Lit85]   Diane Litman. Plan recognition and discourse analysis: An integrated approach for understanding dialogues. Ph.D. thesis, University of Rochester, Rochester, New York, 1985.

[Lit86a]   Diane Litman. Linguistic coherence: A plan-based alternative. In *Proceedings of the Twenty-Fourth Annual Meeting of the Association for Computational Linguistics*, pages 215–223, New York, 1986.

[Lit86b]   Diane J. Litman. Understanding plan ellipsis. In *Proceedings of the Fifth National Conference on Artificial Intelligence*, pages 619–624, Philadelphia, 1986.

[May80a]   E. Mays. Correcting misconceptions about database structure. In *Proceedings of the Third Canadian Conference on Artificial Intelligence*, Victoria, Canada, 1980.

[May80b]   E. Mays. Failures in natural language systems: Applications to data base query systems. In *Proceedings of the First National Conference on Artificial Intelligence*, pages 327–330, Stanford, 1980.

[McC86]   Kathleen F. McCoy. The ROMPER system: Responding to object-related misconceptions using perspective. In *Proceedings of the Twenty-Fourth Annual Meeting of the Association for Computational Linguistics*, pages 97–105, New York, 1986.

[McC88]   Kathleen F. McCoy. Reasoning on a highlighted user model to respond to misconceptions. *Computational Linguistics* 14(3):52–63, 1988.

[McK82]   K. McKeown. Generating natural language text in response to questions about database structure. Ph.D. thesis, University of Pennsylvania, 1982.

[McK83]   Kathleen R. McKeown. Focus constraints on language generation. In *Proceedings of the Third National Conference on Artificial Intelligence*, pages 582–587, Washington, D.C., 1983.

[McK85a]   Kathleen R. McKeown. Discourse strategies for generating natural-language text. *Artificial Intelligence* 27:1–41, 1985.

[McK85b]   Kathleen R. McKeown. *Text Generation.* Cambridge University Press, Cambridge, England, 1985.

[MH69]   John McCarthy and Patrick J. Hayes. Some philosophical problems from the standpoint of artificial intelligence. In B. Meltzer and D. Michie, editors, *Machine Intelligence*, pages 463–502, American Elsevier, New York, 1969.

[MML77]   William Mann, James Morre, and James Levin. A comprehension model for human dialogue. In *Proceedings of the Fifth International Joint Conference on Artificial Intelligence*, pages 77–87, Cambridge, Masssachusetts, 1977.

[MWM85]   K. McKeown, M. Wish, and K. Matthews. Tailoring explanations for the user. In *Proceedings of the Ninth International Joint Conference on Artificial Intelligence*, pages 794–798, Los Angeles, 1985.

[Nil80]   Nils J. Nilsson. *Principles of Artificial Intelligence*. Tioga Publishers, Palo Alto, California, 1980.

[PA80]   R. Perrault and J. Allen. A plan-based analysis of indirect speech acts. *American Journal of Computational Linguistics* 6(3–4):167–182, 1980.

[Par88]   Cecile L. Paris. Tailoring object descriptions to a user's level of expertise. *Computational Linguistics* 14(3):64–78, 1988.

[PHW82]   M. Pollack, J. Hirschberg, and B. Webber. User participation in the reasoning processes of expert systems. In *Proceedings of the Second National Conference on Artificial Intelligence*, pages 358–361, Pittsburgh, Pennsylvania, 1982.

[Pol86a]   M. Pollack. Inferring domain plans in question-answering. Ph.D. thesis, University of Pennsylvania, 1986.

[Pol86b]   Martha Pollack. A model of plan inference that distinguishes between the beliefs of actors and observers. In *Proceedings of the Twenty-Fourth Annual Meeting of the Association for Computationa Linguistics*, pages 207–214, New York, 1986.

[Pol87a]   Livia Polanyi. The linguistic discourse model: Towards a formal theory of discourse structure. Technical report 6409, Bolt Beranek and Newman Laboratories, Cambridge, Massachusetts, 1987.

[Pol87b]   M. Pollack. Some requirements for a model of the plan-inference process in conversation. In Ronan Reilly, editor, *Communication Failure in Dialogue*, pages 245–256, North-Holland, Amsterdam, 1987.

[PS83]   Livia Polanyi and Remko Scha. The syntax of discourse. *TEXT* 3(3): 271–290, 1983.

[QDF88]   Alexander Quilici, Michael Dyer, and Margot Flowers. Recognizing and responding to plan-oriented misconceptions. *Computational Linguistics* 14(3):38–51, 1988.

[Qui89]   Alexander Quilici. Detecting and responding to plan-oriented misconceptions. In Alfred Kobsa and Wolfgang Wahlster, editors, *User Models in Dialog Systems*, pages 108–132, Springer Verlag, Berlin, 1989.

[Ram89a]   Lance A. Ramshaw. A metaplan model for problem-solving discourse. In *Proceedings of the Fourth Conference of the European Chapter of the Association for Computational Linguistics*, pages 35–42, Manchester, England, 1989.

[Ram89b]   Lance A. Ramshaw. Pragmatic knowledge for resolving ill-formedness. Ph.D. thesis, University of Delaware, 1989.

[Rei78a]   Rachel Reichman. Conversational coherency. *Cognitive Science* 2:283–327, 1978.

[Rei78b]   R. Reiter. On closed world data bases. In H. Gallaire and J. Minker, editors, *Logic and Data Bases*, pages 55–76, Plenum Press, New York, 1978.

[Rei84]   Rachel Reichman. Extended person-machine interface. *Artificial Intelligence* 22:157–218, 1984.

[Rei85]   Raymond Reiter. On reasoning by default. In Ronald Brachman and Hector Levesque, editors, *Readings in Knowledge Representation*, pages 401–410, Morgan Kaufmann, Los Altos, California, 1985.

[Rob81]   Ann Robinson. Determining verb phrase referents in dialogs. *American Journal of Computational Linguistics* 7(1):1–18, 1981.

[SA75]   R. Schank and R. Abelson. Scripts, plans, and knowledge. In *Proceedings of the Fourth International Joint Conference on Artificial Intelligence*, pages 151–157, Georgia, USSR, 1975.

[SA77]   Roger C. Schank and Robert P. Abelson. *Scripts, Plans, Goals and Understanding*. Lawrence Erlbaum Associates, Hinsdale, New Jersey, 1977.

[Sac74]   Earl D. Sacerdoti. Planning in a hierarchy of abstraction spaces. *Artificial Intelligence* 5:115–135, 1974.

[Sac75]   Earl D. Sacerdoti. The nonlinear nature of plans. In *Proceedings of the Fourth International Joint Conference on Artificial Intelligence*, pages 206–214, Georgia, USSR, 1975.

[Sac77]   Earl D. Sacerdoti. *A Structure for Plans and Behavior*. American Elsevier, New York, 1977.

[SC88]   Margaret H. Sarner and Sandra Carberry. A new strategy for providing definitions in task-oriented dialogues. In *Proceedings of the Twelfth International Conference on Computational Linguistics*, pages 567–572, Budapest, 1988.

[Sea70]   John R. Searle. *Speech Acts: An Essay in the Philosophy of Language*. Cambridge University Press, Cambridge, England, 1970.

[Sea75]   John R. Searle. Indirect speech acts. In Peter Cole and Jerry Morgan, editors, *Syntax and Semantics*, vol. 3, *Speech Acts*, pages 59–82, Academic Press, New York, 1975.

[SI81]   C. L. Sidner and D. Israel. Recognizing intended meaning and speakers' plans. In *Proceedings of the Seventh International Joint Conference on Artificial Intelligence*, pages 203–208, Vancouver, 1981.

[Sid81]   Candace L. Sidner. Focusing for interpretation of pronouns. *American Journal of Computational Linuistics* 7(4):217–231, 1981.

[Sid83a]   C. L. Sidner. Focusing in the comprehension of definite anaphora. In Michael Brady and Robert Berwick, editors, *Computational Models of Discourse*, pages 267–330, MIT Press, Cambridge, 1983.

[Sid83b]   Candace L. Sidner. What the speaker means: The recognition of speakers' plans in discourse. *Computers and Mathematics with Applications* 9(1):71–82, 1983.

[Sid85]   Candace L. Sidner. Plan parsing for intended response recognition in discourse. *Computational Intelligence* 1:1–10, 1985.

[Sow76]   J. F. Sowa. Conceptual graphs for a database interface. *IBM Journal of Research and Development* 336–357, 1976.

[SSG78]   C. F. Schmidt, N. S. Sridharan, and J. L. Goodson. The plan recognition problem: An intersection of psychology and artificial intelligence. *Artificial Intelligence* 11:45–82, 1978.

[SSJ74]   H. Sacks, E. A. Schegloff, and G. Jefferson. A simplest systematics for the organization of turn-taking for conversation. *Language* 50:696–735, 1974.

[Ste81]   Mark Stefik. Planning and meta-planning: MOLGEN, part 2. *Artificial Intelligence* 16:141–170, 1981.

[SW80]   Norman Sondheimer and Ralph Weischedel. A rule-based approach to ill-formed input. In *Proceedings of the Eighth International Conference on Computational Linguistics*, pages 46–53, Tokyo, 1980.

[Tho80]   Bozena H. Thompson. Linguistic analysis of natural language communication with computers. In *Proceedings of the Eighth International Conference on Computational Linguistics*, pages 190–201, Tokyo, 1980.

[vB87]   Peter van Beek. A model for generating better explanations. In *Proceedings of the Twenty-Fifth Annual Meeting of the Association for Computational Linguistics*, pages 215–220, Stanford, 1987.

[vBC86]   Peter van Beek and Robin Cohen. Towards user specific explanations from expert systems. In *Proceedings of the Sixth Canadian Conference on Artificial Intelligence*, pages 194–198, Montreal, 1986.

[VD87]   Y. M. Visetti and P. Dague. Plan inference and student modeling in
            ICAI. In *Proceedings of the Sixth National Conference on Artificial
            Intelligence*, 77–81, Seattle, 1987.

[Wal78]   David Waltz. An English language question answering system for a
            large relational database. *Communications of the Association for Com-
            puting Machinery* 21(7):526–539, 1978.

[WCL*88]   Robert Wilensky, David Chin, Marc Luria, James Martin, James May-
            field, and Dekai Wu. The Berkeley UNIX consultant project. *Compu-
            tational Linguistics* 14(4):35–84, 1988.

[Web83]   Bonnie L. Webber. Varieties of user misconceptions: Detection and
            correction. In *Proceedings of the Eighth International Joint Conference
            on Artificial Intelligence*, pages 850–852, Karlsruhe, 1983.

[Web86]   B. L. Webber. Questions, answers, and responses: Interacting with
            knowledge base systems. In Michael Brodie and John Mylopoulos,
            editors, *On Knowledge Base Management Systems*, pages 365–402,
            Springer Verlag, New York, 1986.

[Wil78]   Robert Wilensky. Why John married Mary: Understanding stories in-
            volving recurring goals. *Cognitive Science* 2:235–266, 1978.

[Wil80]   Robert Wilensky. Meta-planning. In *Proceedings of the First National
            Conference on Artificial Intelligence*, pages 334–336, Stanford, 1980.

[Wil81]   Robert Wilensky. Meta-planning: Representing and using knowledge
            about planning in problem solving and natural language understanding.
            Cognitive Science 5:197–233, 1981.

[Wil83]   Robert Wilensky. *Planning and Understanding: A Computational Ap-
            proach to Human Reasoning*. Addison-Wesley, Reading, Massachusetts,
            1983.

[Wil84]   D. E. Wilkins. Domain-independent planning: Representation and plan
            generation. *Artificial Intelligence* 22:269–301, 1984.

[WS82]   Ralph Weischedel and Norman K. Sondheimer. An improved heuristic
            for ellipsis processing. In *Proceedings of the Twentieth Annual Meeting
            of the Association for Computational Linguistics*, pages 85–88, Toronto,
            1982.

Index